ISBN: 978-0996625258
LCCN: 2016931686

Legit Styles Publishing
16501 Shady Grove Rd, Suite# 7562
Gaithersburg, MD 20898

info@legitstylespublishing.com
legitstylespublishing.com

This is a work of fiction. Any names historical events, real people, living and dead, or locales are intended only to give the fiction a setting in historic reality. Other names, characters, places, businesses and incidents are either the product of the author's imagination or are used fictitiously, and their resemblance, if any, to real life counterparts is entirely coincidental.

DEDICATIONS

This book is dedicated to my grandmother, Ruby Gardner, and Uncle Richard Burns. I miss you two very much. May ya'll continue to watch over me from above. Love ya'll.

SPECIAL DEDICATIONS

To Ma' Dukes, the one who laced my boots, the queen of all queens. You've always held me down and I'm forever blessed to have you as a mother. To my Pops, for giving me so much without even realizing it, I love you O.G. To wifey, thank you for putting up with all my shit through the years and riding strong through this 20 year bid. I love you baby girl. Last but not least, my son and daughter, DeSean Jr. and Ashanti. Daddy love ya'll truly and will be home shortly.

ACKNOWLEDGEMENTS

First and foremost, I'd like to thank God for life and watching over me while I go through this world and this game. To my nigga, Byron "CEO" Grey, who I've had the pleasure of walking the yard with and a real nigga. Thanks for allowing me to bring my talents to Legit Styles. To the homie, DonTwan, we done did it again. Thanks for showing me how to turn sugar from shit. Keep ya head up homie, we almost home.

SHOUT OUTS

Big ups to both of my brothers, Nate G and Band-Aide. Continue to hold shit down til lil bruh get home. To my sisters: Starrprina, Yvette, and Jolynn, love ya'll. To all my nieces and nephews, love ya'll.

Shout out to all my niggas on lockdown. Free my nephew Nail and my brother from another, M-San from B-Town. My niggas Chest, J-Fitch, and Lad, ya'll hold it down. My niggas from the Haystack, Raiders,DJ, and James, ya'll already know. My town niggas: LiL D, Sheist, and DP all from Ice City. S'up with my East Oakland niggas, G.I.B, what's good though? Black ass Curt, I see ya! My burn out niggas, B.I, LiL T, and T-Bow. Joc holla at yo boy. Dre what's good?

My B-town niggas: Speedy, Sean, Whoo, And Dewhite. My niggas Tone, Squeeze, Crash, And Cedio Bo from the Rich. My nigga Fade from the Valley. AJ, Baby Ken, Tee Lee, Chevy, T, And Al all from Sac. My city niggas, Geez and Juan from Kirkwood. Hard and Big Learn, what's really good? LiL QB get at ya boy! Lambo Lou, I ain't forgot about ya. My niggas from D-Block, Fella, and Cut. My Sonnydale niggas, Noodles and Dog. O, what's good?

My L.A niggas, L.B.C's Down "Rolling 20's," C-Nutty "Ocean Side," Capone "Hub City NHC," LiL Young Meech "YFC," E-Rida "East Coast," Cheese from Vegas and Don. Say So and Fat Dawg . Blood gang, Face from San Diego, Rusty, and RVE from Sac. Stock Town, twin from the east side. Keek, Chump, Villian, and Ty. My niggas King Dave and Chop from Milwakee. Yak from Pontiac. To all my E.P.A niggas on lock, S'up Rogues. Free Young Bunk and DJ. Rest in peace Tha Jacka.

CHAPTER ONE

"Boy, wake yo' lazy ass up and get ready fo' school," Donminique yelled at her son.

Lamonte laid stone cold still, buried beneath his covers.

"You know damned well you hear me! If I got to tell you one mo' time I'mma come in there and knock lightning out cho ass!"

Although the room was dark from the closed blinds and curtains, she still made out the clutter that existed in the room. Piles of clothes and boxes of Nike Air Jordan's laid scattered on the floor.

In a slow tired voice Lamonte said, "Come on wit' all that yelling, ma."

"Boy, this my house and I'll yell if I want to," she said with a hand on her hip. "I done told your ass about stayin' up on school nights, watchin' them Bernie Mac re-runs."

Lamonte tossed in his bed. "Alright, just five more—"

Donminique took one step into the room with intentions of snatching his ass up. Instead, she stepped barefoot on his PlayStation 4's wireless controller. "Got DAMMNIT! Boy, clean this damn room," she hollered before slamming his door.

Lamonte bust out laughing.

Despite her frustration towards her son lack of motivation in school, she loved him dearly. She was only hard on him because she knew it would only help him down the road. Every time she looked at him, she was reminded of his father; the man she loved with all her

1

heart. With his chocolate complexion and slanted hazel-brown eyes, her son was the splitting image of Jack, all the way down to the bald-fade he sported.

He was the man's fucking twin.

The birth of Lamonte was also a turning point for her. Before him, her life was going in a million directions. She was young, running the streets, and going out. Then she met Jack, who was a young hustler and a member of the Gangster Disciples, one of Chicago's most feared street organizations. But for Donminique there was nothing to fear for, especially with Jack. Nicknamed Black Jack, her man became one of the G.D's headmen. With many under him, and the organizations street dealings in his control, Black Jack asked her to bear his child. His reason was simple; the family life was the only savior for a Gangster.

So she agreed.

Putting all her partying days behind her, 18 year old Donminique looked to impress her man by being what he needed her to be. She was soon pregnant and Lamonte was born. At times she feared Black Jack's interest in her would leave, once she had her son, but he proved loyal to his word, which made her love him even more.

From what she saw, he loved his son and thought the world of him. He made sure they had the best of everything and never wanted for anything. He moved them right outside of Chicago to a suburb called Maywood. There he raised his son, who went through the public school system. On the weekends, he'd hang with his father, who would give him the ends and outs of the streets and life.

Donminique didn't mind her husband showing their son the street life. She wanted him to be both book and street smart. It wasn't long before everyone started calling Lamonte by his own nickname. A name she really didn't like, but she knew was fitting for him.

Pretty Black

Her whole life had been a struggle. From her father being shot and killed in a gang related incident when she was fifteen, to her mother's heroin addiction and turning to prostitution two years thereafter. Donminique suffered through it all. Black Jack had rescued her, providing his wife a comfortable life and she would make sure her son benefited greatly from it.

He will not struggle like I had to, she promised herself.

3

The three bedrooms, 2-bathroom brick house sat on 2,800 square feet on a quiet street in a very nice community. Donminique held nothing back when Black Jack gave her permission to decorate it how she saw fit. Of course, she left the extra room for her husband's office space and Lamonte's room alone. But everything else, she went all the way in on.

She had plush wall-to-wall carpeting, new aged fashionable paint designs, and colors decorated each room in a vibe she coordinated with leather couches, drapes, and throw rugs. Black art donned the living room walls amongst cherry oak end tables and glass shelf casings, topping areas off with plant life and colorful flowers gave her home a fresh, lively feel.

Another area she held precious was her kitchen. With its granite countertops, stainless steel stove and oak cabinets, it was her laboratory for all the exotic dishes she experimented with along with a 32-inch flat screen that she'd placed next to the sink allowed her to prepare all the things she learned from the Food Network.

She pulled a carton of eggs out of the refrigerator, along with a slab of turkey bacon. She smiled. No one took motherhood as a blessing like she did. She was so thankful.

←——————————————————————→

At 11 years old, Lamonte was treated like a king. When he rolled over and tossed the comforter from his body, he stretched and got up. Stepping over toward the light switch, he hit it, and then looked around his room.

Yea, he thought. *I need to clean up.*

Wasting no time, he started picking up and straightening his room. He cut his CD player on to give him some morning inspiration. Soulja Boy's *Pretty Boy Swag* song came blasting through his system as he rapped along.

Hopped up out da beeed, turned my swag on....... looked in the mirror, said what's up!!

Yeeeeahh, I'm gettin' Mon' eeee...Ahhhh!

Bouncing in his room, Lamonte's task moved quickly. He picked up a scrap piece of paper he used to do his math homework with and crumbled it. The life-sized poster of Michael Jordan that decorated his wall gave him new inspiration as he shot the paperball toward the wastebasket. With pure form, tongue out, and a wrist extension, he made the shot.

Swishh!

He went back to bouncing.

After stacking his boxes of Jordan's next to his bed, Lamonte went to his closet and picked out an outfit for the day. He settled on a pair of black True Religion jeans and a white Polo shirt with the black horse to match his black and white patent leather number Eleven Space Jam Jordan's.

"Yea, " he said nodding his head.

Once he got dressed, he checked himself out in the full-length mirror mounted on the back of his door. Turning to the side, he checked out his footwork. The clear gum sole of the Jordan's looked extra fly. He raised his pant leg to check out the Roman numeral 23 on the side.

He nodded again. Extra fly indeed.

After brushing his teeth, Lamonte walked towards the kitchen where he smelled the wonderful aroma of his mother's cooking. Taking his place on one of the stools at the granite countertop, he smiled. "Excuse me, miss. Can I have the number two?"

His mother's head snapped back as she looked at him. "Ol smart ass! This ain't Denny's." Then she scooped some eggs and turkey bacon on a plate, dropping it down in front of him. "And hurry up. You got ten minutes before you gotta be out of here."

The side door to the kitchen opened and in walked Black Jack.

"What's up, pops?"

"What's up, Pretty Black," he responded to Lamonte.

"That lil nigga ain't pretty," his mother responded. "That's his problem now. He thinks he's too damn fly."

Lamonte nodded and gave his dad some dap. "Just like my ol' man."

"That's right son. You almost ready?"

Lamonte took two quick bites and pushed his plate to the side.

"Yea, you takin' me? Let's go."

"Boy, finish yo' food!"

"Nique, he's cool."

"Yea ma, I'm good. Don't be buggin'."

Just when Lamonte jumped down off the stool, his father's cell phone rang.

"Hello.... yea.... No shit? Alright. Nigga I said alright! Don't trip, I'll be there." He ended the call and looked at Lamonte. "Your mom's gonna have to drop you off. I've got an emergency."

Lamonte's disappointment showed all over his face. He looked forward to rolling up to the school in his dad's H2, sitting on 28 chrome wheels. "Man," was all he said.

"Don't trip," Black Jack told him. "I promise. I'll pick you up when you get out. Then we'll grab somethin' to eat."

He smiled. "Cool."

"Do you want me to make you an egg sandwich to take with you?" Donminique asked her husband.

"Nah babe. I'm good."

She turned to Lamonte. "Now hop yo pretty ass back on that stool and finish yo breakfast. Somebody gone eat this shit. I ain't playin' Chief Boy R' D for my health."

Lamonte did as he was told as his father gave his mother a kiss goodbye. What none of them knew was that would be their last morning as a complete and happy family.

CHAPTER TWO

Although Lamonte received good grades in school, he hated attending class. Usually he came in late and took a seat at the back so his teacher, Mr. Chapman, wouldn't call on him to answer any questions. He was only there because his parents made him. He would sit, watch, listen, and take the tests when asked. Other than that, all he did was wait until lunchtime and recess to run the playground.

6th grade was the best. The schools in Maywood weren't as bad like in Chicago, but there was still some action. Most of the kids came from money and unlike Lamonte, they weren't used to the gangster's lifestyle. They knew about G.D.'s and Vice Lords, and a few pretended the roles. As long as they were down for the G.D's, he wasn't tripping.

Another thing he loved was chasing girls. For some reason they loved his swag and he never let off the gas when he got on them. Maybe it was the confidence he had. Even in class, they gave him googly eyes. Lamonte was always a young gentleman; smiling and pulling out chairs for them. He was a charmer naturally.

Today Mr. Chapman had the whole class taking a math test. Lamonte was good with numbers and he ran through the fifty questions in no time. Once he was finished, he opened his folder and took out some lined paper so he could jot down a few bars.

Catch Pretty Black in somethin' all black/ Bitches know I'm all that/the Vice Lord niggas betta fall back/Before they get their heads cracked.

After laying down a quick two bars, he sat back in his chair and focused on the clock. He couldn't wait until the 3 o'clock bell rang, announcing the end of the school day. He anticipated his pops picking him up and going to get something to eat.

"Yo Black! Wat up wit' it folks?"

When Lamonte turned around, he saw his homeboy, Tae-Tae, from the Wild Hundreds throwing up the universal sign for the G.D's, a pitchfork made with the thumb, middle, and pointing finger.

"Wassup Tae," he said giving the sign back.

Tae-Tae was a young G like Lamonte. At the same age, the youngster sported shoulder length french braids with the flyest gear. The two of them found each other after Tae-Tae relocated to Maywood to live with his grandma.

"Ya boy try'nah get them answers," he told Lamonte.

"Damn nigga. You always try'nah copy a nigga shit. Wha' you need to do is start studyin', wit cho dumb ass."

Tae-Tae shot him a defensive look. "I did study but I still ain't gettin' this fraction shit. You know how my G-Ma be about my grades. C'mon nigga, hook ya' folks up one mo' time."

Although Lamonte didn't like letting his homeboy copy his work, he went along with it. "You know I got'chu. But if you can't count, how you expect to be ballin'?"

Tae-Tae smiled. "I'll make it, you count it. Nigga, that's what I got chu for!"

Lamonte just shook his head because he knew his homeboy was serious.

"Just make sure Mr. Chapman doesn't catch you."

Thirty minutes later the bell rung and Lamonte grabbed his backpack, and headed out of the class. The hall monitor, Mr. Scott, was standing in the hallway directing the flow of traffic. He was trying to keep the kids from running, while also making sure they didn't loiter around the lockers.

"Mr. Gibbson, pull your pants up!"

Lamonte looked back at Mr. Scott, shouldered his backpack, and chunked the pitchfork up with his fingers.

When Lamonte got outside, he shot a glance around the front of the school, looking for his dad's Hummer. Not seeing the truck anywhere, his eyes locked on this young chick named Shannon, who was standing by the bus stop talking to her friends.

"Nigga, what 'chu doing?"

Lamonte turned and saw that it was Tae-Tae. "Oh, whut up folks?" As if automatic, they both shook hands, performing the ritual G.D shake.

"Who you lookin' at?" Tae-Tae asked.

Tossing a head nod towards the bus stop, Lamonte said, "Shannon's fine ass. I'm tellin' you when she gets older I'ma make her mine."

Tae-Tae looked at the tight jeans Shannon wore. "Yea, she's the finest at the whole school. Why you ain't over there try'nah holla?"

Shannon shot him a glance and smiled.

"Oh, she knows what's up. She already told me I gotta wait until she's 16."

The two of them stood silent for a moment, admiring Shannon and her crew.

"Anyway, why you posted up out here?"

Lamonte turned his attention back towards the entrance of the school. "I'm waitin' for my pops."

"He's scoopin' you in the Hummer?"

"Fo sho'."

Tae-Tae nodded. Then seeing his bus coming, he said, "Alright, imma see you tomorrow."

"Alright."

The two friends embraced. Once Tae-Tae was gone, Lamonte pulled his cellphone from his pocket and called his dad.

◄──────────────────────►

The day was prime for getting money, something Black Jack was dead serious about. After he got the call from his lieutenant, Rashawn, he headed over to the Altgeld Garden Projects to pick up the money he had. Being that the G.D's controlled that area, security on their business was tight and efficient.

Just how Black Jack liked it.

Standing out, the 6' 2", jet-black governor eyed the enterprise he oversaw. As he posted up next to his H2, sweat perspired from his head. The sun beaming down from the black top scorched the area, but that wasn't the only thing hot.

The police were rolling up and down the block, but his crew was rolling harder.

They called Chicago "Chi-Raq" because of all the killing going down. Black Jack knew the dangers that came with being G.D, as well as one of their top ranking members. There really wasn't a need to be out there but he liked to show up now and then and didn't mind getting out there with the young runners.

"I told you it was rollin'," Rashawn told him as he walked up with two Gucci bags.

"It's all there?" he asked taking the bags.

"Yea folks and we'll need to re-up before the sun drops."

Black Jack looked at his watch. It was 3 o'clock. He had been out there for hours and knew he could bring another kilo, and it would be done before the sun came back up the next day. "I'll call you in about forty-five minutes."

Rashawn nodded.

Tossing the bags inside the truck, Black Jack was just hopping in when his iPhone rang. He looked at the caller I.D. and saw it was his son.

"Wut up?"

"Where you at pops? School is out and I'm standin' out front waitin' on you."

He started the ignition. The six 15's knocked, pumping pure bass throughout the projects. "Shit, I'm runnin' a few minutes behind, but I'm on my way now."

"Alright."

Black Jack disconnected and maneuvered out of the parking lot. A group of his homeboys chunked up the pitchfork as he wheeled into traffic. Sticking his arm out the window, he gave it up back to them.

For him, this was the boss life.

← ⎯⎯⎯⎯⎯⎯⎯⎯⎯⎯⎯⎯ →

Nobody noticed the black van parked just outside the west wing of the project's parking lot. In it were four members of the notorious gang called Vice Lords. They were an equal rival to the G.D's, aiding in the blood bath the deadly streets of Chicago was experiencing. Rock, the leader of the four, sat in the passenger's side with a pair of binoculars glued to his eyes, watching Black Jack's every move.

Jay sat behind the wheel of the vehicle. The 300 plus man kept his eyes peeled for anyone looking in their direction. A Glock .40 sat in his lap. "These nigga is makin' a killin' out in this bitch!"

In the cargo area of the van sat T-MAC and Shortie, two stone cold killers. Both of them held AK-47 assault rifles.

Rock gathered this crew together because he felt they'd be the most effective in his mission. For days, they cased out the projects, waiting on Black Jack to make his rounds. Rock's intent was simple; to murder the nigga but the projects kept G.D soldiers on deck, so he wanted to wait until he left to put his move down.

"Look at all this traffic," Jay continued about the drug clientele coming and going in the projects. "How much do you think these niggas makin'?"

Rock put the binoculars down. "That nigga Black is sitting on somethin' cool that's for sure. Hopefully he'll head home so we can see what he got in the stash. Look at 'em. He doesn't even know a cloud of death is hovering over him right now."

Everyone watched as Black Jack accepted two bags from one of his homeboys before tossing them in his truck.

Rock racked a round into the .9mm he held. His blood shot eyes were like small red beads underneath his dreadlocks. They shined brightly in the shadows of the dark van. "Fuck that nigga! And the rest of the G.D niggas. I swear, before I blow that niggas head off I'ma make him look me in my eyes. I want to make sure he knows who gave him his one-way ticket to hell." Everybody in the van catapulted into deep thoughts by Rock's statement. His hatred for Black was far beyond some gang shit.

Rock's only son was deceased because of Black and his goons; that twisted Rock's whole world around. He'd long since made up his mind that his life wouldn't mean shit again until he bodied Black Jack's bitch ass. The only reason he didn't jump out gunning at him in that moment

11

was because he wanted the complete ups on him. He didn't want the nigga to have the slightest of help from his boys.

Just like his son didn't have a chance.

When Rock picked up his binoculars again, he saw Black Jack getting into his Hummer.

"It's ShowTime Five," he said to his crew.

Everything was going according to plan so far.

Rock prayed the hit wouldn't occur until they had a chance to locate Black Jack's stash house. Jay started the van and pulled out after the Hummer pulled into traffic.

Rock gripped the .9mm tighter. "Make sure you stay a few cars back," he said to his homeboy.

"Fa sho."

The van grew silent as everyone concentrated on the mission at hand.

⟵————————————⟶

Lamonte was about to give up on his pops when he heard the rumbling of bass vibrating through the air. Everybody out front looked as the Hummer pulling into the lot.

"Heey Pretty Black," a cute girl called him. "I see you."

Shouldering his backpack, he gave her a head nod. "And I see you baby girl."

He was such a player.

When his dad pulled up, he hopped in. "Wut up pops?"

"Nothin'. How was school?"

He shrugged. "It was cool. We did a test on fractions."

"How do you think you did?"

"I aced it. You know me, numbers is my thang. I mean, you can't count money if your math ain't right."

Black Jack laughed. "That's right. I like that."

As he drove, Black Jack kept glancing back in his rearview mirror. He noticed that the same black van he saw two lights ago was still behind him.

"Dad, can we stop at McDonald's?"

He nodded. "Yea, sounds like a good idea."

Pulling into the righthand lane, Black Jack headed towards a McDonald's one block up. But when he saw the black van change as well he passed it up.

"Dad, you just ...."

"I know, hold your horses lil' man. I got to check somethin' real quick."

Maybe the van was a coincidence the second time he saw it. However, when he turned down a residential street, he knew it was following him.

Who the fuck is in that van? he asked himself. It was obviously trying to keep its distance to remain unnoticed. He was a vet, spotting it immediately.

He wasn't freightened being followed because he always stayed strapped. But his son being with him caused him to be alarmed.

Man, who the fuck is that? he wondered. *Is it some jack boys or them fuckin' people?*

Black Jack turned on another street, circling completely back in the direction of the Altgeld Garden Projects. His eyes stayed glued to the rearview, and like he figured, the van stayed on his trail.

"Hold on 'Monte!"

Flooring the truck, Black Jack sped towards the projects. This was the only solution to losing whoever it was. He knew that if they kept following him, once they saw him in that territory, they'd either pull back, or pull him over. That's if it was the police.

Jay accelerated hard trying to keep up with the Hummer. Although he wasn't trying to draw attention, it seemed Black Jack made them out.

"Fuck," Rock cursed out loud. "That nigga headed back to the Gardens. Fuck that, we still gon' light his ass up."

Rock was extra frustrated because killing a kid wasn't something he wanted on his conscience. When he saw Black Jack picking his son up at school, he thought to let it go for another day. But then he thought of his son and how he died that day while playing in the park. He thought about how Black and his boys opened fired on them as they all congregated and barbequed.

"Speed up," he ordered Jay. "We gon' get him before he gets back to the projects."

The metallic *click-clack* sound came from the cargo area as T-Mac and Shortie racked rounds into their assault rifles.

When Jay drew closer to the Hummer, Rock rolled down his window. Leaning out, he took aim at the truck's tires rattling off a barrage of bullets.

Pop... Pop... Pop... Pop... Pop

When Black Jack saw the nigga lean out the window, his heart skipped a beat. "Get down Lamonte!"

The sound of gunfire then the ricochet of bullets on the truck, caused him to swerve. With his foot firmly planted on the gas pedal, Black Jack gripped his .40 Glock just as his back window shattered.

"Who is that!" Lamonte screamed.

"Just stay down," he ordered.

With one hand on the steering wheel and the other on his cannon, he took aim, busting back at the van. He dumped, emptying the clip into the windshield of the vehicle. Smoke was seeping from his barrel as he bought enough time to round another corner.

He took a look at his son, who was crouched low at the truck's floorboard.

Once he came to another street, he accelerated as hard as the truck would go. He raced, trying to separate himself from the van as much as possible. To his surprise, the gunfire from the van came again. This time, a bullet hit home, striking his back tire, and sending him swerving into a hard impact with a parked car.

The impact caused the Hummer's front end to climb the Regal's trunk, sending the truck to sit lopsided. The air bags deployed and the driver's side bag struck Black Jack with so much force that it dazed him for a few seconds. Through his blurry eyes, he saw his son scrambling beneath the seat.

"Run Lamonte! Pretty Black, run," he said in a groggy voice.

"But dad .... I don't wanna leave you."

14

"Run! They're comin'! Just run and knock on one of those doors... Tell'em you need help," he said breathing hard. He looked at his rearview and saw the van screeching to a halt. "Go!"

Lamonte was jolted by his dad's command. Moving with speed, he snatched the door open and hopped out. The angle of the truck caused him to have a step down from the trunk of the Regal. The sound of screeching tires put fire under him as his legs pumped hard into the grassy lawn of the house before him.

As soon as he darted up the driveway, and toward the side of the house, he heard the sound of doors slamming. Lamonte looked back and saw four men with guns approaching his dad's truck. His eyes grew wide as they all raised their weapons.

"Nooooo!" he screamed at the top of his lungs.

Like an ill patterned drum roll, the sound of bullets exploding and striking the armor of the vehicle filled the air; sparks from the truck jumped as fire exploded from the muzzles of each killers' gun. Paralyzed, Lamonte watched in fear as hundreds of bullets riddled the Hummer. In his mind, he knew there was no way his father could ever survive such a horrific incident.

In the end, he was right.

CHAPTER THREE

Black Jack's funeral was crowded with Gangsta Disciples, family members, and associates from all around the world; everyone came to pay their respects to the hood legend. Donminique and Lamonte was escorted to the funeral home by an entourage of G.D's. Seeing his father laying in a box in front of the church changed Lamonte's life forever.

From the whispers and speculations, Lamonte concluded it was some niggas from the Vice Lords who'd made the hit that almost claimed his life as well. Looking on in pain and disbelief, there wasn't anything left in his heart but anger. The only thing on his mind was revenge, retaliation, and pay back. Something inside of him died that day and he never once shed a tear.

He watched as people stood in his father's honor. It seemed everyone had a speech to say about how good 'ole Jack was. Even his Uncle Buck flew in from Cali. Lamonte didn't speak to him much but he knew his uncle was hurt by this.

Most of the gang in attendance was hooping and hollering, and talking about how they were going to do this and that. The looks on their faces was menacing to say the least.

Lamonte searched the church desperately looking for a familiar face among the group. He spotted Rashawn, a good friend of his dad. He'd been around Rashawn on numerous occasions with his dad and considered him an uncle.

"S'up Unk?" Lamonte said firmly, as he walked towards where Rashawn sat with a couple of his runners.

Rashawn noticed Lamonte as he approached with dry eyes. "Hey, how's it goin' Neph?"

"Man, I'm holdin' up but something gotta be done 'bout this real soon," Lamonte said in a hushed tone. His eyes were blank. His young soul was filled with nothing but hatred. In his own way, he was asking to be a part of any retaliation.

Rashawn gave him a look, recognizing Lamonte to be beyond his years.

"I want in Unk," he whispered frantically.

Rashawn's heart went out to the little man standing in front of him asking to be put on. Lamonte was the son of the man he loved and respected. The man who'd brought him in and put him on. He respected the courage of Lamonte to the utmost.

"I'm sorry Pretty Black but I can't disrespect ya pops like that. He never wanted this life for you. I will promise you this though...whoever is responsible fo' this shit gon' get it brought to 'em. Now here's my phone number. Call me if you ever need anything."

Rashawn stood after handing Lamonte his number, then walked down the center aisle of the church to view Black Jack's body.

Lamonte waited five minutes before going to say his final farewells to his pops.

"Hey pops. How's it goin' up there where you at? I miss you so much. Still can't believe you're gone. I know you told me you didn't want me to get involved with the gang, and I promised I'd at least wait until I got a little older. But there's nothin' in life I want mo', than to find the niggas who did this to you, and kill 'em. I promise I won't rest 'til they're resting in piss. I love you, Big Guy."

He took one last look at his father's lifeless body and reluctantly walked away to go find his mom.

After the funeral, Lamonte got into the car with his mother. He said farewell to his young sweet soul and hello to the beast he'd soon become. He sat in the passenger's seat and stared despondently out of the window.

Once they arrived back home, Lamonte went straight to his room and let out all the emotions he had boxed inside for days. Throwing an enraged fit, he kicked things over in his room, yelled, and finally cried. His father was gone and no matter how big of a commotion he caused, he was never coming back.

After throwing a tantrum, until he was too tired to do anything else, he laid down and cried himself to sleep.

CHAPTER FOUR

Six years later...

Six years had passed and Lamonte was causing havoc on the streets of Chicago. Now at seventeen years old, with no fatherly figure to guide him, he was a monster.

He and his mother moved out of the house in Maywood shortly after Black Jack passed due to mortgage issues. Donminique found a job as a secretary on the south side of Chicago and immediately moved them into a rundown two-bedroom apartment. The crime infested neighborhood was run by the Vice Lords and Four Corner Hustlers.

Lamonte felt incomplete in his new surroundings. He was forever getting into trouble with the law, fighting in the streets, using drugs, and not going to school. His heart was completely empty; cold on the inside and hot on the outside. He often wished he had died because the day his father died was the day he stopped giving the fuck about life.

Bam! Bam! Bam! Bam!

Donminique banged on Lamonte's bedroom door.

"Lamonte! Get yo' black ass up and ready for school! I am not playin' either! If I find out you ditched school again, Im'a beat the black off yo' ass! So Im'a be beatin' fo' days!"

It was like things near changed.

"Miss me wit' that Ma'! I'm gettin' up now! And how many times have I asked you not to call me Lamonte! It's Pretty Black or Black!" he blurted out.

"Wha'ever Black! Just make sure that ass gets to school!"

Lamonte wanted to open the door and give his mom a piece of his mind. However, out of respect, he decided against it. Even though she bugged out at times, he knew it was out of love.

19

He turned on his stereo and blasted the new LEP song featuring Gucci Mane, *Handlin My Business,* while getting dressed. Today he went with a pair of tan khakis with a White Sox's jersey and fitted cap. All black low top Air Force 1's complemented his feet.

Lamonte was G.D. born and raised, so in the new neighborhood he kept to himself. He hadn't met any friends to clique up with, so he was always running into trouble. Even though Tae-Tae lived in Maywood, he would come to visit him in the Roseland neighborhood. He'd already been stabbed twice and sliced by a razor on a couple different occasions by rival gang members. After the second incident, he phoned Rashawn and received a pretty, little chrome plated .380 for safety. He learned really quick that it was better to be caught with than without.

He knew the spots his rival gang members hung around and usually he avoided them. But today he was looking to spill some of the Vice Lord's blood in the name of his pops.

Today marked the 6 year anniversary of his death. A date he held near and dear to his heart.

Lamonte was dressed and out the door in thirty minutes. He walked down a garbage littered street smoking the last of a blunt. After tossing the roach, he reached into the pockets of his triple fat goose coat to warm his hands. In ritualistic fashion, he gripped the handle of the .380 and felt a sense of security sweep over him. The sensation of the kush had him ready to bag anyone who looked at him wrong. Every so often, he'd peeked down alleyways looking for any sign of a Vice Lord.

Up to this point, he had not retaliated against the Vice Lords for his father's death. But the urge tore at him daily and today it was even stronger.

Despite the cold air cutting at his new stocky frame, Lamonte's insides were on fire. The act of violence was racing through his system faster than a thorough bred horse at the Kentucky Derby. His whole body trembled with uncontrolled intensity. It wasn't the cold weather, but the fact that he'd made up his mind.

He was about to claim his first body. He was past the point of no return and completely over the edge. The Vice Lords had brutally stripped away his father's life for no reason in which he understood. There was no understanding in his mind, only pay back.

Lamonte strolled down W. 95th street huddled beneath the cloak of the wintery weather. With his hood draped over his head, he held his head down inconspicuously. He noticed a couple of niggas on a corner hustling with the Louis Vuitton logo airbrushed on their hoodies. He knew this was the logo worn by Vice Lords to confirm their affiliation with the gang. As soon as he saw it, his right hand gripped the .380 even tighter.

Revenge, retaliation, and payback rushed through his mind, making him colder than the weather. He started breathing harder as his eyes grew to slits and his pace increased. All he could think of was the day he witnessed his father being gunned down.

By the time the two hustlers noticed Lamonte, he was upon them with his pistol aimed.

"What it is folk?"

In ritual fashion, they turned and banged back. "Vice Lords!"

He squeezed the trigger.

Pop! Pop! Pop! Pop!

The loud sound of the gunfire caused the two Vice Lords to scramble. That's until a bullet struck one in the back, head, and side. Seeing his partner hit, and convulsing on the concrete, the other hustler tried to dart into the traffic. Lamonte was on his heels, sending slugs to chase him down.

Pop! Pop! Pop!

A bullet struck him in the leg and hip causing him to fall in the street. Lamonte skipped into the road and took his place above the dude.

"Please," he begged Lamonte. "Please man, don't kill me."

Blinded by his emotions, Lamonte raised the barrel of the .380 and aimed it at the air brushed logo. "Anybody Can Get it," was all he said before unloading the rest of the clip.

Lamonte was stuck in a trance until an oncoming car screeched to a halt. When he looked up, an old black lady sat in shock behind the wheel of a late model sedan.

"Somebody call the police," someone yelled from a storefront.

Turning on his heels Lamonte took off up 95th, headed in the direction of his school. His adrenaline pumped with the thrill of finally getting some revenge on the Vice Lords. The closer he got to Fenger

21

High school the louder the blares of sirens grew in the distance. He picked up his pace.

When he got to the hallway, he grabbed his book bag out of the locker and tossed it over his shoulder. When the bell sounded, he was in his seat, in first period, with time to spare.

CHAPTER FIVE

Two days after the killing, Lamonte sat in his living room with Tae-Tae. Tasha and Nicole, two girls from his high school, were in the kitchen hooking up something to eat. Tasha was indeed a dime. Lamonte met her and her best friend, Nicole, his freshman year at Fenger almost four years ago. If he had any feelings in his heart, one could assume he was in love with the girl. But since he was heartless, she was just something to pass the time. Tasha was as beautiful as she was smart. Standing at 5'4" with mocha skin, jet-black curly hair that hung past her shoulders and round hazel green eyes; she was the baddest in school. Her body was banging and her ass looked like the rapper Lola Monroe. She got her complexion and good hair from her mother who was Spanish. Her father on the other hand was Black. Every nigga at school was trying to get with Tasha and although Lamonte was feeling her also, he never tried to holler. He fell back and waited for the right opportunity for her to notice him, and that's exactly what happened. He still remembers that day...

$$\longleftarrow\longrightarrow$$

It was lunchtime and the cafeteria was crowded as always when Lamonte made his way inside and took up a place in line. As he reached the food counter, and picked up his tray, he turned and was bumped hard against his side, making him spill his food all over the floor and his shoes. When he turned to face whoever was responsible for not watching where the fuck they were going, he came face to face with three seniors standing behind him laughing. Now, one thing Lamonte wouldn't tolerate was somebody embarrassing him in front of

*the whole school, seniors or not; approaching him in a full cafeteria
like that definitely meant trouble.*

*"S'up! You muthafuckas got a problem wit' walkin'?" he snapped
loud enough for everyone to hear. The tallest of the three eyebrows
were suddenly wrinkled out of confusion and shock.*

*"Lil' nigga wha'?" By this time a crowd began to surround them,
waiting on something to jump off. Now it was one thing Lamonte's dad
taught him before he passed away, and that was how to fight.*

*"You heard me nigga! Did I stu...tter or maybe one of them
bitches wit you heard me!"*

*Lamonte could tell the niggas wasn't bout it by the looks in their
eyes.*

"Lil' nigga, you betta get tha fuck outta my face before I.."

*That was all he got to say before Lamonte grabbed him by his
shirt and punched him in the jaw, making him stumble before losing
his balance. The dude on his left tried to swing on him, but Lamonte
saw that shit coming. He ducked and gave him a quick right to his left
eye, closing it shut.*

*See, most dudes hid behind a gun so they weren't good with their
hands, but Lamonte was a beast. When he connected again with the
boy's temple, he fell unconscious; the third nigga took off running
long before that.*

*Lamonte started to stomp the first dude's skull in, but was
interrupted by someone pulling on his shirt.*

"Get the fuck off me!" he barked, trying to get a good stomp in.

*"That's enough Pretty Black. They got exactly wha' they
deserved. Now you gotta leave before the school police shows up," she
said, grabbing his arm.*

*Lamonte turned to find Tasha standing in a sexy ass tennis skirt
that clung to her thick ass hips. When he didn't respond, she pulled
him by his arm again and said, "Let's go!"*

*Before walking away, Lamonte stomped the first dude in the
stomach and said, "That's fo'fuckin' up my Timbs!"*

*Once they were outside Tasha said, "They were so stupid, I can't
believe you kicked their asses."*

"Yeah, well believe that shit," he nonchalantly shrugged.

They left campus and had been fucking ever since.

⟵——————————————⟶

During this time, his mother was out of town for the weekend so Lamonte took full advantage of the situation by inviting Tae-Tae and the girls over to kick it. Rapping along with the words from Meek Mill's song, *I'm a Boss*, while bobbing his head, Tae-Tae passed him the blunt. Tae-Tae was his best friend for real. They'd been rolling tight with each other since the days they played in the sand box. Even though Tae-Tae was the oldest, Lamonte was far more aggressive.

Maybe it was the look in his eyes, or the way he was feeling himself, bobbing his head and rapping the words of every song that came through the speakers.

Whatever it was, Tae-Tae caught onto it and instantly realized he'd put in some work. Looking at Lamonte with a devilish smile on his face, he said, "S'up nigga? You got that look in your eyes. What's really hood? Let me find out you popped your cherry."

Them Vice Lords ain't ready. I pack that heavy. A nightmare, so I be in their dreams like Freddy.

Lamonte rapped along with Beanie Sigel changing the lyrics around to better suit him.

"Nah nigga, it ain't even like that," he laughed, inhaling the kush smoke before letting it out hard. "You know tha kid gets down fo' his A-B-C-G- Anybody Can Get It!" Grabbing the bottle of Hennessey and taking a swig, he continued. "But off top, I put in some work. Caught a couple of them Vice Lord niggas slippin' and it was rocka-bye-baby."

Tae-Tae pondered his words. "No shit!" He'd already suspected that, but hearing it come from Lamonte's mouth confirmed any doubts. "Nigga I wish I was there. I wouldn't mind rockin' one of them bitches myself."

After taking a few seconds to grasp what Tae-Tae was saying, Lamonte passed the blunt back to him. "Nigga, you know you aren't ready fo' no 1-8-7...Stop it! Wha' you know 'bout that?"

Tae-Tae hit the blunt then blew a thick cloud of smoke in Lamonte's face.

"Nigga, I stay down fo' whatever. Don't get it twisted, Anybody Can Get It!"

Letting out a laugh, Lamonte took another swig of the Hennessey. "I hear that shit, but we'll see."

Passing the blunt back to Lamonte, while grabbing the bottle of Hennessey, Tae-Tae took a swig. "No doubt my nigga, but what's takin' them broads so long? I'm hungrier than a muthafucker!"

"Tasha! Nicole! What's goin' on in there? We out here starving'!" Lamonte yelled into the kitchen.

"We almost done! Give us a couple mo' minutes," Tasha yelled back.

Lamonte sighed, passing the blunt back to Tae-Tae. "Man, after we eat, we gon' shake these broads and hit the block and see what's crackin' with them fools on 155th street. I heard they be holdin'. I hope that we can catch a couple of 'em slippin' and get 'em off some stacks."

"Off top! I can use some extra change."

At first Lamonte was worried he'd made a mistake by telling Tae-Tae about the murders. He suddenly realized he was acting like a complete fool trying to keep Tae-Tae in the closet about it. They'd been tight for far too long and Lamonte trusted him with his life. The lick on 155th was something he'd been plotting for some time. With times being hard on his mom, a burning desire to do something ate at him day and night.

After finishing their grilled cheese sandwiches with the girls, they discussed the possibilities of the lick. It got so good to them that they decided right then and there to go ahead with it immediately.

$$\longleftarrow\!\!\!\longrightarrow$$

Lamonte and Tae-Tae walked up the street and headed towards the pool hall located on the corner of 155th street. They were both armed with baby .380's concealed within their baggy jeans. Moving up the block, Lamonte started up a conversation.

"You know it's goin' to be bout three to four niggas hangin' out in front of the hall right? Dem four corner niggas be makin' a killin' 'round that bitch. I'm just sayin', if it gets ugly, we may have to body a muthafucka." Lamonte shrugged, caressing the cold steel inside his jeans. "I hope you really ready fo' some gangsta shit, 'cause shit you never know."

26

"Fa'sho. Nigga I'm ready!" his partner shot back as they passed an elderly couple who reminded him of his grandparents. "A-B-C-G...Anybody Can Get It!"

"Now that's exactly what I was thinkin'! And if the rumors are true, we should get somethin' cool off them fools when we run up on 'em. If one of 'em start trippin'-A.B.C.G!"

Tae-Tae nodded his head while feeling the .380 on his hip. Looking over, Lamonte saw the scowl on Tae-Tae's face. The expression alone caused a smile to form. This was the exact reason he always fucked with Tae-Tae. He'd proven he was loyal from day one and he never ran his mouth about shit they did together. He always stayed on point about his surroundings, something Lamonte had long since mastered, and it was definitely needed to survive in the streets.

The Chicago streets were covered with snow and small puffs of forest clouds escaped their mouths as they marched ahead like two soldiers on a mission.

As they reached the pool hall, Kanye's *Thru the Wire* could be heard booming through the stereo system inside. A few cats were posted out front, looking as if they were making money.

They immediately approached the hustlers who were wearing light green clothing. A few were sporting skullcaps and mittens and making sells, while others stood around watching. A tall husky nigga with a long ass razor scar across his face gave them a suspicious look as they got closer. By the look on his face, Lamonte could tell he was calling all the shots.

Lamonte gripped the handle of the .380 that was now tucked inside his hoodie pocket as he casually approached Scarface. Beanie Sigel's lyrics were still floating through his head as he walked in step with the music coming from the pool hall.

This would be his second mission but he felt like a vet.

When he got within a few feet of the crowd, he pulled the pistol out and pointed it directly at Scarface. Tae-Tae followed suit, pointing his pistol at the rest of the hustlers.

"Ya'll know wha' it is! Get down or lay down! Dope, money, and bling!" Lamonte said, sneering viciously at Scarface.

This muthafucka may have to get it, he thought noticing no sign of fear in the man's eyes.

Tae-Tae chimed right in. "You muthafuckas heard 'em! Up that shit, fo' I bust this bitch!"

Scarface was obviously stunned. His eyes bounced back and forth between Lamonte and Tae-Tae. Suddenly, he gave his boys a head nod, indicating to come off their valuables.

Although two of the them were strapped, they were caught slipping and knew better to even think about going for their weapons. One by one, Tae-Tae walked up on each of them with his .380 aimed, patting them down. He took a .9mm off one dude and a .45 off another before tucking them both in his waist. Next, he pulled out a brown paper bag and started filling it up with their goods.

When Lamonte was sure Tae-Tae had gotten everything that was of value, he turned back to Scarface with the .380 to his head.

Still nothing.

He had to admit, the nigga was holding up well, never blinking, or looking away at all. After the stare down, and grill face game, Lamonte stepped back and said, "Rocka-bye-baby!" Before firing the pistol.

PLLOWW!

The blast struck Scarface with so much force that his head snapped back, shooting brain matter, and blood to spray the sidewalk and brick wall of the pool hall.

Tae-Tae followed suit with hysterical speed firing at the three remaining men.

Pop! Pop! Pop! Pop! Pop! Pop! Pop! Pop!

Despite them scattering like roaches, he hit everyone, killing two and critically wounding the others.

Moments later, they were running down the street at top speed as if they were competing in a race. They reached an alleyway around the same time police cars passed, speeding in the direction of the pool hall. Coming upon a dumpster, they wiped down the .380's and tossed them inside. With the .45 and .9mm tucked under their shirts and brown paper bag under Lamonte's arm, they ran as fast as they could back to Lamonte's apartment.

CHAPTER SIX

Lamonte and Tae-Tae entered the apartment amped up on adrenaline. Tae-Tae sat down on the sofa and reached into the ashtray to blaze up the last remnants of a blunt they'd put out earlier. Lamonte sat down beside him and dumped the contents of the brown bag onto the coffee table.

Everything went well. That is, with the exception of having to blaze those fools. *But hey, Scarface had it coming.* Lamonte thought, while also wanting to see Tae-Tae in action.

"Boy, you a wild nigga, Black. I didn't even know you were gon' blaze that fool," Tae-Tae said, inhaling the last of the blunt.

"Man, that nigga had it coming. Did you see the look in his eyes? That nigga was definitely trouble. But shit, I was impressed by the way you handled yours. Guess you are 'bout it after all," he playfully replied, giving Tae-Tae some dap.

Upon seeing all the money, dope, and jewels, they instantly began celebrating.

"Yeah, that definitely was a nice one. It gotta be at least 10 stacks in this bitch! Believe that shit," Lamonte said in delight.

It took them about twenty minutes to count and separate all the money, which they concluded was $11,568. They also had eight ounces of crack, three ounces of heroine, some kush and a couple pieces of jewelry.

Still juiced from the lick, they were now ready to have some fun and party the night away.

Looking at the time on his iPhone, Lamonte noticed it was going on 5 o'clock. He decided to call Tasha and tell her and Nicole to come back over

Knock! Knock! Knock! Knock!

Lamonte stood straight up when he heard the knocking at his front door. He figured it was the girls since he wasn't expecting anyone else. His mother rarely had visitors. He grabbed the .45 off the table and walked towards the door. He couldn't allow himself to be caught slipping if there were actually some gun totting lunatic on the other side of the door.

"Who that is!"

"It's us! Let us in already, dang!" Tasha shot back.

"Hold on!"

Lamonte unlocked the door then he turned and placed the .45 back on the coffee table, before sitting back down.

Tasha and Nicole entered the living room where the boys sat, smoking kush, and drinking liquor. Both pistols lay in plainview within reach. Tasha smiled, reaching for the blunt Tae-Tae was holding before squeezing her fat ass next to Lamonte. Meanwhile, Nicole took a seat next to Tae-Tae.

Even though Nicole's butt wasn't as big as Tasha's was, it was still nice in size. Tae-Tae had been trying to get with her for over a year now. Finally, he had a chance since she was no longer seeing that square ass boyfriend of hers.

Tae-Tae gave Lamonte a look that suggested he'd be getting his skeet on tonight.

Lamonte sparked up another blunt while thumbing through the channels with the remote control.

"Ooh! Ooh! Let's watch this!" Tasha pressed, referring to the movie *The Janky Promoters* playing on B.E.T.

"You like this shit, huh?" Lamonte laughed, blowing smoke out of his nostrils.

"Hell yes! Mike Epps a fool!" Tasha smiled mockingly.

"Black, may I use your bathroom?" Nicole asked.

"Gon' head... You know where it's at."

Tae-Tae's eyes were fixed on Nicole's rear as she got up and walked to the bathroom. Her throwback daisy duke shorts showed nothing but ass cheeks protruding from the bottoms.

Man, I can't wait to check that! he thought eagerly.

When Nicole returned, they were all laughing their asses off to a part in the movie. Tasha was hitting the blunt and the sight of her juicy MAC covered lips had Lamonte's dick harder than a muthafucker.

He smiled. "Damn girl. You gon' fuck 'round and make me jealous of that blunt."

"Boy stop it," she coughed. "You so nasty," she replied, passing the blunt to Nicole.

For hours they sat, drank, smoked, and watched movies. Now, high as a kite, Lamonte was ready to fuck. For him, there was nothing left to do at 10:30 at night. If it weren't for entertaining his friends, he would have headed up to his room hours ago.

Tasha looked over at him. "Black, you aight?"

"Yeah, I'm cool. Just higher than a muthafucka, that's all," he said, drawing in a deep breath before letting it out. "Let's go in my room and give these two some privacy."

Lamonte stood, grabbing the .45 off the table like a true gangsta. He had to get Tasha out of the room so Tae-Tae could bust his move. Plus, he wanted to blow his high and fucking seemed to work every time.

Tasha simply smiled. She knew what Lamonte was up to by leaving the two alone. But shit, she was ready to get her freak on as well.

"I'm following you, babe."

Lamonte gave Tae-Tae a look that said handle yo' business before heading down the hallway to his room.

The moment they entered his room, Tasha started peeling off her clothes. She stood in front of him in a cherry-laced thong and matching bra. Lamonte licked his lips as his manhood stood at full attention, ready to be released from its cage. He hurried up out of his clothes, kicking them across the room.

Standing only in his birthday suit, Lamonte grabbed Tasha by her waist and started kissing and caressing her body, while pulling her towards his bed. With the quickness of his fingers, he reached around her back and unclipped her bra.

Tasha's perky titties bounced slightly as she threw her bra to the floor. Grabbing hold of her breasts, he slowly massaged her nipples with his tongue. He could smell the scent of her sweet pussy oozing through her thong. It was intoxicating and driving him crazy.

Sliding off her panties, while kissing her inner thighs, he slid two fingers inside of her in a circular motion while playing with her clitoris.

She twitched, easing her legs apart. "Mmmmmm...mmm," she moaned, trying to guide his face to her crevice.

Lamonte was young, but definitely knew how to please a female. Using his tongue, he probed, up and down, in and out, playing with her G-spot. Her pleasure was his motivation.

Tired of foreplay, he spread her legs and stepped between them. Lifting her back up slightly, Lamonte slid inside with his hard shaft.

"Umph," she grunted, feeling every inch of him inside her. "Ooh! Black."

Lamonte dug in hard, while she moved her hips back and forth. Her moans and groans had him on the verge of cumming.

"Mmmm.Oh! Ahhh!" she moaned loudly, not caring if Tae-Tae or Nicole heard her.

Twenty-minutes later, Lamonte exploded inside of her as she came for the third time. He laid down beside her, panting and sweating. They were both out of breath.

"Damn Black, you beat this pussy up!" She managed to say in between breaths.

He smiled, knowing he'd knocked dust of that pussy.

CHAPTER SEVEN

After spending the weekend away in St. Louis, on a business trip for her boss, Donminique was happy to finally be home. Although she longed for the luxury she had with her husband, she managed to adjust back to the Southside.

As she walked through the door, she immediately noticed that the place reeked of marijuana. *That goddamn boy! I told 'em 'bout smokin' that shit in my house!* she thought.

Lamonte's antics had been causing gray hairs to appear on her head. He was getting too big and out of control.

Whatever happened to the sweet lil boy who used to do what I asked? Oh yeah! He died the same day his father died, she thought, answering her own question.

Before Black Jack passed away, Lamonte was easygoing and well mannered. They'd gotten along perfectly. She never had to ask him to do his chores and hardly ever had to raise her voice. In a serious manner, that is.

But now, she was certain he was headed for destruction. She could sense it in the air around him, and hear it in his voice. Something definitely had to give.

"Black! Get yo' ass out here!" she yelled down the hallway.

No answer...

"Boy, don't make me come back there! I'm extremely tired!" she said impatiently as she threw her purse and keys on the table and kicked off her heels.

Still no answer...

A quick trip to his room confirmed he wasn't home.

"Ooh! Im'a kill that boy!" she mumbled to herself.

Lamonte's room was a complete mess and he'd left a pair of his stinky ass boxers in the middle of the floor. She was suddenly overtaken by the odor of sex in the air. Pulling back his comforter, she noticed a big wet spot on his sheets.

Ewww! I told that boy 'bout bringing them fast ass girls in my house, she said to herself. *And I don't know how many times I warned him about using protection. Lawd knows, this boy gon' send me to an early grave.*

Lamonte was getting out of control and Donminique was getting sick of his shit. She walked into the kitchen and poured herself a glass of orange juice, wondering what she was going to have to do to that boy. Picking up her cell phone, she gave him a call. As she waited for him to pick up, she looked around the kitchen and noticed the trash hadn't been taken out and the dishes hadn't been washed.

Could at least have the little tramp clean up!

Lamonte picked up after the third ring.

"S'up Ma?"

"Don't s'up me! Yo ass supposed to be here at the house. Now where tha hell are you, Black!" Her voice was full of anger.

"Calm down Ma! I'm on my way back from walkin' Tae-Tae to the L-Train. I should be there in 'bout ten minutes."

"Hurry up and get yo ass here! We gotta talk and damnit we gotta do it now! I'm sooo tired of yo shit!"

"Okay Ma, I'll be there in a minute...Bye."

If it ain't one thing it's another, he thought.

When Lamonte made his way through the door, he was surprised to see his mom sitting in a chair, backwards, in the middle of the living room. One hand rested on the back of the chair, while the other clenched a frying pan. She was ready to go upside his head.

His pupils, which were once dilated from the two blunts he'd smoked, while walking back from the L-Train, were now as big as saucers from the sight of the frying pan in her hands.

Donminique smelled the marijuana smoke on his clothes the moment he stepped through the door and instantly wanted to go upside his head with the pan. "Sit yo' ass down, fo' I go upside yo god damn head wit' this pan!" she barked.

She figured if he'd had a glimpse of her violent nature, he definitely wouldn't be in a rush to test her again.

"Boy, wha' I told you 'bout smokin' that shit in my fuckin' house!

"But Ma'-"

"Black...Shut tha fuck up and listen! Not only did you fuck some lil' tramp up in here, yo' stupid ass didn't use any protection either! And don't try to lie; I done already saw that big ass stain on your sheets! And look at this place. You could'a at least made tha tramp clean up! I see you had her cook up!" She gestured with the frying pan pointing it towards the kitchen.

"Ma'...Uh...My bad. Im'a clean it up now," he stuttered.

"So let's get this straight. You smokin' weed in my house now? Wha' tha fuck else you doin' that I asked you not to do?"

"Ma' my bad. Me and Tae-Tae was just chillin'. I promise it won't happen again. Now can you please put down that pan already?"

"Boy I'm tellin' you, you gon' fuck 'round and make me kill you one of these days," she said firmly, keeping her voice down for once.

Dominique's rage didn't go unnoticed by Lamonte. She was ready to show him that the hood was still in her and never had left.

"Boy, if yo' father was still alive you wouldn't be disrespecting me. So don't start now."

She stood and put the chair and pan back where she'd gotten them from. Then she went to the cabinet and get out a glass, and pour herself a shot of Ciroc.

When Donminique went to sleep that night she had the worst feeling a mother could ever have about her child. The streets had definitely played a key role in Lamonte's life. She knew where it could lead. Hopefully it wouldn't, but still it could. There was no way she was ready to bury another loved one. She had to get Lamonte out of Chicago before it was too late.

CHAPTER EIGHT

Thing started looking reasonably good for Lamonte about two months after the pool hall robbery. He was hitting petty licks all over the Southside, some with Tae-Tae, and others by himself. He showed no emotions when dealing with muthafuckas on the streets. His bloodline bred gangsters, hustlas, and criminals and he wasn't going to be any different.

In his mother's eyes, he was still her baby boy, but everyone else saw him as a cold-blooded vicious little nigga. He had to protect himself and his mom. Being the man of the house now, he knew she needed him.

His plan was to stack enough money to move his mother back to Maywood, even if he had to rob every mothafucker in the city to get his stacks up. So far, he managed to save $22,000, which was a far cry from what he needed. He was running wild in the streets, but kept his word with his mother and continued to attend his last year of school.

Sitting in class, Lamonte rubbed his temple with the back of a pencil trying to concentrate on laying down another verse of a rap he was working on. Ms. Williams, his third period teacher, stood in front of the class doing math problems on the chalkboard. Math was his favorite subject, so he already knew the answer to the problem. To keep himself occupied, he dropped a couple of lines into his notebook.

Up against me, you must be fucking mad/I do ya lil' ass like Fabulous, and throw you in a bag/Treat you like a candle, put tha wax off in ya ass/Lil' nigga, you ain't bigger then the rims that's on the mag/And like that four 15's, I'm blasting on niggas like you, who mo' pussy then the playboy mansion/Fuck 'round, I'll turn you to a has been/Wit 1 clip and 1 aim, I can put an ending to ya last name/Tryna fuck wit' me, now that's insane/Matter of fact it's ludicrous, I never heard of 'em/Tell me who this is/Gon' and ask around, I really do this shit/Ain't rappin' fo' tha fan base, I wrap after I fan base, then count 100 stacks, that's what a pack of rubber bands make.

After tossing around a few potential verses, Lamonte closed his notebook and focused on other matters. He was thinking about who would be his next victim to rob. He smiled at just the thought of it. Every time he thought about a lick, it thrilled him. He thought it was easy to sell dope but to pull that burner and demand it took heart.

His daydreaming was interrupted when he heard Ms. Williams calling his name.

"Excuse me, Lamonte. I'm talking to you!"

"Oh! My bad teach. I kind of drifted off fo' a second."

"My name is Ms. Williams, not teach. I'm glad you decided to come back and join us. Now, if you don't mind, I would like you to complete this next problem."

Completing the word problem with ease, he turned and headed back to his seat. Making his way, he noticed Keisha sitting at her desk behind his looking finer than ever. She had on a little yellow Bebe skirt and matching shirt. Her legs were slightly open, giving him a tiny glimpse of her pink panties.

He quickly took his seat before his dick got hard. Leaning back in his chair, he whispered, "Slow down girl you killin' 'em." Repeating a piece of Biggie's verse from Total's, *Can't You See.*

"I can't tell. Tha way you be avoidin' me and all," she said sarcastically.

"Nah, it ain't even like that. I just been busy and shit. But I still got yo' number in my phone and I plan on using it."

Lamonte had to talk really low because if Ms. Williams caught them they'd have to hear her mouth. Not to mention all the hating ass niggas and bitches who would love to run back and tell Tasha some bullshit.

When the bell rang, announcing lunchtime, Lamonte was out the door and waiting for his new homie Tres, who was from his father's old stomping ground—Altgeld Gardens. Tres recently transferred to Fenger High after his mom moved to the Roseland neighborhood. The sudden zone shift caused him to get into beef with students from the Ville, a neighborhood around Fenger High.

Two weeks after transferring to Fenger, Tres was cornered in the hallway by a bunch of Ville niggas. A brawl broke out and Lamonte immediately made himself a part of it in Tres' defense. A true bond between the two was formed ever since that day.

Chicago wasn't called the windy city for nothing. The cold air felt like ice on Lamonte' s skin, as he stepped out of the classroom, allowing the wind to hit his face. He pulled his White Sox's cap down to his eyes in attempt to shield the wind.

Moments later, he was greeted by a freezing Tres, who was wearing only a black hoodie.

"Nigga, I know you cold!" Lamont said shaking.

"Hell yeah!" Tres replied shaking as well. My lil brother took my coat this morning without me knowing and I'ma kill 'em when he gets home from school."

"Damn, like that?" Lamonte laughed. "You ain't got no other coat?"

"Nah, moms ain't got it like that."

"Yeah well, fuck that shit! It's time you got down wit' that get down."

"Shit, I'm down fo' whatever," Tres said, sensing what Lamonte was referring to.

"Well then...A-B-C-G! "

"A-B-C-G? Wha' that mean? Tres asked, clueless.

"It mean, anybody can get it!" Lamonte said, hoping he'd gotten the message.

"Oh...okay. No doubt!"

They continued their conversation on the way to get something to eat off campus.

Making it back to school, just as the bell sounded for the start of fourth period, Lamonte gave Tres dap before going to their separate classes. He was building not only a band but a squad and there was no doubt who the leader was.

A-B-C-G was for real!

CHAPTER NINE

It was 10 o'clock at night when they entered the tenement building, which housed a profitable trap spot. Lamonte was kind of shakey because this was Tres' first lick.

Although Tres promised not to ever mention anything they did with anybody, Lamonte was was still a little apprehensive. Tae-Tae promised if he got wind of Tres breaking that promise he'd be the first to give him a permanent dirt nap.

Tonight's drug spot was operated by some Latin Kings who were making a killing even on a bad day. If what they had planned went off successfully, they'd be up like never before. Just the thought of it alone made Lamonte that much more eager to put it down.

Entering the building, noise could be heard coming from the upper level. Lamonte and his crew quickly pulled and positioned their guns as they crept up the stairs. The odor of piss could be smelled throughout the stairway.

Reaching the second floor, which housed the dope spot, Lamonte peeked around the corner and saw two Latino men sitting on chairs in front of the spot; one had a bottle of corona to his lips, while the other held a Bic lighter in his hand and fired up a joint. Loud laughter could be heard after one of the men said something in spanish.

Lamonte turned to Tae-Tae and Tres, then gave them a head nod. It was time to move while they had the upper hand.

Lamonte quickly came around the corner of the dimly lit hallway with his glock .45 aimed and ready. Tae-Tae came up the rear with a Mac-11 followed by the .9mm Tres was holding.

"Don't fuckin' move," Lamonte whispered with pure venom in his voice. "Open your mouth and you a dead man."

The man, who had the corona to his mouth, spilled beer all down his shirt. His eyes were wide and showed signs of fear as he stared at them. The joint that was on his friend's lip hung loosely as he stared down the barrels of their guns.

Smiling as he looked down at the Latinos, Lamonte stepped up to the one who was drinking the corona and stuck the barrel of the .45 down his throat.

"Mu'fucka, you understand english now? I said how many—"

The man tried to open his mouth to respond, but the barrel eased its way deeper down his throat, causing him to gag. With the .45 pressed to his tonsils he gestured with his hands, holding up three fingers.

Lamonte pulled the gun out of his mouth just as he started coughing up beer. "Okay, knock on that door and tell 'em you gotta use the bathroom. If you try anything slick, you'll be the first to get it," he said, pointing the gun back to his lips. The man flinched into full attention.

After patting down each man, Lamonte nodded over to Corona and told him, "Let's go."

They positioned themselves on each side of the door, away from the peephole as Corona began to knock. When someone came to the door, Corona said, "BAIJO," which means bathroom in Spanish. That was one of the things Lamonte liked most about Tasha being half-Spanish; she always kept him hip to understanding certain words.

As the door opened, they pushed both Latinos inside while shouting.

"Everybody on the mu'fuckin' floor!"

Lamonte slapped the Mexican in the face with his gun. The blow was so hard that the man's head collided against the wall. As he cringed in agony, Tae-Tae and Tres went about searching the apartment.

Just as Lamonte's eyes took in the interior of the apartment, machine gunfire exploded from the backroom.

Tac!Tac!Tac!Tac!Tac!Tac!Tac!Tac!Tac!

Without looking to see what was going on, Lamonte scrambled for cover. With his .45 still aimed at the three Mexicans lying on the floor, he opened fire, looking to lessen the opposition.

Boom! Boom! Boom! Boom! Boom!

Tae-Tae flinched when the machine gun started spitting out bullets. He stayed low, while firing away at the backroom.

40

Tat!Tat!Tat!Tat!Tat!Tat!Tat!

The three men on the floor gave a torrent of grunts, moans, and terror-stricken screams of pain, each suffering from their issue of gunshot wounds.

Lamonte pumped one more bullet in each of their heads.

Boom!Boom!Boom!

Lamonte estimated that at least two Mexicans were somewhere in the apartment and time was of the essence. Figuring his clip was getting low, he quickly reloaded the .45 with lightning speed.

Tac!Tac!Tac!Tac!Tac!Tac!

The sound of gunfire came from the backroom.

By the time Tres heard the movement and sprang around, it was too late. A wave of bullets battered his chest and a nearby wall, sweeping him clean off his feet.

Clutching his wound, he shouted. "Help! Help! I'm hit!"

Glancing over to his right, Tae-Tae saw that Tres was down and holding his chest. Simultaneously, he heard him let out a moan stricken with pain. Just as he was about to run to Tres' side, out of his peripheral vision, he noticed movement. He aimed his Mac-11, but wasn't quick enough.

Tac!Tac!Tac!Tac!Tac!Tac!

Two bullets ripped through Tres' head, spraying brain matter, bone fragment, and blood all over the already bullet riddled wall.

Tae-Tae saw the shooter trying to creep back into his hiding spot. With the shooter positioned perfectly behind some dry wall, Tae-Tae unleashed a barrage of Mac-11 bullets.

Boom! Boom! Boom! Boom! Boom!

Uggg, was the sound the culprit made as he crumbled to his death.

Meanwhile, Lamonte fired the .45 at the back room while crouching behind a sofa.

Fuck, he mumbled to himself. He had to get that dude in the back room. His mind was doing somersaults. He knew Tres was dead and they still hadn't searched the apartment for money and drugs.

Tac!Tac!Tac!Tac!Tac!Tac!

The shooter in the backroom opened fire again just as Lamonte appeared from behind the sofa. When he heard the shooter's gun click, he knew it was his best time to rush the room before he reloaded. In a bold and daring move, Lamonte jumped up and ran towards the room firing off shots.

Boom! Boom! Boom! Boom!

Flames were spitting from his gun as he ran with remarkable speed.

In blind rays, he suddenly felt a huge blow to his left shoulder, which slowed him down for a second. Before the shooter could squeeze off another burst of bullets, Lamonte was on top of him.

Boom! Boom!

The two shots, which he aimed at his dome, found its mark successfully.

Looking at all the blood running down his hoodie, Lamonte felt a searing burning sensation from the bullet's impact. Grabbing his shoulder, he shouted to Tae-Tae. "I got 'em! Let's find the money and work!" He knew it was only a matter of time before someone called the police.

Tae-Tae ran into the kitchen and started running through the cabinets. It didn't take long for him to locate where the dope was stashed. Pulling out a tote bag, he immediately began filling it up.

Searching the backroom, Lamonte came across a duffle bag filled with money. Each bundle was rubber band wrapped in thick stacks.

Mu'fucka wasn't tryna let us get to this, he thought, looking at all the big faces.

The sensation of seeing all that money caused Lamonte to forget about the pain in his shoulder. The sounds of sirens shook him out of his deep thoughts.

"Got it! Let's roll!" he yelled to Tae-Tae as he ran out of the back with the duffel bag wrapped around his good shoulder.

The sirens grew louder as they ran out of the building disappearing into the night.

CHAPTER TEN

D onminique arrived at the hospital and from the look on her face, you could tell she was distraught. Her son, her baby, the last soul in the world to love her unconditionally was currently undergoing surgery

Lamonte was shot and that was all the information she had, not how many times he'd been shot, or whereabout. She had the slightest idea how he ended up like this.

The waiting room was crowded with people eagerly awaiting doctors. Donminique took a seat on an empty chair in the far corner. The look on her face clearly reflected the stress she was experiencing. An hour earlier she was awakened by her cell phone ringing, right in the middle of a romantic dream about her deceased husband. To her surprise, it was Tae-Tae calling to inform her that Lamonte had been shot and was in route to the hospital by the way of an ambulance. She didn't even want to think about what in the world Lamonte had gotten involved with to get himself shot. She was just thankful he'd made it to the hospital alive. Lord knows if her son died, she'd be ready to end her own life.

She was barely holding it together as it was. People in the waiting room kept eyeing her as if any second she'd pass out. All the crying and screaming she could handle was done earlier on her way there. Now, she simply waited to question doctors and nurses on the welfare of her son.

Donminique rose to her feet as a doctor approached. He was a tall black man in his late fifties; clean shaven with salt and pepper hair, who reminded her of Bill Cosby. He walked over with a pen and clipboard in his hand.

"Anyone here for Lamonte Gibbson?" the doctor asked.

"Yes! Yes! That's my son. How's he doing? When can I see him?" Donminique asked as she immediately rushed over towards him.

"Well Ms. Gibbson. Your son is a very strong young man. The bullet entered his upper left shoulder and traveled downward towards his abdomen. But I'm pleased to say we've recovered all the fragments from the bullet and he should recover perfectly. Let me show you to his room."

Escorting Donminique beyond the ICU doors he'd just came out from, the doctor stopped in front of a room number 3C.

"Now Ms. Gibbson, before you go inside, I want you to know that in cases like this, it's our procedure to notify the police." There was a short pause. "And it seems the police are very interested in your son here. They feel he may have been involved in a robbery and homicides. They're on their way now to question him." There was another short pause as the doctor looked around before continuing. "Let's just say this is a heads up from me to you."

"Thank you," Donminique exclaimed before the doctor walked off.

When she entered the room, the smell of medicine and antiseptics was thick in the air. She noticed Lamonte was hooked up to all kind of tubes and monitors. Her heart went out to her son who laid in front of her looking so innocent, yet severely battered. This was the reason she hated hospitals so much. She felt this was a place of great pain and suffering; a place where people came to die.

Hearing his mother enter the room, Lamonte turned and opened his eyes. The moment he saw her face he knew she'd been worried to death.

"Hey baby, glad to see you're okay. You had me worried for a second there. Just 'bout drove me to an early grave, boy."

"My bad Ma', it ain't nothin' but a flesh wound." He smiled.

"Flesh wound my ass. I could've lost you boy. So how the hell this happen anyway?"

"All I remember is walkin' up the street wit Tae-Tae when a car pulled up shootin'."

Donminique stared him straight in his eyes.

"Now boy, I hope that's what really happened because the police think differently. In fact, they think you had somethin' to do with a robbery, and some homicides. They're on the way here now to talk to you. So I hope you got your story straight."

44

Lamonte's eyes squinted as he pondered her words. He wasn't so much worried about the police. All he had to do was stick to his story, but Tres' body was left in that apartment along with the Mexicans, and that did bother him. It wouldn't be hard for them to discover the two hung together at school.

Fuck! Why he had to get smoked?

When Tres' predicament came to mind, Lamonte focused his attention to Tres' mother, and how she would take the news of his death.

Stick to tha story...stick to tha story.

After repeatedly telling himself to stick to the story because the cops didn't have any witnesses who could identify him and place him at the crime scenes, he relaxed. The duffel bag full of money came to mind causing a smile to creep to his face. He figured it had to be at last 50 to 80 stacks inside.

Off top! It's definitely on! he thought.

"Black! Black! Boy did you hear anything I just said!"

Lamonte snapped out of his deep thought and regained his composure. "Yeah Ma', that's how it happened. I ain't worried bout no police. They probably just wanna see if I know who shot me or not. See if I'll snitch and shit... Oops! I mean stuff."

Donminique just shook her head. She knew there was more to it than he was saying. She was no fool.

Twenty minutes later, two detectives entered Lamonte's room. Lamonte instantly became nervous as the thought of the tv show *First 48* came to mind.

Stick to tha story... stick to tha story...

The first to enter was a tall black detective with a bald, clean-shaven head with a muscular build; he kind of resembled the actor Idris Elba. He didn't wear a suit or tie. Instead, he dressed like an ordinary man on the streets of Chicago, in his black Sean John jeans. He had a black leather puff coat over a black Sean John sweatshirt. A fresh pair of black Timbs was on his feet. The only way one could tell he was an officer was from the gold badge hanging from a chain around his neck.

The second detective was light skinned and resembled the rapper Drake. He was slim with a caesar bald fade and stood a couple inches beneath his partner. Like the first detective, he too was dressed in street attire; leather coat, jeans, and Timbs.

45

These clowns must think they're on some New York Undercover shit.

"Mrs. Gibbson, can you please excuse us for a moment? We have a couple of questions we'd like to ask your son," the dark skinned detective asked, pulling up a chair.

"No! My son is still a minor. So whatever you have to speak with him about, you can discuss in front of me!" she said with disgust.

"I'm sorry if my partner appears to be rude. I'm Detective Moore and this is my partner, Detective Bailey. We're investigating a robbery gone bad that left multiple people dead and we both haven't had much rest," the Drake looking officer said.

Donminique didn't respond. She just gave him a cold stare.

Detective Bailey said firmly, "So Mr. Gibbson, I understand you were shot somewhere on 95th. Street, while walking with a friend. Is that correct?"

"Yeah, that's right. We were on our way to the L-Train when a car pulled up and opened fire. I got hit once in the left shoulder and that's all I remember. I didn't see the shooter or make of the vehicle."

Detective Bailey just sat there staring into Lamonte's eyes, as if he was looking into his soul. The demeanor on his face said bullshit as he retorted, "Does this *friend* of yours have a name?"

Lamonte knew that question was coming and decided not to involve Tae-Tae. Not only was the money, dope, and pistols stashed at his house, it was the code of the streets. He'd never mention a name. If the detective wanted to know his name, it damn sure wouldn't be through him.

"Nah, he ain't got no name. Im'a leave 'em outta this. He kinda don't like police, if you know wha' I'm sayin'?" After saying this, he gave them his most innocent face.

The detectives looked at each other then over towards Donminique to see if she'd persuade him into giving up that information. But they received nothing from her.

"But Mr. Gibbson, you're the victim here I thought. Surely you wouldn't have anything to hide, would you?"

Lamonte knew it was time to take a few steps back. He'd already drawn suspicion to himself. With that in mind, he decided he was done talking. If they had any evidence they wouldn't be there to talk, they'd be there to arrest him.

He cleared his throat. "I'm sorry I can't help you detectives on your case. I'm tired and would like to get some rest. So if you don't mind."

"I'm sorry, but we have one more question for you," said Det. Moore, flipping through his notepad. "Do you know a Mr. Tresvon Coleman?"

The look on Lamonte's face must have had guilty written all over it because the detective smirked.

"That name doesn't ring a bell but it could be somebody from my school. I do know somebody named Tres who goes to my school. But I'on know if Tresvon is his first name or Coleman's his last name. Why?"

Detective Bailey chimed in when he saw the look on Lamonte's face.

"I do believe he goes by the name Tres, and yes he was a student at Fenger High. And oh! He was killed last night along with five other men-all Latinos in what looks like a robbery gone bad."

Now it was Detective Moore's turn to clear his throat for a dramatic emphasis and said, "You know we found blood at the scene. And there's this little thing called DNA, just like fingerprints, no two are alike."

Lamonte felt pain erupt through his system as he was caught off guard by the news of his blood possibly being left at the scene.

Fuck! he cursed himself for getting shot.

Leaning forward in his chair, Detective Bailey whispered, "You know you done fucked up don't cha? When the tests come back with your blood at the scene, where six bodies were discovered murdered, including someone who went to the same school as you, it's so over for you."

"Excuse me detectives, but I think that's enough. My son already told ya'll how he got shot and as far as this Tresvon victim goes, whether my son knew him or not, doesn't mean he knew about his whereabouts last night. If you found blood at the scene like you claim, then I suggest you wait until them test come back before you start accusing my son. Now, unless ya'll have some kind of warrant for his arrest, Im'a have to ask ya'll to leave now…Thank you." Donminique was now infuriated.

"Okay, have it your way. But we will be back with that warrant. That I can bet cha!" Detective Bailey blurted out before standing up.

47

CHAPTER ELEVEN

It had been three days since Lamonte was shot. Going to school wasn't priority so Donminique called in to the school and informed them that he wouldn't be returning to finish the last month of the school year.

As for Lamonte, he was under a lot of pressure. He expected the detectives to come any day kicking down their front door with a warrant for his arrest. To make matters worse, his mother was now aware of his involvements in the robbery and homicides.

The same night Lamonte was released from the hospital, she entered his room at 1:30 a.m. in the morning.

"Black, Black. Wake up baby. We gotta talk."

Lamonte felt a soft yet firm touch shaking him. "S'up wit' it Ma'?"

"You ready to tell me what really went on the other night? And don't bullshit me; I know you had somethin' to do with them murders." As she spoke, she balanced a firm, but loving demeanor.

Lamonte heard her clearly, but in a sense he didn't. He knew he couldn't pull a fast one on her, she was just too slick. She probably suspected him the moment he wouldn't give the detectives Tae-Tae's name. He loved his mother more than anything in the world and feared she'd love him less from what he was about to tell her.

"Ma', I fucked up. I mean, messed up. Everythin' got outta control and I got shot while Tres got killed. I'll probably be goin' away fo' tha rest of my life. I'm so sorry mom. I'on know wha' to do." This was the first time since his father passed he was emotional.

"Who else was with you? Tae-Tae?" she asked leaning over him and placing a hand on top of his.

It's like he had blacked out and went back to the night of the shooting.

"Anyone else? Does anybody know about this besides you, me, and Tae-Tae?" she pressed patiently.

"Nah, nobody else," he said finally. "I'm scared to lose you, Ma. I only wanted to make things better. Get it back like it used to be when pops was here."

"Where's the murder weapons and clothes you wore that morning? We gotta get rid of anything that connects ya'll to the murder scene." Donminique felt her son but she knew she needed to help him out of this. Lamonte was amazed by his mother.

Damn! Where did all of this come from?

He knew his dad used to talk about how down his mother was but this was something entirely new to him. Here he was thinking she's about to flip out on him. Instead, here she was helping him and worried about forensics and shit.

"Uh, we put the clothes in a dumpster, and Tae-Tae got the guns and money from the robbery."

"Good Black. Now first thing you gotta do is get in touch with Tae-Tae and get rid of them guns. Next, you gotta make sure he sticks to the same story as you just in case those detectives go snooping around. Finally, you goin' get yo share of that money and I'm goin' to get you the hell outta Chicago before them tests come back."

"Okay Ma," he said in muffled words. He began to feel some security knowing she had his back.

"No matter what, we're going to get through this together. You ain't no cookie, so you don't crumble. Stay strong and remember no one is untouchable. In this world, and this game, anybody can get it."

Her words shook him back to reality. His mother was a G for real.

She stood from his bed and started for the door before turning to look him over once more. "Boy, you know that I love you right? And will do anything in my power to make sure you're safe?"

Lamonte let out a half smile before Donminique opened the door. "Yeah I know. And love you too, Ma."

←――――――――――――――――→

The moment Lamonte stepped out from the building, the cold air slammed across his face. He rubbed his cold arms, trying to warm up a little. He was on his way to the L-Train subway to meet up with Tae-Tae and get his half of the take. He still hadn't discussed the guns, detectives, or conversation he had with his mom to his friend. He was waiting to see him face to face to tell him everything. Lamonte couldn't wait to see the scowl on Tae-Tae's face when he told him about the detectives. He wanted to see if Tae-Tae would show any signs of weakness.

He spotted Tae-Tae the moment he stepped from the train. Tae-Tae was sporting a Walter Payton Chicago Bears throwback jersey, with a navy blue hoodie underneath, which was pulled over his Chicago Bears skully. Blue Enyce jeans and a fresh pair of navy blue Timbs finished off his attire. Noticing Lamonte step from the train, Tae-Tae strolled over towards him.

"S'up wit' my nigga? Wha' it be like? How's tha shoulder?" Tae-Tae said, playfully punching at Lamonte's wounded shoulder.

"You know, some mo' of it. Same shit, different day. But the shoulder is straight. That shit was nothing."

"Oh word! Could've fooled me. Tha way you were hollerin' and screaming," Tae-Tae laughed.

Lamonte paused for a moment as he glared at Tae-Tae in shock. Staring at him with tight menacing eyes he said, "Fuck you folks! That shit did hurt. Nigga, when you finally get hit up, we gon' see who's laughin' then."

"Ah nigga, I was just kiddin'. You ain't gotta be starin' a nigga down like that either. You know I'm yo boy."

"Yeah, okay. Let me find out you on some funny shit." Lamonte playfully replied as they walked off down the street.

"So wha' happened at tha hospital? Did them people come see you or wha'?" Tae-Tae asked, keeping his pace.

"Hell yeah, the people showed up with a gang of questions and shit. That's one of the things I needed to talk with you about. They were actin' like they knew I was involved with them murders. Said they had some blood samples and shit and was just waitin' on some test to come back. Them muthafuckas even know Tres went to my school. Shit, by now, I'm sure they know the two of us hung tight."

As they walked and talked, the Chicago commuters whizzed by oblivious to the talk of murder.

"Damn! Folks, I forgot all 'bout the possibility of you leavin' yo' DNA in that bitch after getting' shot. So wha' now?" Tae-Tae asked.

"Shid, I ain't bout to wait fo' them tests to come back. I talked to my mom 'bout everythin'. And befo' you say anythin', she was real gansta 'bout the situation. She told me to make sure we got rid of them burners and any clothing that could connect us to that scene. After that, she got in touch with some of my father's relatives out west. It looks like I'm goin' to Cali fo' a while."

"Wha'? Nigga you leavin'!" Disappointment etched on Tae-Tae's face.

"I gotta. They don't know nothing 'bout you. And as far as I'm concerned, it's gon' stay that way. Anyways, you already know when I get shit poppin' out west, Im'a send fo' you."

Tae-Tae gave Lamonte dap and smiled a little harder than usual with the thought of going to California. He'd watched so many videos on tv about California, its good weather, and bad bitches.

"Well," he said turning towards Lamonte, "I guess you gotta do, wha' you gotta do. Just don't fo'get 'bout a nigga when you get shit crackin' out there."

"No doubt," Lamonte said, confirming his intentions.

"Look folks. There goes Shannon's fine ass," Tae-Tae gestured with his hands pointed to a white Mustang GT pulling up to a store across the street.

Lamonte looked in the direction Tae-Tae was pointing and sure enough, Shannon was getting out of a white Mustang GT on matching 22 inch rims. She looked finer than ever, rocking a pair of Guess skinny jeans and white open toe heels, despite it being freezing outside. The snow-white bubble coat complemented her thick ass hips.

"Damn! I ain't seen shawty in years. She's still badder than a mu'fucka and even thicker," Lamonte said focusing his concentration on Shannon. "I see she's riding clean. That's her shit or her niggas?"

"I think that's her shit. Her peoples got that money."

"So who's she fuckin' wit' now days?"

"I hear she fuckin' wit' some square-ass ball player at her school. But I'on know."

"Like that, huh? Well then, let me go see s'up wit' her then. I'll be right back."

"Off top!" Tae-Tae said, as he leaned up against a building, putting one foot behind him for support.

Lamonte walked over towards the store wondering how he was going to approach her. As usual, he walked with the confidence of a boss playa.

Once inside, he stepped straight to her. "S'up wit' Ms. Thang?"

Shannon turned to see who was behind her and immediately flashed him her brightest smile.

"Hey Pretty Black. I ain't seen you in years. How's it goin'? Last I heard, you moved to the south side."

"Yeah, we did move after my dad got killed. But I'm good though shawty. I was just walkin' up the street wit' Tae-Tae when he pointed you out. So I had to come say s'up."

Shannon started laughing. "I see you two are still rollin' tighter than my jeans. But I'm glad you came over to say hi. I've always wondered if I'd see you again."

"Is that right? Well look, I'm 'bout to move to Cali fo' a while on some music shit, but I'd like to keep in touch. You got a number or somethin' where I can call you?"

"Yes," she said. "Let me put my number in your cell phone."

After getting Shannon's number and promising he'd keep in touch, Lamonte strolled back over to where Tae-Tae was waiting. Then they continued up the street to Tae-Tae's house.

"S'up nigga, you got tha number or wha'?" Tae-Tae asked, speaking through a balled fist as he tried to warm up his hands.

"No doubt." Lamonte laughed turning to face him. "Fo' real doe. Nigga you that cold?"

"Nigga, I'm freezing."

Back at Tae-Tae's house, it took them 30 minutes to separate the money and dope. When they were finished they had close to $48,000 a piece. Plus three kilos of pure fish scale cocaine.

"Damn nigga! We came off phat!"

"No doubt. I knew you'd like it," Tae-Tae agreed

"Shid...wit' this type of money, a nigga gon' get it poppin' fo' real out in Cali."

"Off-fuckin'-top! Everything's big from here on out. No mo' petty shit."

Lamonte became on the defensive. "Aw...Nigga. That petty shit put money in yo' pockets! Didn't it? All of a sudden you big Willie! Nigga, I gets mine however...A-B-C-G anybody can get it."

"There you go wit' that bullshit. All I'm sayin is we on like shit, that's all. And wit' you movin' to Cali and all, a nigga ain't 'bout to be hittin' anymore licks. Fuck that! I'm 'bout to flip this work."

"Nigga, wha' you know 'bout pushin' some work?"

"I know my cousin Derrion got a spot over on tha westside. I'm thinkin' 'bout getting in touch wit' 'em and seeing how much he's paying fo' a brick."

"That's wassup! Just make sure you set my issue to tha side."

"C'mon folks, you already know doe," Tae-Tae assured him.

After chopping it up with Tae-Tae a little while longer, and making sure he understood the seriousness of getting rid of the guns, Lamonte was back on the train headed home $48,000 richer. In the morning, he'd be on a plane headed for the Sunshine State of California.

Something that intrigued him like a motherfucker.

CHAPTER TWELVE

The next day, Donminique and Lamonte stood outside of the airport embracing each other. They'd spent most of the night talking about the good old days. Donminique knew they would always be close at heart, but due to her son's unfortunate circumstances, he had to move on. Chicago was a big city and soon enough his shit would catch up to him. He'd done far too much dirt to too many niggas. If it weren't Jonny Law taking him down, surely it'd be someone looking to retaliate for something he'd either done or been a part of.

Before grabbing his bags to board the plane, he kissed his mother on the cheek and said, "I love you Ma. Don't you go worrin' 'bout me. Im'a be good."

"I love you too, baby," she said almost in tears. "Have a safe trip. Call me when you land. You got yo' Uncle's number locked in your phone, right?"

He nodded. "Yeah."

"Okay, now go before you miss yo' plane."

Lamonte knew his mother was worried about him making it out west. But shit, like Young Jeezy, he was a soul survivor. After hiding $10,000 in her top drawer, he was headed out west with close to $60,000 in his pocket.

After the long plane ride to Oakland's International Airport, Lamonte immediately called his mom to tell her he made it safely. Next, he called his Uncle Buck, while walking to the baggage claim to retrieve his luggage.

Lamonte met Buck outside in the pickup area. Buck wasn't how he imagined him to be. He was tall, early thirties looking, with long dread locks hanging down his back, and he was as black as the night.

He pulled up in a candy apple red Chevy van on matching 26 inch floaters. Lamonte hopped in, setting his bags in the back. "Wha' it dew young nigga?" Buck said, exposing twelve platinum fronts that sat with crushed diamonds.

"S'up wit' it Unk?"

"Nah, fuck that shit, call me Buck. That Unk shit makes me feel old."

"Fasho!" Lamonte smirked, liking his uncle's style already. He also noticed that his eyes were red as the paint on his van.

On the way to his house, Buck brought Lamonte up to speed on how to survive in East Oakland.

←—————————————————————→

The smell of good weed clouded the living room of Buck's house. His girlfriend, Desiree, was sitting on a sofa dumping ashes into an ashtray, while watching Maury on T.V., when they walked through the door.

"Desiree, this is my nephew Black. Black this Desiree," Buck said, smacking Desiree on her thick thighs.

Desiree looked up at Lamonte with low red eyes. "Hey Black, nice to meet you. Ya'll wanna hit this blunt?"

Buck grabbed the blunt and said, "That's yo' room at the end of the hallway to yo' left."

"So that's the famous Black Jack's son, huh?" Desiree asked, after Lamonte headed down the hall.

"Mmm Hmm," Buck nodded, exhaling the purple smoke.

Buck's house was located on Walnut Street, right off of 98th Avenue. From the outside, it looked like all the other houses on the street. It was with dents and in dire need of a makeover.

But the inside was totally laid out. The interior was covered in a plush light brown carpet that felt like it cost a grip. The leather sofa had a matching love seat with a two tone brown and cream blend. A large brown marble coffee table sat in front of the sofa, while a matching bar

55

took up the far wall. A sixty-inch plasma screen television was mounted above the fireplace, Scarface posters hung throughout the house along with pictures of hood legends like Felix Mitchell, Little D, Tupac, and the Flower Boys.

Buck was definitely doing his thing.

Lamonte walked down the hallway to his new bedroom. When he swung the door open, for a brief moment, he was surprised at how well put together the room was. A queen size bed sat in the middle next to a desk that held a top of the line computer and printer. A large dresser took up one side of the wall with a forty-two inch flat screen sitting on top of it.

I can definitely get used to this, he thought, sitting his bags down on the bed.

Next, he went to the closet. It was huge and he thought of all the clothes and boxes of shoes he'd store inside. He also entertained the thought of installing a small safe.

"You straight, lil' nigga?" Buck peeked in, puffing on a blunt. He took a drag and blew the smoke out inside the room.

"Off top," Lamonte responded, opening his luggage and pulling out clothes. "I'm just gettin' settled, that's all."

"Cool. When you finished gettin' situated, meet me outside. I gotta run a few errands, so I might as well show you around while I'm at it."

"A'ight Buck...and thanks again."

"Aw nigga, it's nothin'. We family. If I'm straight, you straight."

"Fo' sho'. Give me a couple of minutes and I'll be out there."

After Buck left out of the doorway, Lamonte's face lit up. He had a good feeling about Buck and East Oakland.

Coming out of the house, Lamonte was smiling from ear to ear. Buck looked him over, wondering what he was thinking. This was the first time Buck had seen Lamonte since the funeral, yet still he felt a connection to him.

"What's all the cheesin' 'bout, Lil' nigga?" Buck asked.

"Nothin'," Lamonte started. "I just think things are goin' to work out fo' me here."

"No doubt. Now c'mon so I can show you tha hood."

CHAPTER THIRTEEN

Lamonte felt like an outsider as Buck took him on a tour around East Oakland. He sat on the passenger's side of Buck's Candy-Green '96 Buick Park Avenue, staring out at International Blvd. From what Buck told him, the popular strip was changing by the minute. There was still hustling and prostitution going on up and down the avenue but not how it used to be back in the day when International Blvd was known as E. 14th. The Feds were picking up all the cases in the town, making it almost impossible for a nigga to make some money. Buck laid out all the details and he just soaked up game.

Passing a few corner stores, Buck pointed out the new era pimps. Tennis Shoes Pimps was what the news labeled them; young men who wore tennis shoes and jeans, instead of reptile-skinned shoes and cashmere coats. But they were still familiar with the trade of sending a bitch to get that dough.

Lamonte noticed that, like in Chicago, the black folks were still in control of the hustle game.

"This right here is where The Dragons, a local motorcycle club, throw parties every Friday," Buck said before passing Lamonte a blunt.

"Over there's where they be havin' one of tha many side shows every weekend."

"Buck," Lamonte started. "What's a side show?"

"Oh, it's just a place where a lot of people gather to drink, smoke and show off their rides."

"Okay, I see."

Buck took Lamonte to JJ's, a fish and chips joint on International Blvd, for something to eat. It had been so long since Lamonte had some good 'ole soul food, and JJ's was the spot.

Once inside, Lamonte piled his plate with chicken wings, prawns, french fries, a side of potato salad, and macaroni & cheese. After finishing his meal, he had a piece of chocolate cake for dessert.

By the time they left JJ's, Lamonte felt like he was going to explode. "Man Buck. That was off the hook!"

"Now I know, they ain't got no prawns like that in tha Chi," Buck said playfully.

"They got prawns, but not like those. Them thangs were bangin'!"

"Next time I'm a take you to this joint called The Southern Café. Now they got some good food."

Their conversation was interrupted by an exchange of cars swerving in and out of the lanes with their doors open. Lamonte looked on as people stood on top of the hoods dancing. The driver in the second car jumped out shaking his dread locks, while the car kept rolling. Loud music could be heard from the speakers that was mounted to the grills of each car.

"What's that all 'bout?" he asked dumbfounded.

"Man, that ain't 'bout shit. Just some young niggas getting hyphy and goin' dumb. That's wha' they do out here in tha Bay. You see them cars?"

"Yeah."

"They're called Scrappers. That's wha' this is a Scrapper. And when that nigga jumped outta that car while it was still movin', that's Ghost Ridin' ya whip. These youngstas out here be thizzin'," Buck concluded, while shaking his head as if to say they were crazy.

"Thizzin'?"

"Yeah, poppin' pills, rollin'...you know, Ecstasy."

"Oh, okay. But shit, don't tha law be trippin' off that shit? I mean, it can't be legal."

"Do they? This shits so serious, they got everybody and they mommas tryin' to stop it. Tha news is always reportin' 'bout it and tha Mayor been breathin' down tha police chief's back try'na get 'em to form some kinda task force. But that shit ain't gon' stop nothin' ma' fucka's gon' stay getting' hyphy."

58

The back to back blunts Buck kept firing up had Lamonte light headed, so he cracked the window and reclined his seat. He felt good. What started out as a clueless journey had turned out as a lesson in Bay Area-ology.

"So," Buck said blowing out more smoke. "Wha' you think so far?"

"I most definitely could get used to this," he replied, sitting up and reaching for the blunt. "I mean it's definitely not tha Chi. But now, same shit, different hoods."

They rode in the car for hours chopping it up like old school buddies, while passing blunts back and forth. Buck laced Lamonte up on just about everything that went on in Oakland. He also told his story on how he was his dad's half-brother, born with the same father but different mothers and how he came up hustling for an old head back in the days, who he later killed and he took over his empire.

That shit sounded like a movie script to Lamonte. After taking another hit, he passed the blunt back to Buck, and immediately thought of Tae-Tae.

Im'a have to call my folks and let 'em know it's all good.

After riding for a while, Buck pulled into an apartment complex on Alingroom Court, right off MacArthur Blvd. He double parked his Scrapper in a no parking zone.

"Im'a be right back," he said before hopping out.

He nodded his head to a few youngstas standing around the curb serving in coke white tees, blue jeans, and Nikes.

"Kay," Lamonte nodded as he pulled out his cell phone and began to call Tae-Tae.

'Wha' the deal fam?" Tae-Tae said, picking up on the first ring.

"Shit, out her kickin' it in tha Sunshine State."

"Like that! I know you havin' a ball. Speaking 'of ballin', I got in touch wit' my cousin Derrion. He said tha goin' rate for a key of good coke is $30,000. I told 'em, I'll set it out to 'em for $25,000. Wha' you think 'bout shootin' him those we got for that price?"

"Shid, it's all good. I see you wasn't bullshitin' huh?"

"I told you. I'm tryn'a get this paper."

"Fasho. Hustle 24/7."

"Feel me? Can't sleep on tha bread."

Lamonte looked up in the rearview mirror and released the phone from his grip, letting it fall freely to his feet, denying him any chance to continue his conversation. What he saw was a black Camero Z-28 screech to halt behind the boys out hustling. A man jumped out of the passenger's side carrying an AK-47. Dark sunglasses covered his eyes while a red bandana was tied around the lower half of his face, making it hard to identify him.

The four hustlers out there looked on in shock, as the man approached. Before they could flee or reach for the weapons they carried, the masked man let loose with the chopper.

Doom! Doom! Doomm! Doooomm!

.223 bullets ripped through each of their bodies, knocking chunks of flesh, and leaving them mortally wounded. Lamonte watched on in amazement as the deadly assault rifle left their bodies with missing holes like swish cheese.

Buck was coming out of the apartment when he heard the shooting. Ducking for cover, he immediately pulled out his .45 from his lower back. He then took off to his car, afraid he'd find his nephew hit. Looking up in time, he saw the shooter who jumped into the Camero, before speeding out of the complex.

Lamonte had jumped behind the wheel of the Buick when he saw Buck coming.

"Roll out!" Buck hollered, jumping in the passenger's seat.

Hitting the gas Lamonte, fish tailed out of the parking lot leaving a trail of smoke behind them.

CHAPTER FOURTEEN

The next day, right after Desiree left for work, Buck entered the kitchen to begin his weekly routine of cooking up coke. The kitchen looked like a crack lab, with boxes of baking soda, Glad sandwich bags, scales, and Pyrex bowls everywhere. It was time for him to put his Chef Boy-R-Dee down.

Buck supplied a good number of blocks in East Oakland and was well respected throughout the East, West, and North. Knowing that the dope game was a cutthroat business, and thinking back to how he'd come up in it, caused him to keep little to no company around him. He trusted no one. But it was something different about his nephew that intrigued him.

←――――――――――――――――――――→

Lamonte was drawn out of his sleep by the sound of a blender operating in the kitchen. He glanced over at the bedside clock that displayed *8:35a.m.*

Damn! Looks like they're early birds, he thought as he prepared to get up and make his way to the bathroom.

Throwing on a pair of sweats and a white tee, he strolled to the bathroom, washed up, and then headed for the kitchen.

Upon entering, he noticed a big pile of coke spread across the table. He immediately turned on his heels.

"My bad, I didn't know you were in here handlin' yo' business," he said, heading back down the hall.

Buck looked at him and laughed. "It's all good lil' nigga. Ever seen anyone cook up work?"

"Nah," Lamonte said as he re-entered the kitchen taking in all of the paraphernalia Buck was using to cook with.

"Well shit, wha' betta time than now. Sit down and take notes on how to fry chickens. Shid, KFC, Popeyes, and Churches combined can't fuck wit' me."

Lamonte watched as Buck weighed out 250 grams of coke. He then weighed out 75 grams of baking soda before dumping them both into a blender. After blending it on low for a couple of minutes to make sure it was properly mixed, he poured the powder into a Pyrex bowl. Mixing in four teaspoons of water, he placed the bowl on the stove. Cooking it on a low flame, Lamonte watched as the powder broke down into a paste like substance before turning into a gel.

"Tha object is to make sure you don't overcook it while continuously stirrin'. You see how it looks like gel? That's when you know it's ready to come off tha stove."

Buck took the bowl off the stove and ran some cold water from the faucet over the gel until it began to harden. He sat the bowl in the ice-filled sink for a moment before twisting the cookie loose. Placing the cookie on some paper towel, he sat it under a fan so it would dry quicker.

Turning to Lamonte, Buck asked, "Nigga, you took notes?"

"Uhhh-yeah! I got it."

"Well alright, let me see you try. We'll start you off with a little."

Although Lamonte was hesitant, he got up and tried his hand. Before he knew it, he was cooking up. After cooking up the remainder of the brick, weighing, and bagging up ounces, Lamonte was exhausted. It took close to three hours for them to cut and weigh up 52 ounces. The thought of all the money that would be flipped from the work had Lamonte motivated to invest some money into the business himself.

Once the kitchen was clean, and all the paraphernalia was stored away, Lamonte went into the living room and turned on the T.V. Buck followed behind him, firing up a blunt.

"Yo, Buck. I'm not try'na be all up in your business and stuff, but I was wondering wha' them bricks go fo' out here in the Bay?"

Buck hit the blunt and then passed it off to Lamonte while responding.

"Shid...They go fo' 'bout $18.5. But I can get 'em fo' $16. Why? Wha' you got up yo sleeves?"

Before Lamonte could reply, Buck pointed at the T.V. screen.

"Turn that up!"

Lamonte grabbed the remote and turned the volume up. On the screen were three pictures of young men with their names underneath, then the pictures were replaced by a reporter standing in front of a building. Lamonte immediately recognized the apartment complex they were at yesterday.

The reporter was saying...

"I'm standing in front of an East Oakland apartment complex in the 2600 block of Alvingroom Court, not far away from Castlemont High School, where gun fire erupted yesterday killing three and critically injuring another. Among the dead are sixteen-year-old Jaquavis Hall, nineteen-year-old Ronnie Harris and twenty-one-year old Gary Jackson, all from Oakland. Witnesses say they heard about twenty to thirty shots ring out from a high powered assault rifle around 7:15 last night, leaving three dead and one fighting for his life in ICU.

Officials say they're looking for two vehicles seen fleeing from the scene. The first vehicle is a dark colored Z-28 Camero. The second vehicle is a late model Buick, with a custom green paint. At this time, officials say they have no motives, but have reasons to believe the incident was gang related.

If you have any information concerning this crime, or any others, please contact

Crime Stoppers at 510-87-CRIME. This is Amber Lee reporting live from Oakland..."

Buck sat with his eyes glued to the screen in shock. "Fuck!" he yelled, reaching for the blunt Lamonte had been trying to pass him for some time now. He inhaled the smoke before exhaling it through his nostrils. "Damn, the fuckin' scrap is hot! I gotta drop that bitch back off at tha paint shop, ASAP."

"Man, whoever did that shit wasn't playin'. Three slumped and another fightin' fo' his life. And just think, we were right there." Lamonte shook his head in disbelief as well. They could have easily been *got* also.

"Yeah, that shit is crazy. I'm just glad nothin' happened to you. 'Cause then it really woulda been on."

"Shit, I wonder wha' the fuck they do?" Lamonte asked more to himself than to Buck.

"I'on know but betta them than us," Buck laughed. "I know one thang... That nigga in ICU must'a had somebody prayin' fo' his ass though. C'mon let's jump in the van and hit tha blocks to check some change."

Lamonte jumped up and followed Buck. *Checkin' some change* sounded like something he'd be well interested in. This Cali idea from his mom turned into the best thing yet and when it was all over he hoped to make it pay out big in the long run.

CHAPTER FIFTEEN

Over the next few months, Lamonte hung with Buck as he networked. The Park Avenue was still in the shop so Buck used Desiree's Lexus SC400 for transportation. They rode with nine ounces down Bancroft Avenue, headed for the 69 village, one of the many projects throughout Oakland.

Buck pulled into a crowded parking lot where niggas stood around hustling while others gathered in a circle shooting dice. He parked in an empty space next to a Dodge Charger on 24-inch rims. Lifting his shirt, he handed Lamonte one of the twin .45's he had tucked in his jeans before they got out of the car.

Noticing the unfamiliar Lexus pull into the parking lot caused many of the young hustlers to reach for their burners they had concealed under their shirts. Recognizing Buck, they immediately left their guns in place and said their wassups.

Buck nodded as they disappeared into the projects. Looking at Lamonte, he shook his head and smirked.

"Them youngstas stay strapped and ready."

"Shid...They ain't tha only ones," Lamonte said, tugging the handle of the .45 through his shirt.

"No doubt," Buck countered before stopping at a door and knocking.

Knock! Knock! Knock! Knock!

Moments later, the door opened. A short stocky man stood on the other side of it. "Buck, wha' it dew my nigga?" Gino greeted, opening up the door for them to enter.

Buck and Lamonte stepped in as Gino shut the door behind them.

"Same shit, different day," Buck shot back. "This is my nephew, Black. You 'gon' be seein' him wit' me fo' awhile. Black, this my main man, Gino."

The two mutually nodded and embraced each other with a dap.

"S'up Buck, you got that same shit?" Gino asked.

"Fa sho. Look, check this," Buck suggested, handing over the nine ounces.

Gino's eyes lit up as he examined the dope, knowing Buck was back on with that butta.

Yeah, this that good-good mu'fuckas been askin' 'bout all day, he thought to himself as he looked over each ounce. When he was finished eye fucking the candy, he said firmly,

"Yep, this that shit! Same price?"

"Off top. $4,500," Buck said.

Moving like speedy Gonzalez, Gino rushed to the back to get his bread. He peeled off the cash making Buck's stop a profitable one.

Leaving the village, Buck decided to hit some corners in the town. They rode down Seminary Ave and stopped at a hoagie shop for something to eat. When they pulled into the parking lot, Lamonte noticed a clean ass candy apple red Benz 600 AMG parked out front. Buck saw Lamonte eye balling the whip and said, "That's tha Gov's shit right there."

"The Gov?" Lamonte asked confused at such a name.

"Yeah Gov...Like Governor."

"You mean a real Governor?"

"Nah, everybody just calls 'em that because he used to have tha town on lock back in tha day. Tha nigga was a real kingpin. One of tha major players out here in tha town. Now all he does is fuck wit' that music shit. That nigga be puttin' out them rappers."

"Is that right? Well he's most definitely sittin' clean," Lamonte replied.

"Gotta say that!" Buck said, as they got out of the Lexus and strolled through the entrance of the shop.

The Gov was a brown-skinned cat who stood 6'4", with 260 pounds of muscles. He sat with two young niggas as they took up a booth by the window facing the door. He looked up as they entered the shop. "S'up wit' it Buck? How's life treatin' ya?"

"S'up Gov. Shit, I can't complain. But if I had yo hand I'd cut mine off," Buck laughed.

"I hear ya," The Gov smiled.

After ordering their sandwiches, Buck and Lamonte took a seat in the booth next to The Gov and his friends.

"Ayo, Buck. This is my new group right here. This is Cash and that's Dolla. Together they're 'Tha Money Gang.' They 'bout to be next big thang to come outta tha town. You watch and see." The Gov had a proud look on his face as he spoke about his new protégés.

"Is that right? So they got gas or wha?"

"Do they? Cash, give my man a bar or two," Tha Gov said to the shorter of the two.

Cash checked his swagger and gave them the look of a nigga preparing for a video shoot.

"I say Maserati stance, get it we disappearing I tell her cut off the phones, there's nothin' to interfere/ She follow my every order, do anything that I dare/ I'm givin' her everything, so all my neighbors can hear/ Scream to her making her fien more/ We be makin' a movie, they think it's Scream 4/ Got that from that nigga Jeezy and then I put Dean on/

I'm seven looking like heaven, I love when them jeans on/

When rollin' get yo' chick stolen. Stand up paper, I can't fold it/ Old bread baby, my money be moldy/ Every time I'm goin' down it's nothin' but roses, yeah I was just on the money, never was on hoes."

"Yeah, I like that. Youngsta's got heat!" Buck chuckled.

"I told you. They goin' to be that hottest thang outta tha town. Hott'a than that nigga Short."

"Like that? Wha' you think Black?" Buck asked.

"He a'ight." Lamonte was obviously unimpressed.

"A'ight? You say that like you can do betta or somethin'?" Cash challenged.

"Somethin' like that," Lamonte shot back.

"Well then, let's hear wha' you got," The Gov chuckled.

Lamonte shrugged his shoulders and said, "Cool. Check it..."

"Last one to leave tha block, first to make it there/ These Jordans, they ain't comin' out til next year/ When it comes to squares, we whip

them whole thangs/ Perform tricks with them bricks like tha X-games/
Mo' money-Mo' money, Mo 'change-Mo' change
   Mo' scrilla mean mo' cocaine-cocaine/ Ask 'em in tha streets, got
that shit on lock/ Could lead tha league in assists how I ditch tha rock/
My jump shot-probably miss/ I take it to the rack, and all I get is bricks/ I
put on fo' that white bitch, whip up two at a time on some dyke shit, dyke
shit/ Cranberry-Apple M6, 160 on tha dash/ Call it blowin' money fast."

When Lamonte finished, he popped his collar like a real vet from the Bay.

"Okay, okay. I like that. What's yo' name kid?" Tha Gov asked, impressed by his flow.

"Pretty Black," he replied, unwrapping the sandwich the waiter had placed in front of him while he was spitting his bars.

"Pretty Black," Tha Gov smirked nodding his head up and down. "Kid you gotta nice flow. Wit a little help, you could be that nigga. Your flow is like none other. Where you from anyway?"

"I'm from tha Chi. I just moved out here a couple months ago to fuck wit' my Uncle Buck."

"Tha Chi, huh?" The Gov responded with a smile spread across his face. He extended his hand and shook Lamonte's, knowing he'd just found his next boy wonder. "Well Pretty Black," Tha Gov affirmed. "If you really serious 'bout this rap shit, put my number in your phone and hit me up so we can talk."

After making sure Lamonte had his phone number stored, Tha Gov and his two rappers departed, making their way back to his Benz.

Later that night, Lamonte laid in his bed excited about the idea of a rap career, hustling dope, and making it in a new city. But he couldn't shake the memories of his days in the Chi out of his head. Picking up his phone, he thumbed through the contacts until he reached his mother's number. He hadn't talked to her in over a week and really wanted to hear her voice.

It had been months since he abandoned his city and every day he thought of his mom, Tae-Tae, or Tasha. He never once thought about all the bodies he'd left behind or the case that was building up against him.

CHAPTER SIXTEEN

Riding through the various hoods of East Oakland, Buck sat behind the wheel of his recently painted candy purple scrapper. As he rode, he surveyed the areas he'd soon be serving with his good quality dope. With Capone being his Mexican connect, he'd been able to flood the town with the best dope possible, while never catching a drought. He'd been fucking with Capone, who had direct ties to the Zeta Cartel for over three years now. Things were beginning to look really good since then.

During that time, he never allowed anyone to meet Capone. He wanted to control the price and distribution of all the dope throughout the town.

Today he rode in deep concentration as he wondered whether or not he'd made the right decision by allowing Lamonte to meet Capone yesterday when he re-uped.

Realizing his phone was ringing, Buck turned down the stereo and answered seconds before the voicemail picked up. "Wha' it dew?" he said into his phone.

"Wha' it don't dew my nigga. A nigga try'na get good. You workin' today?" asked Chop from 77th.

"Off top. I got them C.D.'s all day. Wha' you lookin' fo'?"

"You got that new C.D. from that nigga Eighteen, outta Hayward?" His lingo held the code for 18 ounces.

"No doubt. I just got that shit too. Give me 'bout twenty minutes and I'll be on my way. You at tha spot?"

"Yeah, I'm here."

"A'ight. I'll see you in a sec," he said before hanging up.

Driving down Foothill Blvd, heading towards 98th, Buck called Lamonte to tell him to have eighteen ounces ready. After hanging up, he called Desiree to see if she wanted to go to Chili's for lunch. Desiree loved Chili's and agreed to go immediately. It was something about their cajun steak that always caused her to crave the restaurant.

"Fuck!" he cursed out loud, hanging up in Desiree's face. He noticed the blue and red lights of Oakland's finest in his rearview mirror. Pulling to the side of the road, he placed his hands on the steering wheel. The way police had been killing niggas in the city, he didn't want to give them any reason to pump his body full of lead. So he waited patiently for the officers to approach his window.

"License, registration, and insurance," the cop said as he approached his driver's side window.

Reaching into the glove compartment to get the registration and insurance card, Buck noticed the second cop walking up to the passengers's side with his hand positioned on his gun.

Scary mu'fucka! Buck thought to himself.

Handing his information over to the cop he asked, "What's tha problem officer? Why am I being pulled over?"

The cop informed him that he was being pulled over for talking on the phone while driving; this was a violation in the state of California.

Buck's mind was put to ease at the thought of only receiving a small infraction before being on his way.

Then he saw something that troubled him.

Fuck! Fuck! Fuck! he thought, seeing three more squad cars pull up. *Wha' that fuck they need all this back up fo'. It ain't like I gotta warrant or somethin'...Fuck! And I got this burner on me.*

Two black officers got out of the first car, followed by two latinos in the second.

A fifth officer, who was white, and looking to be the Sergeant, got out of the third vehicle. They were all standing in a huddle talking and looking over toward Buck. After a few minutes, the cop that pulled Buck over came back and tapped on the window asking Buck to step out of the car.

"What's the problem officer?" he calmly asked.

"I ask the questions not you dip shit! Now get out of the vehicle!" the officer snapped, unhosting his weapon.

Buck didn't like the way things were going and knew if he resisted they'd probably open fire on him. He did the smartest thing and got out of the car. Once out, he was ordered to put his hands behind his back. He complied and was immediately cuffed.

After being searched, he was placed in the back seat of a squad car while the officers searched his vehicle.

Fuck, they gon' find that pistol! he thought. The last thing he needed was a Federal case for being a felon in possession of a firearm.

The officers high-fived and celebrated after finding Buck's Glock .40 stashed between the driver's seat. One officer came to the squad car. "Well Mr. Gibson, you wanna tell us about this gun we found in your car? It wouldn't happen to be registered to you, would it?"

"Fuck you! I know my rights. Talk to my lawyer!" he barked

"Oh yea, tough guy," the officer said with a smirk. "We'll be sure to tell that lawyer of yours that you're being investigated in a shooting that left three dead, another fighting for his life, not to mention this possession of a firearm. Looks like you won't be home for the holidays."

Buck sat in the back seat of the squad car and watched as a tow truck arrived, loading his Buick onto its flatbed. It was then that he realized he should've just got rid of the damn scrapper. He feared someone might have gotten a view of his plates. Right then he felt stupid thinking that repainting the car would put him in the clear.

←——————————————→

Down at the Eastmont sub-station on Hegenberger Street, Buck was led into an interrogation room where he was cuffed to a table. Despite the turn of events, he did his best to remain calm. After thirty minutes of waiting, two detectives entered, one took a seat opposite of him while the other remained standing.

"So, Mr. Gibson, I'm Detective Scott," the one sitting said. He was a stocky white man with gold-rimmed glasses. "This is my partner, Sikes."

Sikes, a lean black man in his early forties nodded. Buck could tell he thought he was bad ass.

"We're not gonna waste any time," Scott continued. "What do you have to say about these murders?"

Looking the detective directly in his eyes, he said, "I don't know nothing."

Infuriated by his smugness, Detective Sikes rushed the table, slamming both his fists and making a loud thud. "Mutha fucka, you know damned well what we're talkin' about! Now talk or we're gonna make sure you're buried under the rubble in San Quinten."

Buck looked at Scott, who shook his head at his partner. Buck was an OG in this game and immediately recognized their tactics. Good cop/Bad cop. "Like I said, I'on know S-H-I-T! So, if yall gon' book me then hurry up and do it. I'm tired."

Detective Scott saw Buck wasn't going to give in so he stood up with the manila file folder he brought with him. "Okay, suit yourself."

Both detectives stormed out of the room, leaving Buck cuffed to the table. Sitting there, he thought about his house and what he had in it. He wanted to make sure he didn't leave anything exposed in case they decided to run up in it. He knew no residue was anywhere because he was thorough whenever he cleaned up after cooking up his work. His pistol and choppers were safely stashed.

Buck anticipated that they'd make him sit on ice before finally booking him and sending him to county. He also knew his rights. As soon as someone came in, he'd ask for a lawyer call. Mr. Cooper, his attorney, was the best in Northern California.

Closing his eyes and taking a deep breath, Buck focused. This was a situation he didn't see happening when he woke up that morning.

CHAPTER SEVENTEEN

L amonte glanced at his watch then over toward his phone that was lying on the coffee table beside his propped up feet, as he awaited Buck's return. High as hell from smoking on purple kush, he sat there flicking through channels with the remote. Buck had called over thirty minutes ago and asked him to get eighteen ounces ready for him.

Damn! It's 11:30 a.m. Where this nigga at?

Thirty more minutes passed without a sign of Buck.

Somethin' ain't right. I can feel it.

Picking up his phone, he called Buck's cell. It went straight to his voicemail.

Fuck!

He waited fifteen minutes before trying again. Still his voicemail.

Shit!

He decided to call Desiree to see if she'd heard from him.

"Desiree, what's good?"

"Hey Black. Where's that uncle of yours at? I'm goin' to kill 'em. First, he hung up in my face. He was supposed to take me out to lunch. Now his phone is off. So where the hell are ya'll?" she asked sounding slightly upset.

"Shid, I'm at the house, but Buck ain't here. He phoned me over an hour ago and said he was on his way to pick up somethin' but never showed up. That's why I'm hitting you to see if you heard from him."

"Well, where tha hell is he?" she asked next.

"I...I..I'on know," he stammered nervously.

"A'ight. Let me call our lawyer Mr. Cooper to see if he's been picked up by the police or somethin'. In the meantime, make sure ain't nothin' in the house. I'm on my way there now."

"Yep," he said before hanging up.

With red-rimmed eyes, Desiree waited by the telephone for hours anticipating Buck's call. It had been close to eight hours since the last time she heard from him and the weight of the world was heavy on her shoulders.

She called everywhere, from hospitals to jailhouses, but got nothing. Her instincts were steering her to call any and everybody Buck knew. Helplessness made every second seem like hours, leaving her nothing else to do except pray. She felt as if she was losing her mind and on the brink of insanity. Knowing that anybody can get it in Oakland caused her to fear the worst. But she hoped God wasn't that cruel.

Please Lord, I pray he's alright, she thought kneeling to her knees.

She wasn't used to speaking to God but now was a desperate time. This was the first time she hadn't heard from Buck for this long since they'd met eight years ago. For the first time in her life, she was lost. She was in her purest and rarest state. She faced her greatest fear, which was that her man was somewhere dying if not dead and she couldn't do anything to help him.

When the house phone rang, she rushed over and snatched it up. "Hello," she sobbed into the phone.

"Hey Desiree. I just located Buck. He's at the North County Jail being booked for possession of a firearm and possible homicides. He has a no bail hold right now, but I'm going to try to get him one Thursday at his arraignment," Mr. Cooper said.

"Homicides? Who he supposed to have killed?"

"I'll know a lot more Thursday after his arraignment," he admitted.

"Yea okay, wha' time is his court at?" Desiree asked.

"It's 9:00 a.m., department 26, on the third floor. Now I know you've been worried all day, so try and get some rest. Everything is going to be alright," he said. "I'm disappointed too but I promise I'll do all that I can. I mean, that's what ya'll pay me for."

74

Desiree knew Buck paid him a lot of money for situations like this. So she could only trust the lawyer's word. "Okay. Make sure you call if anything changes."

"I will," he said.

←————————————————————→

"All rise! This court is now in session. The Honorable Matthew P. Hampton presiding," the court deputy announced at the top of his lungs for everybody to hear.

"Thank you. You may all be seated," the Judge said taking a seat on the bench.

"Your Honor, we call matter 37 on today's 9:00 calendar-people vs. Buck T Gibbson. This matter is on calendar for arraignment," stated the court's clerk.

"Thank you, Ms. Smith. State the appearance for the record please," Judge Hampton stated.

"Your Honor, Attorney David Cooper, for Cooper and Associates, appearing on behalf of the defendant, Mr. Buck T. Gibbson, who appears in custody," Mr Cooper spoke professionally, looking the part in his high dollar silk suit.

"Assistant U.S. Attorney Teri McIntosh, appearing on behalf of the state of California." Ms. McIntosh was a boney white woman in her late 40's. Her reputation was brutal for drug dealers. It was said her son overdosed which was the cause of it.

"Thank you. Are we ready to proceed with this arraignment?" asked the Judge.

Both parties agreed.

Buck sat shackled in front of the courtroom. He looked back to make sure the two most important people in his life were present. Seeing them, he smiled.

Lamonte sat in the middle row along with Desiree, awaiting Buck's fate. On the otherside of the courtroom sat spectators along with correspondents from Channel 2 and 4 news.

This was only the beginning of a long journey ahead and Buck prayed that he'd be granted bail. Three deputies stood at the exit doors of the courtroom carrying .45 caliber pistols.

Judge Hampton softened his tone a bit as he asked, "How does the defendant plead?"

"Not guilty," Cooper replied. "Your Honor, we wish to waive time and set a date for motions to dismiss on the grounds that evidence was obtained illegally. I would also like to ask the court to grant my client bail so that he can be with his family during these times."

"Do the people have any objections?" asked Judge Hampton.

"Yes, your Honor. This is not just a simple case of possession of a firearm. Mr. Gibbson is also being arraigned on multiple counts of homicide and attempted homicide. In addition, the defendant is a known drug dealer with a lack of responsibility and any known place of employment."

"I object! Your Honor. There isn't any evidence to substantiate that information," said Mr. Cooper rising from his seat. "My client hasn't been charged with a single drug-related offense."

"Sustained," Judge Hampton said. "Strike it from the record. Let's stick with the facts here Ms. McIntosh."

"Sure thing, your Honor. With the seriousness of his crimes, I feel the defendant poses a flight risk and ask that bail not be granted. Thank you, your Honor."

Ms. McIntosh sat back down in her seat and shot a glance over towards Buck with a smirk on her face.

Buck showed no emotions. He decided he wouldn't play her little games.

Smile now, cry later, he thought.

"Mr. Cooper, do you have anything else to say?" Judge Hampton asked.

"No your Honor."

"Okay then, motions will be sat for May 3rd at 9:00 a.m. on this matter. You can submit all motions to me before then. Bail is denied. You are remanded to stay in custody. This matter is adjourned," Judge Hampton said, slamming down his gavel three times.

Desiree's cries could be heard throughout the courtroom. The bailiff came and escorted Buck back behind the walls.

Lamont looked to console her. "Come on, it's gonna be alright."

"I just can't believe he wouldn't give him bail," Desiree cried. "I want him home."

After gathering their things, they made their way out the door. Outside the courtroom, Mr. Cooper approached Desiree and Lamonte.

"Sorry about today. That D.A.'s a bitch. I just wanted you to know that I'm on my way up to the jailhouse now to see Buck. Do you want me to tell him anything?"

"Yeah, tell 'em I love 'em and that I'll be up there to see 'em tomorrow. Tell 'em I will put some more money on the phone and to call me," Desiree told him.

"Yeah and tell 'em I said to keep his head up and not to worry 'bout nothin'. I'ma hold him down," Lamonte blurted out.

Getting into the car, Lamonte thought about Buck's situation. No matter what, he was gone hold it down and keep them dollars circulating. He owed it to Buck. He wasn't just an uncle who took him in, he was also a friend and teacher. Now, with him gone, Lamonte was back in the world alone.

Ever since coming to Oakland, Buck had been a guiding force in his life, molding him to be the ultimate hustler. Buck knew age wasn't nothing but a number and Lamonte was already living in the fast lane because that's all he'd known.

Thinking about Mr. Cooper, Lamonte settled on the fact that he knew his uncle paid dude a lot of money.

And he couldn't even get him bail, he thought. *That's crazy! Anybody can get it*, he concluded as thoughts of killing Mr. Cooper crossed his mind.

Before Desiree drove off, Lamonte rolled up a blunt, looked in the mirror and made himself a promise to do whatever was necessary to get Buck out of there.

This blunt fo' you, my nigga, he thought before firing up.

CHAPTER EIGHTEEN

As Lamonte rolled over from the position he was sleeping in, the bright sun shining through his bedroom windows awakened him. He spent a long night recording at a studio he came up on. With his uncle's situation, the studio helped to clear his mind. He ended up recording a mix CD in the meantime.

He glanced around the room before getting up, and planting his feet on the plush carpet. Everything in the room had been upgraded. Turning on the 67-inch flat screen TV, he flicked it to BET. With the new Meek Mill's video playing on the tube he threw the remote on the nightstand, picked up the blunt that was in the ashtray, and fired up.

Things were really coming along well for him with the exception of Buck being locked up. Lamonte was getting money and a whole lot of it.

Ever since Mr. Cooper brought him Buck's phone, he was going through two to three kilos a week easily. Not only was he stacking chips, he was knocking bitches left and right thanks to his new status in the streets. He had bitches way older than him willing to do whatever. He was truly in the fast lane with fast money, fast cars, and fast bitches.

He had just cashed out $28,000 on a new Dodge Charger. He had it painted candy-brandy-wine, sitting on matching 24's. He decided to stay at Buck's house a little while longer, just to watch over things while he was away.

A couple of mo' months, then I'm gettin' my own shit, he thought.

Lamonte sat in his boxer shorts holding his crotch with one hand, while smoking the blunt with the other. Picking up his phone from the nightstand, he glanced at the time. *11:30 a.m. Man, I ain't talked to Ma' Dukes in a couple weeks. Let me hit her up.*

Dialing his mother's number, he got up and headed into the bathroom.

"Hey son," she answered on the first ring. "I haven't heard from you in awhile. How's everything going?"

"It's cool...weather is good, beautiful women. What's not to like 'bout it. I just wish you were here."

"Now...there you go. You know I can't just up and leave my job. Besides, what would I do in California?"

"Gon' wit' that ma'. I got enough money saved up fo' tha both of us to live comfortable fo' awhile. You ain't never gotta work again. Plus you'll love it out here."

"I don't know. Maybe I'll come to visit soon. Anyway, how's your uncle? Don't he go to court soon?"

"Nah, it was put off fo' six mo' months. But he's good though. I talk to em' all the time. Hold on ma', let me see who's this callin' on my other line."

He smiled, noticing Tae-Tae's name on the screen.

"Look ma', that's Tae-Tae. He's supposed to be comin' down this weekend so I'ma take his call. But I love you and will call again soon."

"I love you too. Tell Tae-Tae I said hi."

"Okay ma', bye," he said before switching over.

"What's good my nigga?"

"You. I'm 'bout to be on my way to the airport in 'bout an hour. My plane get in at 5:30 p.m yo' time," Tae-Tae announced.

"Off top! I'll be out front in a candy brandy wine Charger on matching 24's.

"Oh, so you rollin' like that huh?"

"Man, that shit ain't nothin'. The way shits rollin' out here, a nigga could cop whatever. Watch, you'll see," he boasted.

"No doubt. I know we hittin' tha club tonight, 'cause I'm try'na knock some of that sunshine pussy. Feel me?"

"Man, I'on really be fuckin' wit' tha clubs like that. But shit, if that's what you tryin' to do, then I'll make an exception since my nigga in town," he responded. "Just make sure you don't miss tha flight."

"Nigga, I wouldn't miss it fo' tha world. I'ma hit you as soon as my plane land."

"Off top."

"One."

"One," he said, ending the call.

←——————————————————————→

After using the toilet, and taking a quick shower, Lamonte got dressed and headed for the kitchen to get something to eat. Returning to the room with two turkey sandwiches and a glass of ice-cold lemonade, Lamonte sat down and finished watching videos before starting his day.

Thirty minutes later, Lamonte was dressed and out the door. Getting into his late model Pontiac GTP, he headed straight to the public storage. This was where he'd been storing dope ever since Buck got locked up. Inside his unit were some old furniture, a few boxes, and a nice sized safe. The safe was where he kept five kilos of cocaine stashed and over eighty ounces of hard. Grabbing 18 of the ounces, he put them in a shopping bag so he could run them over to Chop on 77th. He grabbed nine more ounces and put them in a gift bag for Gino over in the 69 ville. After double locking the unit, he jumped back in the Pontiac and headed for 77th.

Lamonte pulled the Pontiac up to Chop's trap house, which was only about a ten-minute drive from the storage. After grabbing the shopping bag off the passenger's seat, he got out and walked up to the shabby house.

Knock! Knock! Knock! Knock!

"Who that iz?" hollered Chop.

"It's me, Black."

Chop opened the door and the two embraced before Lamonte stepped through the door.

"Wha' it dew, Black? You lookin' fresh to death as always," Chop commented on his choice of flyest gear.

"Shid...some mo' of it. Nothin' new but the day."

"No doubt."

After chopping it up for a few seconds, Lamonte dumped the contents of the shopping bag onto Chop's coffee table. Chop handed him a stack of bills and made sure it was $9,000.

Putting the money in the shopping bag, he gave Chop dap and made his exit. "Make sure you hit me when you're finished," he hollered over his shoulder.

"Fa' sho."

Getting into the Pontiac, he stuffed the shopping bag under the seat and headed to the 69 ville to see Gino.

Pulling into the projects, he parked in Gino's assigned parking space like many other times he'd made drops. He checked the government issued .45 caliber on his waist, to make sure it was locked and loaded. He then grabbed the gift bag off the seat and stepped out of the car.

The moment he opened the car door, yelling could be heard coming from somewhere in the projects.

"And if I catch you back at this mu'fucka again, I'ma kill yo' ass!"

Man, let me hurry up and get tha fuck up outta here, he thought, making his way to Gino's door.

Knock! Knock! Knock!

"Gino! It's me, Black!" he hollered through the door.

A moment later, Gino opened the door, inviting him inside

"Wussup playa?"

"Man, it's dumb ass crazy round here," he cautioned, handing Gino the gift bag.

"Shit, that ain't nothin' but them fiends over there. They go through this every day when one of em' holdin' out on tha other," Gino chuckled looking into the bag.

"I can dig it. But I'm try'na stick and move, feel me?"

"Yeah, I smell you," Gino assured.

Standing next to the living room window, Lamonte could hear the fiends getting louder and louder.

"Nigga, give me a hit!" one yelled to the other.

Man, this nigga needs to hurry up. I'm try'na dip!

Usually when Lamonte made drops to Gino, he'd stay and chop it up with him for a minute. Gino was a cool and wise kind of old head. He was nobody's fool. Most old heads in the city wasn't. They'd lived long enough to master the craft. Gino was full of game and one had to listen in order to hear him.

As Gino finished examining each ounce, something he always did no matter what, he gave Lamonte $4,500.

"Count yo' money," Gino sighed.

"I know it's straight. You always on point," he said.

"Boy, how many times I gotta tell you always count yo' money!" Gino hissed.

"You right," he said counting every bill. When he was finished counting he said, "It's short $1,000!"

"That's 'bout a damn lie! Boy I know I done counted that money 'bout-"

"I'm just kiddin," Lamonte laughed. "Let me know when you ready again."

"Boy, I tell you. You young niggas," Gino chuckled. "But tha way this been movin', it's probably goin' to be tomorrow."

"Off top. I got you." Lamonte continued before turning towards the door.

When he got back in the car, he rolled up a blunt, and decided to hit some corners in the East. Everybody was out. The sun was shining and everybody was profiling. Spotting two girls walking down High Street, he dipped up on them.

"Hey, lil' mama in tha pink. Let me holla at you fo' a sec, if you don't mind," he called out.

The girls stopped walking and looked over in his direction. "Who me?" the girl in the pink asked.

"Yeah you."

She walked over to the car and the two engaged in small conversation. The other girl just looked on with a, *could we please go already,* expression on her face.

"Damn ma'. I didn't mean any disrespect by pullin' up on you like that. But you caught my eye so I had to ask yo' name," Lamonte shot in his Chi-town playa mack mode.

"Where you from? Cause you don't sound like you from tha town."

"Nah Shawty, I'm from Chicago. I just moved out here 'bout a year ago. So do Ms. Beautiful have a name?"

"Candi. But if you try'na holla, I got a man."

"As you should. But just one? I woulda thought a pretty girl like you would have a flock of niggas. Wha' bout friends? You do got those don't you?" The whole time he macked, he posted his elbow up on the window.

"Well kinda," Candi said studying his frame and admitting to herself that he was impressive.

"Well, I'm Black. If it's not asking too much, I'd like to get to know you. I mean, seeing how I'm new in town and all. I'ma need somebody to show me around." Lamonte smirked.

"Boy please. But I guess that'll be alright. You got a number?" She smiled, pulling out her cell phone.

Nodding, he gave her his number. "You sure ya'll don't wanna ride to where ya'll goin'?" he asked.

"Thanks but no thanks. We good. I'ma call you later though so be expectin' me." As she spoke, she gave him a wink.

He smiled.

"Off top, pretty lady."

He watched her as she walked away. Her firm ass cheeks bounced extra hard. Shaking his head he pulled off, continuing to hit corners in the town.

"Wooooooeeeeee!" He let out an excited scream as his imagination ran wild. He couldn't wait to fuck Candi. *Wit' a name like that, I know that thang sweet!*

CHAPTER NINETEEN

Tae-Tae opened his eyes when he felt the plane touchdown in Oakland. He smiled, reflecting on the last time he saw Lamonte and the big score they had on the Latin Kings. Just thinking about that very night caused him to miss his homeboy even more.

This was the first time he'd been out west. He heard a lot of stories, and saw a lot of videos; he couldn't wait to experience it firsthand. He'd been planning this trip for some time now. Since coming up on those bricks, he'd been on his grind stacking chips. Being spoiled growing up, it felt good to be able to finally provide for himself.

Tae-Tae had $50,000 taped to his body. $37,500 of which belonged to Black for his cut in the three bricks he sold to his cousin, Derrion. The other $12,500 was strictly for fucking off.

He stood up and began to walk off the airplane. Making his way through the corridors of the airport, he headed towards the baggage pick up area; the whole time he watched for airport security. When he saw no one watching, he relaxed.

Man, I'm glad to be off that fuckin' plane! he thought.

He couldn't wait to see Lamonte. The two had been running tight and pulling licks together since they were kids. Lamonte had quickly made a name for himself after the death of his father.

Tae-Tae grabbed his luggage while dialing Lamonte's number at the same time. "Where you at nigga?" he asked when Lamonte answered.

"Nigga, I'm circling tha drop off area. Where you at!" Lamonte shot back.

"Cool, I'm comin' outside right now. I'm 'bout to be in front of Jet Blue."

"Alright, well look fo' tha clean ass Charger on 4's."

"Yeah, I see you now," he announced.

The California sunshine was beaming down on him and he had a great feeling about this. Something told him things were in store for them and he couldn't wait to see what it could be.

Lamonte pulled the Charger over, jumped out, and gave Tae-Tae a hug.

"Wat up folk?" he asked, giving him the G.D. shake. "Let me get those bags."

He took his homeboy's luggage and put it in the backseat before they got in and sped off.

"Nigga, this mu'fucka is clean. I see yo black ass done put on some weight too," Tae-Tae teased, noticing the slight pounds Lamonte put on.

Lamonte had gained about forty pounds of muscle from eating good and working out four times a week. "Fuck you nigga. I'm solid as a rock under this shirt," he said playfully as they rode down 98th avenue.

"So what's really good wit' it out here?" Tae-Tae continued. He was inquiring about what all the hype was about he and Lamonte had been discussing on the phone over the past year.

"Man, it's lovely out here. I got shit on lock. Plus the price for them bricks is dirt cheap. I figure we could make a killin' off them back home. Here, fire that up," he said passing Tae-Tae a rolled blunt. "And ya boy been in the studio."

"Now this wha' I'm talkin' 'bout. I see you on that good ass Cali chronic."

"Nah, Folk...That there is Grapes," he corrected.

"Grapes?" Tae-Tae asked dumbfounded, before putting the fire to the blunt.

"Yeah, that's wha' they call this purple weed out here," he said, throwing half an ounce of Grapes onto Tae-Tae's lap.

Inhaling the smoke, Tae-Tae immediately began coughing up his insides, forcing slobber to run down his chin. Picking up the bag of Grapes he asked, "Nigga. Wha', this shit laced or somethin'?"

Lamonte had tears in his eyes from laughing so hard. "Nigga, that shit ain't laced. That's just Grapes...Here, give me that shit b'fo' you hurt yo'self," he laughed while snatching the blunt.

He took a deep pull, then blew the smoke in Tae-Tae's face.

"Yeah, nigga. You ain't ready fo' this. I bet we can make a killin' off this shit back home."

"Definitely can. That's some good shit. Let me hit it again." Tae-Tae tried again, this time he was more careful respecting the potency of the exotic bud.

The aroma of the Grapes had the car reeking and Tae-Tae high as hell. Turning onto Walnut Street, Tae-Tae was so high everything was moving in slow motion. From a distance, Lamonte could see Desiree's SC400 gleaming as it sat perfectly in the driveway.

Good, she's here, he thought, pulling his car behind the Lexus.

"That's yo Lexus too?" Tae-Tae said slowly.

"Nah, that's my Uncle Buck's girlfriend, Desiree, shit," Lamonte said dismissively, as he stepped from the car and grabbed Tae-Tae's luggage.

Walking slowly to the front door, Tae-Tae surveillanced the neighborhood.

Good 'ole Tae-Tae, always on point, Lamonte thought to himself while reaching inside his jean pockets in search of the house keys. He never kept them on the same ring as the car keys for security purposes. He did this in case he ever had to abandon the car running from the police.

"Damn! Where tha mu'fuckas at?" he muttered in frustration, patting all his pockets. "Oh, here they go," he said locating them inside his jacket pocket.

The smell of Grapes greeted them as soon as they stepped inside the door. All the blinds were closed and the T.V. was on.

"Desiree, it's me!" Lamonte yelled, making his way through the house.

"Hey Black," she greeted coming out of the bathroom.

"This is my best friend, Tae-Tae, from Chicago. He's gon' kick it wit' me fo' tha weekend, if that's okay wit' you."

She looked at them and smiled. "No, it's alright. Nice to meet you Tae-Tae."

"Nice to meet you too, miss," he responded respectfully.

Desiree walked back into the living room as the boys entered Lamonte's bedroom. Tae-Tae watched as Lamonte sat on the bed, pulled out the bag of Grapes, and rolled another blunt.

"Nigga, you gon' love it out here, just watch," Lamonte announced, as the unlit blunt hung from the right side of his mouth.

"Nigga, I already love it," Tae-Tae stated, sitting next to him and handing him a lighter. Firing up the blunt, Lamonte hit it a couple times, then passed it off.

Later that night...
Lamonte and Tae-Tae pulled up to Sweet Jimmy's nightclub in Lamonte's freshly detailed Charger. The club was packed and had a line going down the block. When they stepped out, fly bitches and hating ass niggas were all watching.

Lamonte walked over and slid the bouncer, who was in charge of the door, $300 to let them in without being hassled. They made their way through the entrance and strolled in without being searched or carded.

Rocking some black Sean John jeans and a black Gucci button up, Lamonte was killing it. Black Gucci tennis shoes graced his feet while a matching Gucci fitted cap sat on his head. He wore a single diamond chain and cross that completed his outfit.

Once in VIP, Lamonte spotted Red from Funktown, popping bottles of Patron with his crew. Sitting in a booth opposite of Red, Lamonte ordered a bottle of Patron and a bottle of Rose.

Usually, he wouldn't be caught dead at a club. But since Tae-Tae wanted to party the night away he made an exception. Now that he was in the building, he wanted everyone to know that he was indeed *that nigga.*

Their bottles arrived, they sipped lightly to insure they stayed focused and on point. Red took notice of Lamonte and nodded his head before approaching with his hand outstretched to show it was all love.

"S'up wit' it Pretty Black? How's Buck holdin' up?" he asked curiously.

"You know...same shit, different day. That nigga Buck is cool though. S'up wit' you? I see ya'll doin' it up live over there," Lamonte replied as he continued to survey his surroundings.

"Aw that!" Red said, nodding his head towards his booth. "That ain't nothin'. It's my boy b-day so we're helpin' him bring it in, in style. But now, I got a proposition that I think can be beneficial for the both of us."

"Is that right? Like wha'?" Lamonte asked with skepticism.

"I think you already know," Red said. "Look, I respect yo hustle
and product. Tha streets are talkin', and right now I'm lookin' fo' a new
line. If tha price is right, who knows wha' we can accomplish. I assure
you it'll work out for the both of us."

"Yeah, I hear you," Lamonte responded. "Let me lock yo number in
my phone and get back at you later." Removing his phone, he stored
Red's number.

After giving Lamonte dap, Red prepared to step away from the
booth.

"Red!" Lamonte called, stopping him in his tracks.

Red turned around.

"Just remember, I'm young, but far from dumb. All a man has in
this world is his balls and his word. If I feel you're on some shady shit,
there will be consequences and repercussions that come wit' it." As he
spoke, he looked as serious as a heart attack.

Red noticed the tension. "Despite wha' you think, I ain't wit that
bullshit. And I hope you not either."

Lamonte saw the befuddled expression on Red's face. "No doubt."

Red walked off just as a group of girls started dancing on tables
entertaining his crew. Tae-Tae focused his attention on the half-naked
bitches dancing on the tables. He'd never seen asses that big in person.
These were Bay Area beauties, with a different demeanor than the girls
back in the Chi. They were slim in the waist, pretty in the face, and
mixed in their race.

"Man, I'm 'bout to knock me a bitch in this mu'fucka. That bitch
over there wit' the yellow thong showin', she can get it," Tae-Tae
announced.

"Nigga, anybody can get it," Lamonte said with his mind elsewhere

Knowing that they both were strapped in the club, Lamonte decided
to relax a little. It seemed like everybody knew who he was and
respected his hustle. Bitches flocked to them all night, flirting left and
right, hoping to come up with a nigga with some change.

After a couple of hours, Lamonte was ready to go. As they walked
through the crowd, headed for the door, Lamonte bumped into a girl,
spilling her drink all over her blouse.

"Damn it!" she yelled, turning to face him.

"My bad ma', I didn't see-" His words were cut short when he noticed the girl who he bumped into was Candi. "Damn ma', I see I ran into you again, literally this time," he said with a smile. "Let me get that fo' you."

Grabbing the napkins out of Candi's hand, he wiped at her top.

"Oh, it's you," she said surprised. "You look different out of the car!"

"Different like how?" he asked.

She smacked her lips. "Not in a bad way."

He smiled. "So, wha' happened to you callin' me then?" Lamonte asked. That's when he noticed she was with another chick.

"Oh, tha night still young. I was goin' to call you."

"Oh really?" he asked playfully. As he spoke, he discreetly scanned her body from head to toe. Her 7 jeans hugged her fat ass perfectly. The Christian Dior stiletto heels made her that much more enticing as she shifted her weight from leg to leg; oversized Christian Dior stunna shades covered her eyes.

Lamonte slowly took in her look, admiring her shape and beauty. He loved the way her jeans hugged her hips.

"Yes really," she smirked as he sized her up.

"Anyways, you lookin' good."

"Thanks." She blushed, trying to straighten her blouse back out. "You clean up well yo'self."

"Oh this! This nothin'. But check it, wha' ya'll got goin' on after ya'll leave tha club?" Lamonte asked her and her friend.

"Shit, we were thinking about leaving but now we're definitely 'bout to leave. I can't stay up in here lookin' like this," she scoffed to herself in irritation.

Her friend thought she looked a mess. "Yea Candi, we can't stay up in here with you looking like that."

"Well, me and my boy 'bout to bounce too. This his first night out here, he's from Chicago as well. Wha' you say you holla at yo' girl and we all go somewhere and kick it," he offered.

Candi looked at her friend, who was rolling her eyes. "Yeah a'ight...Let me holla at her for a moment."

With that, she turned and whispered something into her friend's ear, obviously hipping her to the game.

"A'ight, she's down," Candi smiled.

Putting Tae-Tea up on the move, the four of them slipped out the club and made their way over towards the Charger. Hitting the button on his keyring, Lamonte deactivated the alarm. The freshly detailed Candy-Brandy-Wine paint glimmered under the moonlit sky.

Sitting inside, Candi's nose was rushed with the smell of Grapes. As soon as Lamonte stuck the key in the ignition, the engine smoothly cranked up and the in-dash touchscreen glowed fluorescent green.

"Ya'll sure ya car gon' be cool where it's parked?" Lamonte asked.

"Yeah, it's cool," Candi's friend, Cristal, answered.

"Fa 'sho. Ya'll might wanna put yo seat belts on though...I drive kinda fast," Lamonte instructed.

"As long as you don't kill us, we all good," Candi assured.

Lamonte shifted the gear to drive and took off out of the parking space, burning rubber. He drove past some bystanders, who stared at him like he was insane.

Messy Marv bumped from the stereo system as he shifted from 2nd to 3rd gear with the slap stick, switching lanes; it was a miracle he didn't run into any cops. Remembering they were riding dirty, he decided to slow down and do the speed limit.

Pulling into the parking lot of the Days Inn, Lamonte put the car in park before hopping out. "Be right back."

As he entered the motel's lobby, he approached the night clerk.

"S 'up Ma'...How much fo' tha night?" he asked.

"Sir, our rooms start at $79.95 plus tax," the pretty young lady said behind the counter. She looked no older than twenty-one.

Lamonte pulled out a wad of money and handed her four crispy hundred-dollar bills. "Let me get two rooms fo' one night. And you can keep tha change 'cause I ain't got no I.D., understand?"

"Yes sir and thank you," the clerk said back to him with a smile on her face.

Lamonte returned to the car and removed the keys from the ignition. Grabbing the bag of Grapes, he said, "C'mon ya'll. I got us a couple of rooms."

After showing Tae-Tae and Cristal to their room, Lamonte led Candi to theirs.

"This is nice," Candi said upon entering the room.

"Yeah, it's straight," he admitted dropping down on the bed, before kicking his shoes off and rolling up a blunt. "You smoke?" he asked.

"Just a little bit...Every now and then," she replied with a look of innocence.

"Well, shit...Smoke wit' a nigga. Cause I ain't try'nah smoke by myself," he suggested.

"Okay, I'll hit it once or twice."

After rolling the blunt, Lamonte stood and patted down his pocket in search of a lighter. "So, yo man ain't goin' to be lookin' fo' you tonight?"

"Why you wanna know?" she asked as she looked around the room "Shit, he's probably wit' yo girl." She smirked.

Lamonte laughed arrogantly. "That's a good one."

Candi glanced over toward him, smiling. She was definitely feeling the kid.

He noticed her staring and playfully asked. "Wha'...you see somethin' you like or somethin'?"

"Maybe," she answered seductively while leaning over and removing the blunt from his lips.

He watched as she grabbed a book of matches off the table and lit up the blunt, taking in her sweet perfume and MAC lip gloss covered lips. The fact that she was hood, yet still classy, was definitely a plus. Everything about her turned Lamonte on.

"Well, I definitely like wha' I see," he said smiling.

Candi slowly blew out the smoke. "I bet you say that to all the girls."

"Nah, not at all. But it's something 'bout you...maybe it's yo smile or tha way you dress or-"

"My fat ass," the words came out along with a puff of smoke as she cut him off, before passing him the blunt.

Lamonte took his time hitting the blunt to buy him some time to think of a response. *This girl is something else,* he thought. *I can't lie, that ass is definitely like that! Not to mention her face and she got cute feet. I'm in love!* His mind was rolling.

The room was filled with the pungent aroma of Grand Daddy Purple as the smoke floated above their heads.

He took another hit before responding. "Yeah, that could be it."

"Uh..huh...I bet." She smiled rubbing her thighs as she stood there checking herself out in the mirror.

After putting out the blunt, Lamonte slid up behind her, kissing her neck gently. Goosebumps magically appeared on her skin. He cupped her breasts with each hand, while slowly massaging her stiff nipples. The feeling caused a low moan to escape her lips. Breathing heavily, she began bitting her lower lip. Seeing that she was fully aroused, Lamonte continued his tongue bath while undressing her.

He removed her blouse and unclasped her bra in one motion. Turning to face him, she began passionately tongue kissing him while unbuttoning his shirt. Working his tongue down to her breasts, he sucked them gently before making his way down south. When he removed her jeans and saw her mohawked trimmed pussy hair. His excitement grew due to the fact that she wasn't wearing any panties.

"How bad do you want this candy?" she asked, inserting two fingers inside herself. Her fingers glistened as she slowly slid them in and out while licking her lip.

The sight of her finger fucking herself caused Lamonte's dick to get super hard. He was dying to get in on the action. He didn't waste any time diving right into her neatly shaped pubic hairs. With her fingers and his tongue, he immediately found her clitoris, parting the fat lips of her pussy. Putting one leg over his shoulders, he licked her slit with skills.

Her knees buckled and her body began to tremble uncontrollably. She'd never felt so good. Lamonte definitely knew what he was doing when putting down his head game.

"Oh yes!...Yes!...Right there!" she moaned, gripping the back of his head.

That's all he needed to hear. Finding her spot, Lamonte used his lips to entrap her clitoris while flicking his tongue against it faster than a rudder on a boat.

"Wait, Wait!...I'm 'bout to cum!" she screamed, rotating her pussy in his face. She looked down and the sight of him smothered in her pussy aroused her even more. "AAAAAHHHHHHHHHHHHH!"

For the first time in her young life, she had an orgasm. Lamonte was eating her pussy so good she couldn't wait to return the favor. Soon his jeans were thrown across the room.

His dick was so hard that it hurt.

"Now, it's my turn to show you a trick or two," she said mischievously. Candi dropped to her knees and hungrily began to give him head. Grabbing a hold of her hair, he guided himself in and out of her mouth.

Candi's head game was like that. She had him on the brink of cumming with her tight jaws. She had more than a mouthful and his dick felt like it was going to explode. Pulling out of her, he reached for his jeans.

"Hold on ma, let me grab a condom," he whispered.

After putting the condom on, he flipped her onto her back and guided himself inside her already wet pussy. She moaned loudly as she massaged her clit with her fingers, causing Lamonte to go nuts from the sight alone.

"Shit! This some good pussy," he told her. He began matching her rhythm with each thrust. Moving her thick hips in unison, Candi matched his every pump as he put his hands underneath her ass, lifting her slightly so he could dig her out.

"Yes! Yes! God damn Daddy! Right there!" she called out as he hit her G-spot, causing her legs to shake.

Pulling out, Lamonte flipped her on her stomach, entering her doggy-style. The juices from her pussy coated his dick, allowing him to slide right in. She squirmed beneath him. Deeper and deeper he pushed himself inside her.

"Black!" she called out in ecstasy as he pounded into her a little harder. He enjoyed the view of her ass bouncing up and down from each of his thrusts.

"Damn, ma, I'm 'bout to cum."

"Ohh shit...me too," she called out.

Lamonte felt her body tense up and when her walls contracted on his dick, he exploded. Candi snuggled underneath him as he collapsed on top of her completely drained. Rolling over, he covered their bodies with blankets before they both passed out.

CHAPTER TWENTY

Ring-Ring!
Ring-Ring!

The sound of Lamonte's cell phone woke him and Candi out of their sleep. Tired from the long night of fucking, Lamonte glanced over at the alarm clock which read *10:01 a.m.*

Groggily he reached for his phone. "Yep," he answered sitting upright.

"Rise and shine, folk. It's just 'bout check out time."

It was Tae-Tae, who sounded like he had a great night as well.

"Yep. Meet us at tha car in like fifteen minutes."

"Fa 'sho," Tae-Tae said, signaling off.

"Get up ma, it's 'bout that time," Lamonte said as he got up and began putting on his clothes.

Candi's face expressed her disappointment. Under no circumstances was she ready to depart. "I'll be ready in a few minutes. I just gotta use the bathroom," she said, slipping on her clothes.

Making it to the parking lot, Lamonte was relieved to find Tae-Tae and Cristal waiting beside the Charger. Once they all were in, he cranked the ignition and drove straight to Broadway Street to drop the girls off at their car.

Pulling up to their Chrysler 300M, everything looked intact. Tae-Tae got out and walked Cristal to the car.

"So when am I goin' to hear from you again?" Candi asked, knowing she should've acted like it didn't matter.

"Shid, you tell me. You the one wit' my number."

"Well, I'll call you later on if I find tha time," she said smiling.

94

A feeling of frustration suddenly covered over Lamonte like a dark cloud. "Wha' do you mean...if you find tha time?"

As she opened the door, he pulled her close, kissing her on the neck. "I see you can't get enough of this candy," she cooed in his ear.

"Make sure you hit me...you hear?" he said dismissively.

Candi chuckled at Lamonte's threat.

"I will...bye." Stepping out of the Charger, she waved before strutting over to the Chrysler.

Tae-Tae hugged Cristal one last time then hopped into the front seat, reaching for the C.D. case.

They drove down Broadway before getting onto 880 South, bobbing their heads to Yo Gotti's new CD. Tae-Tae was quiet and it wasn't until they reached 98th that he spoke.

"Man, let's hit a mall or something. A nigga only out here for a few mo' days. I know they gotta have some gear out here that they ain't got back home," Tae Tae said, admiring the change of scenery that East Oakland offered. "Man, I could get used to this good ass weather."

"Yeah, it's cool. But don't let this weather shit fool you. It's rockin' out here. Niggas be getting it left and right. No doubt it's money out here, but a nigga gotta stay on his toes...feel me? My uncle left me his connect so I'm getting that pure shit fo' tha low-low," Lamonte informed him.

"What's tha number?"

"Shit, right now I'm getting' 'em fo' $16,000. But I know he'll drop tha price once I start cuppin' mo'.'"

"$16,000?" Tae-Tae raised his eyebrows. "Man, we definitely could kill 'em back home."

"You think?" Lamonte teased. "We almost at tha house right now. I just need to take a quick shower before we head to the mall."

***

The two ended up going to Valley Fair Mall in Santa Clara because it had all the high end stores. Lamonte thought it was time for Tae-Tae to step his game up and go back to the Chi with some gear nobody else would have. He definitely would turn a few heads and make a few jaws drop when he got back.

On their way back to Oakland, he stopped at an urban clothing store in Hayward called Manny's, which had all the latest name brands and throw back jerseys.

After making it back to the house, they immediately got dressed and hit the blocks. Tae-Tae decided to rock some yellow and black Coogi shorts with a bumblebee shirt, and jacket to match. All white Creative Recreations graced his feet. Lamonte had on an army green Akoo outfit with the new all black Air Jordan 23 lows.

Lamonte was getting money in Oakland, and it wasn't a secret. Living by the A-B-C-G rules, he knew he was a target for the *jackas* in this new area. It was definitely getting to that point for him to be moving from Buck's house to a more discreet location somewhere in Alameda County.

As he drove through East Oakland, he bumped Tha Jacka's C.D. *Tear Gas*. He cruised slowly up blocks so that his presence could be felt. Pulling onto 28th street, he noticed niggas running around hustling with Murder Dubbs embroidered on their attire. He crept up the block and parked in front of a run-down house.

Before getting out of the car, he punched in the code to his hidden compartment, revealing twin .45's. Removing both guns, he tucked one on his waistband underneath his shirt before tossing the other gun to Tae-Tae.

"Be right back," he said getting out.

As soon as he stepped from the comfort of the A/C, he was greeted by the scorching hot 93 degree heat. With every step he took, the sun seemed to bounce off his diamond chain and cross. He had his army fatigue Oakland A's fitted cap pulled low over his eyes, trying to shield the sun from his face. Everyone had their eyes on him and as he passed, they each greeted with head nods. Even the young kids playing touch football in the streets stopped to admire his presence.

"S'up wit' it, Black?"

"Black, that Hemi thang clean. On Mommas!"

"Wha' it dew Pretty Black?"

"What's really good wit' Tha Dubbs? I see ya'll," he responded, as he headed up the walkway of the run down house.

Knocking on the door in a pattern, Buck showed him a while back, he gained entry. Once inside, the smell of good Grapes instantly filled his nostrils. It was business as usual at the weed house. A couple of dudes sat around smoking blunts while two bitches bagged up trees on the dining room table. Lamonte smiled at the thought of Gene's small weed operation running smoothly in Tha Dubbs.

He walked through the house to the dining room table, where Gene sat with a blunt hanging out of his mouth.

At twenty, Gene wasn't that much older than Lamonte. He was also already on top of his game. He grew up under his big brother, T, who was now serving a 10 year bid in the Feds.

Gene was so busy watching the women weigh and bag up the trees, he didn't even notice Lamonte enter the room.

"Wha' it dew, my nigga. What's really good?" Lamonte asked, walking towards the table.

"Oh shit! My nigga, Black. Wha' brought you to Tha Dubbs besides these bomb ass Grapes?" Gene chuckled, giving Lamonte daps.

"You know, just hittin' some corners in tha town. Since I was in tha area, I decided I could use a zip or two of that Grand Daddy, feel me?"

"No doubt. I got that fo' you all day," Gene boasted, referring to the many pounds he had laid out on the table.

"Yeah, I need to holla at you 'bout some serious weight also. Wha' you'll let me get a couple of them P's fo'?"

"You serious? How many we talkin' 'bout?"

"Shid, probably 'bout three or four fo' now. But imma need mo' later."

Gene couldn't believe Lamonte was getting involved in the weed game being that he already had the town on lock with work. "Damn Black. You try'na push Grapes now? I thought tha dope game was treatin' a nigga good."

"Yeah fam, it's good. But I'm try'na get some Grapes to send back home."

Lamonte figured the money that could be made back home was far more than what Gene was making in Oakland.

"Shid...In that case, I can give 'em to you at $3,500 a piece. As long as you're getting at least three at a time."

"Yep...off top, I could fuck wit' that. You ready now or wha'?"

"I stay ready, just let me know when you need 'em."

ABC6

"Shit, give me a minute to go grab tha paper. I'll be back in 'bout an hour. Let me get one of them zips fo' now though. I need somethin' to smoke."

"Yep, I got cha."

Gene supplied him what he needed and he was out the door in no time.

Getting back inside his car, Lamonte tossed the zip of weed on Tae-Tae's lap and prepared to pull off. Once they were in motion, Tae-Tae immediately began to roll up. Anxious to bend some more corners, Lamonte hit the gas, bobbing his head to *Tha Jacka*.

He steadied his driving and eased off the gas pedal a little to grab the blunt Tae-Tae was passing him. Noticing an Oakland P.D. cruiser parked on the right side of the road, he tucked the blunt, closed the sunroof, and blasted the A/C. His adrenaline was uncontrollable as he passed the parked cruiser. The song '*Glamorous Lifestyle*' filled the interior of the car as Lamonte's cell phone began to vibrate. Turning down the stereo, and glancing at the caller I.D., he saw it was Lil' Pookie from 90th.

Pookie was a kid Lamonte had met from around the way, and like himself, Pookie didn't have much family. Lamonte ran into him about eight months ago hanging outside of Booker's Liquor Store on 90th, bumming for change. He was yet another victim born in Oakland to drug addicted parents leaving him to take care of himself at the young age of fifteen.

Lamonte could tell the kid had a grind from the way he hustled up change all day outside that store. He simply needed to be put on. When Lamonte first laid eyes on the kid, he reminded him of himself because of the hunger he saw in his eyes. Lamonte immediately decide to put the kid under his wings.

"Yo, what's good?" Lamonte spoke into his phone.

"Ain't nothin' bra," Lil Pookie responded. "Nigga out here on the block try'na get good."

Lamonte knew Lil Pookie needed more work. "Where you at?"

"Shid...at tha store right now."

"Like that. Didn't somebody get knocked down over there last night? That spot's hot. You shouldn't even be up there."

98

"Nah, I just came up here to grab some blunts. Then I'm goin' back over to Verdest Ave."

"Cool, I'll meet you over there in 'bout twenty-minutes."

"Yep, good lookin' too, Black. I'on think you know how much I owe you."

"Nah, lil nigga. You don't owe me nothin'. I do wha' I do, 'cause I know if tha shoes were on the other foot, you'd do the same fo' me."

"Off top. See you in twenty. One!"

"One."

Man, that lil nigga doin' his thang. I'm proud of my Lil' protégé fo' getting on his grind, he thought to himself.

"I see duty calls," Tae-Tae smirked, firing back up the blunt.

"Always!" Lamonte replied, driving down International Blvd.

The feeling Lamonte had as he maneuvered the Charger through the city streets was better than anything he'd felt in a long time. The six 12's in the trunk knocked so hard, the ashes from the blunt kept falling on Tae-Tae's new outfit.

"Fuck!" Tae-Tae cursed passing the blunt off.

Taking the blunt, Lamonte inhaled deeply before letting out the smoke. "Bruh, we just gotta make a few stops then go back to the house we just left, and pick up a couple P's of Grapes fo' you to have back home."

"Shid...It's all good. Do you fam."

Hitting the blunt, Lamonte took a long, slow pull before he exhaled a thick cloud of purple smoke into the air. "Damn! This some good shit," he said more to himself than to Tac-Tac.

"I can't tell! Can I smoke wit' you?" Tae-Tae laughed, knowing Lamonte had lungs like a Hoover vacuum cleaner.

Lamonte passed the blunt off to Tae-Tae and he took a long drag, reclined his seat and thought about his return back to Chicago in a couple of days.

As Tae-Tae stared out the window, he thought aloud. "Man...Im'a have to come back out here ASAP."

Lamonte heard him and knew exactly where he was coming from. "No doubt, my nigga. We 'bout to really get this money. Once you touchdown in tha Chi, all you have to do is get me the addresses to where

I'm goin' send tha work. My nigga who works at Fed-Ex will do tha rest."

"Off top, that shit gon' move quick too. Then I'm on tha next thang smokin' back out here."

Lamonte looked at Tae-Tae, thinking about how far they'd come and how far they were going. *Sky's the limit. Our future is definitely looking bright.*

CHAPTER TWENTY-ONE

During the ride to the airport, Tae-Tae looked out at all the passing buildings and cars, realizing he was going to miss Oakland. He asked Lamonte to drive down International Blvd so he could grab an order of prawns to go from JJ's Fish and Chip.

Pulling into the restaurant's parking lot, Lamonte slowly cruised through the aisles until he found a place to park. After retrieving the two pistols from the stash box, they made their way inside.

Out on International Blvd, black and white police cars sped up the block with sirens blaring, rushing to lord knows where. Walking over to the counter, they placed their orders of prawns and fries to go. After their orders were processed and paid for, they moved over to the window to stare out on International until they received their food.

"Here you go sir. Ya'll have a nice day," the woman working the register said.

"Good lookin' Ma, you too," Lamonte told her.

They exited the restaurant and made their way back to the car. As soon as they got inside, Tae-Tae immediately got busy attacking his food like he hadn't eaten in days.

"God damn nigga! Take it easy," Lamonte laughed.

"Fuck you nigga. I'm hungry than a mu'fucka. Plus we ain't got too long fo' we at tha airport," Tae-Tae replied, dipping a prawn in some tarter sauce.

The rest of the ride was silent except for the music playing. Lamonte had his mind focused on how much money was going to be made off the five kilos of coke and three pounds of Grapes he was shipping to Tae-Tae.

The dope game was just as addictive as the drug itself. Once you start stacking dollars, you chased the next buck like a fiend chase their next fix. Lamonte was locked in. Even if he left the game, the game would always be in him.

Tae-Tae's flight was due to depart at 2:00 p.m. They arrived at Oakland International at about 12:15 p.m., with an hour and forty-five minutes for Tae-Tae to spare.

"A'ight nigga, be safe and hit me up ASAP with them addresses so I can get them boxes in tha air," Lamonte said as Tae-Tae grabbed his luggage from the backseat.

"No doubt. Im'a have that as soon as I touchdown in tha Chi. Be easy out here nigga and watch yo'self...A-B-C-G!" Tae-Tae leaned in and gave Lamonte some dap through the window.

"No doubt," Lamonte replied, as they embraced briefly. "Get at me, folk."

Lamonte pulled off and headed back to the house.

$$\longleftrightarrow$$

Paranoia seeped in as Tae-Tae made his way through the security checkpoints. Now it seemed like every white person with shades on were watching him.

Damn, I got this half ounce of Grapes stuffed in my underwear. I should have just waited for the package to arrive back home in a couple of days. But nooo, I had to have somethin' to smoke after I got off tha plane.

If he happened to get busted with the trees, he'd definitely be looking at a federal sentence. His palms started to sweat and his temple throbbed uncontrollably as he was called next.

Approaching a metal detector stick, Tae-Tae prayed the attendant didn't smell the odor of the potent weed. As he walked through, his feet were heavy as bricks; even he thought he smelled the Grapes.

To his surprise, everything went smoothly at the checkpoint and Tae-Tae boarded the plane, sat in his first class seat, and headed for Chicago.

He exhaled.

I knew I'd be alright, he assured himself. Although he was scared as a mothafucker.

————————————————▶

After pulling into the driveway, Lamonte tucked one .45 in his waist, while leaving the other in the stash box. Grabbing his phone and the box of swishers, his mind drifted off.

I got to remember to hit that nigga Red up. I'll do it when I get inside, he thought before going in the house.

Once inside, he went straight to his room to roll up. After twisting up the blunt, he headed into the kitchen to warm up his food in the microwave. When the food was done, he went to sit down on his bed and turned on the flat screen to 106 and Park. He began knocking down prawns and fries, while getting his thoughts in order. He kept thinking about the tasks at hand; vacuum sealing the work, unstitching the stuffed animals, and then restitching them back up with the work inside and then getting the boxes to his boy at Fed-Ex.

While daydreaming, his attention was drawn to the TV screen. The fine ass girl, Shannon, who he had a crush on for many years was rapping in a video with Ludacris.

Oh shit. I never knew shawty had skills. Look at her, he said to himself.

"Damn!" He jumped up to get closer to the screen when she started doing a booty bounce.

Damn, that thang even fatter!

Sitting back down, he took a sip from his water bottle before reaching for the blunt. Putting fire to the tip, he inhaled deeply.

Damn, I wonder if shawty still got that same number? He thought to himself as he let the smoke curl from his mouth into his nostrils before exhaling. Just as he was ashing the blunt, his phone rang. He looked at the caller ID before he answered it.

"What's good?"

"S'up nigga, you good or wha'?" E from Seminary spoke.

"Off top," Lamonte assured, dragging on the blunt. "Wha' you try 'na do?"

"The same as last time."

"That Tech-9 C.D, huh?" Lamonte asked, in reference to the nine zips he sold him a week ago.

"Yes siirr!" E sighed.

"Give me 'bout thirty-minutes."

"Yep, I'm over here on tha block."

"Off top. See you in thirty." Lamonte ended the call thinking it would be best if he knocked out two birds with one stone by hooking up with Red while he was in that area.

After taking his trash to the kitchen, he grabbed his phone and dialed Red's number. "Wha' up nigga?"

"Wha' up. Who tha fuck is this?" Red asked with disgust.

"It's Black. You in tha hood?"

"Oh, s'up wit' it, Black? Yeah I'm local."

"Shid, I'm 'bout to be 'round yo way. Try'na see if you wanna hook up to discuss that little business venture?"

"Shid...Where you try'na meet at?"

"Im'a be on Seminary and Mac in 'bout thirty-minutes. If you want, we can meet at tha Hoagie shop."

"It's good. Call me when you're five minutes away."

"Yep," Lamonte told him before hanging up.

After serving E, Lamonte rode down to MacArthur Street and pulled into the strip mall, which housed a Hoagie Shop. Seminary and MacArthur was yet another hot spot in East Oakland. As he pulled up, he noticed Red leaning against his white Range Rover Sport with his arm tucked underneath his shirt.

"S'up Black?" Red said, walking up to the driver's side window.

"Let me hop in 'cause I'on fuck wit' these niggaz out here."

Red kept his hand under his shirt, gripping his pistol. He knew how niggas from around that way got down and he vowed not to be caught slipping. "It's all good. I'on fuck wit' too many of these niggas either."

Lamonte opened his stash box and took out two chrome .45's and placed them on his lap to show Red that he too was strapped. Then he pushed to unlock the door.

Once Red was seated in the car, he began explaining his situation, eager to get his hands on some of that good dope Lamonte had.

"Man, Im'a get straight to tha point. I hear you got some good shit right now and I need a plug on them thangs fo' a good number. I got some niggas from outta town who try'na get good. But tha last shit I got 'em wasn't right," Red explained.

"S'up with yo' connect? I know you got a dumb ass line already," Lamonte said, wanting him to know he was up on his info.

"Yeah, but my peoples ain't been feelin' their shit. I need a new line. Nah mean? I figure if I cop tha same amount you're copping that would double your order. So you should get an even better number than you're gettin' now," he explained moving his hands to emphasize his point.

As Lamont listened, he could relate to what Red was saying. Lamonte knew that if he doubled his shipment from Capone, the plug would definitely come down on the numbers. His mind began to race. Doing the math in his head, he realized he'd be making a shit load of money.

They sat in that same spot for over twenty minutes, checking the mirrors while discussing prices. Lamonte fired up a blunt with Red, while they sat and talked.

"Yeah, I'm goin' through 'bout ten a week, nah mean?" Lamonte said, passing the blunt.

"Damn, like that huh?" Red said impressed. "Well, I'm only goin' through 'bout five a week. But wit' my outta town niggaz, that's like another five mo'. So ten a week should be right up my alley."

"Off top. I just gotta holla at my dude and see what's tha best number he can give me on twenty a week. Shid, That's damn near a hundred a month. But as soon as I get tha number Im'a holla back." Lamonte reached out his arm to give Red some dap, sealing the deal.

"Sounds like a plan. Hit me as soon as you know something, 'cause I got people waitin'," Red told him as he exited the car, before making his way back to his truck.

Once he started the car and put both .45's back in the stash, Lamonte maneuvered through the parking lot. The whole while he kept his eyes peeled for the Jack boys and the police.

Pulling out into traffic, Lamonte cruised down MacArthur towards Castlemont High School. He was headed to Alvingroom Court to holla at Tina, the lady Buck was serving when that triple homicide occurred.

He stopped at a liquor store on his way there because he needed some Swishers.

Walking out of the store, Lamonte noticed a new school Buick with tinted windows idling across the street. It could have been a coincidence, but his street instinct told him differently.

A-B-C-G! He got in his car and decided not to head to Alvingroom court. Thinking back to the day his father was killed and how they'd been followed, he decided to make a right turn on the first street he came upon. He looked into his rearview mirror and just as he suspected, the Buick turned down the same street. Lamonte turned left onto the next street and sure enough, the Buick followed.

Oh, these niggas think they got somethin' sweet. Well I got somethin' fo' they ass! Ole' obvious ass niggas. I been doin' this, he thought, popping open the stash box and removing his pistols, while periodically checking the rearview mirror.

Maneuvering the Charger down crowded streets, he searched for one that was deserted. He wondered if the niggas in the Buick even knew that he was aware of them following him. Either way, he was about to ruin their intentions. He just needed to find a deserted street so he could do the damn thang.

Nearing 82nd and Bancroft, he sped through an intersection, running a yellow light and barely avoiding a collision. He sped down 82nd and made a left on the first street he came upon. Stopping the car, he jumped out with both .45's in hand. He ran to the corner and ducked behind a parked car, waiting for the Buick.

$$\longleftrightarrow$$

They'd heard a lot about a nigga named Black from Chicago. Word was he was moving a lot of weight in the town. The word on the street was that he had shit on lock and was the next Lil' D. Through the grapevine, they found out he had one of the cleanest Chargers in the town on matching 24 inch Ashanti rims. Also, his local mixtape was starting to make a buzz.

They'd been trying to run into him for over two weeks now. They finally got their break when one of them noticed his car parked outside a liquor store on MacArthur. They immediately put together a plan to kidnap him when they saw him exit the store alone. The plan was to follow him to his destination then jump out and grab him.

Everything was going smoothly until they reached Bancroft. That's when the Charger sped through a yellow light, almost hitting a car.

"Look at that nigga. You think he knows we on em'?" the passenger asked the driver, while playing with the Tech-9 that was on his lap.

"Nah, we good. He ain't goin' nowhere," the driver assured, watching as Black made a left turn on the very next street.

When the light turned green, the driver of the Buick sped through the intersection, racing down 82nd. Coming upon the first street, he made the same left turn as the Charger.

$$\longleftarrow\hspace{3cm}\longrightarrow$$

Lamonte peered over the trunk of the car he was hiding behind in time to see the Buick slowly turning the corner. It was only yards away so he had a clear shot. As the Buick neared, Lamonte came from behind the parked car with both .45's aimed high, letting off shots.

Pop!Pop!Pop!Pop!Pop!Pop!

He yanked both guns with rapid succession, shattering the driver's side window instantly. He was still spitting shots when he noticed the driver lean over towards the passenger. After emptying both clips into the Buick, Lamonte ran back to his car. The Buick sped off down the street swerving from left to right before colliding into an Infiniti Q45.

Moments later, Lamonte was speeding off in the opposite direction. Before turning off the street, he looked into his rearview mirror and saw the passenger jump out running.

As soon as they made a left turn, the driver's side window exploded as a hail of bullets riddled the car. The passenger tried to lift the Tec-9 and return fire but the driver was leaning on him in a way that prevented him from doing so.

"Nigga, get yo scary ass off me! I can't bust tha Tec!" the passenger yelled.

He tried to push the driver off him again, but to no avail. Hearing bullets whizzing through the car, he tried mercifully to snatch up the Tec. Once again, he tried to push the driver over. That's when he saw the gun shot wound and leaking blood from the side of the driver's head. The car sped out of control, due to the driver being dead.

Blamm!

The Buick smashed into a parked car. The impact of the crash caused the dead weight of the driver to jolt forward, giving the passenger enough room to wiggle free.

The passenger looked over at his little brother who had taken the head shot and was unmistakably dead.

"Fuck!" he screamed, snatching up the Tec-9 before getting out and fleeing.

CHAPTER TWENTY-TWO

Throwing the two empty .45's into his secret compartment, Lamonte's adrenaline pumped like a muthafucker. He knew he had bodied the driver when he saw him fall over onto the passenger. He was trying to hit any and everyone, but it looked as if the passenger had gotten lucky.

Fuck boys thought somethin' was sweet, he thought to himself as he slowed to normal speed.

He took Foothill all the way to the Public Storage, where he kept his work. Not knowing if his car was hot or not, he decided to rent a garage size unit to store it away for a while.

Noticing his phone vibrating, Lamonte checked the caller ID and saw it was Desiree. "S'up sis. I was just 'bout to call you."

"Oh really? Well I was just callin' to see if you wanted somethin' from Ed's Bar-B-Q?"

"Nah, I'm good. But I do need a ride. I'm havin' car troubles."

"Boy, where you at? And where's yo car?"

"It's a long story. But I'm at the Public Storage on Foothill. You know where it's at?"

"Boy, I'm sure I'll find it," she said sarcastically.

"Good lookin'. Bye," he said before hanging up.

Fifteen minutes later Desiree pulled up and Lamonte got into the passenger's seat smiling.

"Good lookin' again sis. I owe you one," he said reclining the seat.

Without hesitation, Desiree put the Lexus in gear and pulled out of the parking lot. "Yeah, yeah, yeah. It's all good," she said jokingly. "So where's yo' car anyway?"

"Man, you'd never believe what happened to me today. Some niggas called themselves try'na jack me."

'Wha'! Are you fuckin' serious?" she said in amazement.

"Check this though. Peep how these niggas tried to play yo boy."

Lamonte replayed the event of the day. He didn't remember seeing anyone on the street at the time, so he was hopeful no one had seen him. He knew somebody had gotten slumped for sure and another one had gotten away. He wasn't worried about the police finding fingerprints on the shells because he always used gloves when loading his guns.

Damn! I wish I'd gotten the passenger too. Now I gotta be on the look out fo' somebody tryin' to retaliate. Fuck it! It is what it is. I definitely gotta catch tha 10 o'clock news to find out wha' they know, he thought.

"Man, I can't believe some fools would jeopardize their lives by tryin' to rob you," she replied in shock after hearing what had taken place.

"Well, it just goes to show just 'cause you're try'na creep doesn't mean you can't get crept on. Shid...Anybody can get it. But now, ta hell wit' them fuck boys. S'up wit' Buck? You hear from 'em today?"

"Boy, you know that nigga a phone bandit. He called me three times already today. He says Cooper is goin' to be needin' another $30,000 and then he should be good."

"Yep. Tell 'em it's handled," he said. "Oh yeah can you stop over at Fed-Ex so I can grab a couple boxes?"

"Yeah, I got cha'," Desiree said.

Later that night, Lamonte sat in his room, vacuum sealing five kilos of cocaine and three pounds of Grapes. After making sure he had enough fabric softners inserted to block the smell, he put each bag into different size stuffed animals before stitching them back up.

Once he was finished putting the animals into two boxes and taping them shut, he lit a blunt and smoked until his eyelids got heavy. He exhaled a cloud of smoke and thought. *Today was crazy!*

He was thinking about the Buick when his cell phone started ringing, awakening him from his thoughts. Reaching over to his nightstand, he answered in a tired voice.

"What's good?"

"S'up nigga. Get yo' high ass up and take down these addresses."

It was Tae-Tae.

"Off top. How was yo' trip?" he asked hitting the blunt and glancing at the time." 10:15 p.m.

Damn! I almost missed the news.

"It was cool. Damn nigga, you stay smoking," Tae-Tae said jokingly.

"And you know this!" Lamonte said, looking for something to write with. "I'm ready, go'head."

While writing down the addresses, Lamonte turned the T.V. to the news. Afterwards he continued on. "Boy, you ain't gon' believe wha' happened to me today."

Lamonte told Tae-Tae everything from him seeing Shannon in Ludacris video, to hooking up with Red and last but damn sure not least, the Buick following him.

Tae-Tae listened without saying a word until Lamonte was finished. "Damn, Black! Niggas tried to catch you slippin', huh? I'm glad you recognized game and got at 'em first. You straight though? Or do you need me to do a turn around?"

"Nah, I'm straight. Good lookin' though. You just be on tha look out fo' these boxes I'm sendin' tomorrow."

"No question." Tae-Tae agreed.

Lamonte hollered at his partner for a little while longer before he hung up. Knowing he had a long day ahead of him, he stretched out on the bed and decided to call it a night.

<hr>

Wacko's entire world had been shattered like the driver's side window of the Buick when the bullet flew through it and struck his little brother, Nine, in the head.

Nine was the only person he cared about; the only family he had left in this world. And now he was dead.

Wacko's emotions were at an all-time high. There was nothing in the world that he wanted more than the nigga they called Black. He kept pacing the floor back and forth, shifting positions because the Tec-9 in his waistband was uncomfortable. He couldn't wait to kill Black and anyone else around him. He'd been stressing and crying all day. The death of his little brother was beating him down. The only thing on Wacko's mind was sweet revenge.

CHAPTER TWENTY-THREE

The next few weeks were business as usual for Lamonte. He was shipping out packages and dropping off work throughout the town.

He spoke to Tae-Tae just about everyday. Whenever the boxes arrived, he received a phone call. The plan was to Fed-Ex the boxes to the addresses Tae-Tae set him up with, unbeknownst to the residents of the homes. While the owners were probably away at work, they would use their front porches as drop off spots for the product. Tae-Tae would then cruise down the street, jump out of the vehicle, grab the boxes, and then keep it moving. Tony, Lamonte's inside connect who worked at Fed-Ex, helped Lamonte get the boxes to Chicago without any disturbance from law officials. In return, Lamonte gave Tony $2,500 a box.

So far, shit was going sweet.

After the shooting, Lamonte decided it was best to stay out of the Charger and Pontiac, and got himself a rental car for a while. Not knowing if it was paranoia or what, he switched rentals every couple of days. He'd been expecting retaliation so he tried to stay as discreet as possible. It had been over three weeks and although things seemed to have died down, he was still playing it safe. Since he had no idea who was behind the attempt, he never spoke a word about it to anyone besides Desiree and Tae-Tae. Just in case someone happened to try and gain any information about it from him, his red flag would immediately go up.

Today he was headed to Cooper's office to drop off the remaining $30,000 for Buck's case. His uncle was due in court in just a couple of days.

When he arrived in Berkeley, it was a sunny Monday afternoon. It was so hot it felt like the devil was riding shotgun in the car with him. The rental he was driving was a black Maxima with black leather interior so the sun was trapped inside the car. His legs stuck to the leather seat because he was wearing shorts.

Even though the A/C was on blast, it was still hotter than a mothafucker. The thermostat on the dashboard read 103 degrees, a record-breaking temperature for that time of the month. As he drove, his head began to throb from either the heat or lack of food in his stomache.

"Fuck!" he cursed himself for not picking up some Excedrins when he stopped and grabbed some blunts from the gas station before hitting the freeway.

⟵──────────────────⟶

When he walked into Cooper's office building, it was as if all eyes were on him, as a few people stared at him as if he didn't belong.

Fuck these crackas starin' at? They act like they ain't neva seen a nigga before, Lamonte thought, as he entered Cooper's office wearing a red, white, and black Akademiks short outfit with some all black low top Prada tennis shoes. A White Sox's fitted cap sat on his head, while a black mini Gucci bag with a red and green strap hung from his right shoulder.

"Hi sir, you must be Mr. Gibson. Have a seat, Mr. Cooper will be with you in a moment," said the secretary, as she discreetly looked him over.

She was a middle aged, blonde haired white woman, who resembled the sexy tennis player Anna Kournikova. This was Lamonte's first time at Cooper's office so she had no idea who he was.

Lamonte decided she'd know a lot about him before he left. "Thank you, Mrs.?"

"Ms. O'Neil. And you're very welcome," she corrected.

"In that case, I wonder if I could take you out to lunch some time?" he shot, while leaning over her desk and checking her out.

"I don't think so. Don't you think you're too young to be hitting on grown women?" she asked frankly.

"Not at all. I ain't that young. I'm legal. You'd be surprised. Anyway, you can't be that much older than me. What you twenty-two, twenty-three," he teased, knowing she was well into her thirties.

Ms. O'Neill beamed with a bright smile. "I wish! Let's just say I'm probably old enough to be your mother."

"And she too is a lovely lady. That just makes me like you even mo'," he said with a wink. Then he let his eyes travel to the robust cleavage she flaunted.

Before she could respond, Cooper's office door opened and he waved Lamonte inside.

David Cooper was a forty-something Jewish defense attorney who stood just past five feet and looked like he had one too many cheeseburgers in his life. His jet-black hair was thinning so he wore a comb over. Clear Cartier frames sat on his face as he sported a dark Armani suit with alligator shoes. He wore a nice watch and diamond ring, which Lamonte could tell cost a fortune.

"Hey Black, How's it going?" Cooper asked, once the door was closed.

It took Lamonte a minute to respond. He was too busy taking in the lavish interior of his office. The desk and bookshelf was cherry wood, to the right was a matching burgundy leather sofa with a wall length tropical aquarium displayed behind it. Accented by a custom-made burgundy carpet with Cooper and Associates logo in gold trim, sat directly in the middle of the floor.

"You know, same 'ole, same 'ole," Lamonte responded taking a seat on the opposite side of the desk, from which Cooper was seated. "How's the case looking?"

"Well, hopefully this motion I put in will do us some justice. I'm not really worried about the homicides. The D.A.'s got no evidence whatsoever, except a witness who saw Buck's car leaving from the scene. I'm more worried about the felon in possession of a firearm charge. With Buck's record, if he's convicted in trial, he's looking at 5-9 tops. That's why I'm hoping this motion is granted on Friday. If we get the possession charge thrown out, then the D.A. is not going to have a case."

Cooper was leaning his fat ass back into his chair. Lamonte just knew he would tumble over any second as he eyed the bag around Lamonte's shoulder while awaiting a response.

Lamonte understood what he was saying without him really saying it. Lawyers were the biggest hustlers on earth. They spoke in circles. What Cooper was really saying was, *you got that money for me?*

"Well look, I got that lil' change fo' you," Lamonte said, sitting the Gucci bag down on his desk.

He unzipped the bag and pulled out three neatly rubber-banded stacks of hundreds. Each stack was $10,000.

"Do whateve' you gotta do to get 'em home."

Cooper opened one of his desk drawers and extracted a yellow manila envelope, before grabbing the stacks and placing them inside. Once he sealed the envelope, he dropped it back in his drawer and pushed it shut.

"Black, you know I'm going to do everything possible to bring Buck home. These things just take time."

Yeah, and a shit load of money, Lamonte thought. "A'ight, so do you think he got a chance Friday with the motions?" he asked.

"Right now, I really can't say. It's hard to tell with these judges now days. And Hampton, well let's just say we're not the best of friends. If you know what I'm saying."

After giving Cooper the money and finding out all the insight concerning Buck's court date that Friday, Lamonte was ready to leave. As Cooper escorted him out of his office, Lamonte made a beeline towards Ms. O'Neil's desk and left her a note.

Ms. O'Neil, my older Mami or should I say hottie (smile). Damn, I don't even know your fist name. Anyhow, I couldn't run outta this office without dropping you a line or two to let you know you're running through my mind. Even though you're a lil older than I am, I still would like to get to know you if you don't mind. Here's my cell number, call me if you feel like getting away. (510) 555-2637.
-Black

After that, he walked out into the hot sun with a smile, feeling like a playa.

***

116

DESEAN GARDNER

Friday came and Buck sat comfortably behind the defense table completely confident in winning his motion. So far, Cooper had been successful in proving that the Oakland P.D. had no legal right to search his vehicle. After catching the arresting officer in multiple lies, Ms. McIntosh was desperate to keep the case alive.

Cooper was rolling up his sleeves and earning his pay as he challenged the state's prosecutor, accusing the Oakland Police Department of illegally searching and seizing Buck's property.

"Your Honor, it's clear that my client wasn't on any form of probation or parole. Nor was there any probable cause whatsoever to search and detain my client," Cooper stated.

"Well your Honor, Mr. Gibson was under investigation after witnesses described the car he was driving fleeing away from the scene of a triple homicide. An APB was put out for his car, which by the way was green at the time. Three weeks later, Oakland P.D. ran the plates of a purple Buick, in which Mr. Gibson was driving, and got a hit. Even though Mr. Gibson wasn't on any form of probation or parole, there had been an APB out on the car he was driving, which was registered in his name, giving the officers all rights to search his vehicle, which successfully turned up a loaded firearm," Ms. McIntosh replied.

"Excuse me your Honor, but it's stated in the report of the Oakland P.D. that my client was pulled over simply for a traffic violation of talking on a cell phone while driving. A violation that is only punishable of a fine. There's nowhere in the report that states my client was under some kind of investigation, making it illegal for officers to have searched his vehicle," Cooper shot back.

"Yeah, well he was originally stopped for the traffic violation, but a quick run of his plates uncovered the APB. Had the car remained in its original color it was in the months prior, I'm sure the arresting officer would have discovered that the vehicle was involved in a triple homicide!" Ms. McIntosh shouted sarcastically.

Cooper stood to argue more, but was interrupted by the banging of Judge Hampton's gavel.

"I think I've heard enough. I've had the pleasure of briefly reading through each party's complaint. Although Mr. Gibbson wasn't on any form of probation or parole, the laws say that any kind of state or federal official may stop, detain, and search all occupants of a vehicle that's been up on an All Points Bulletin, giving the officers all right to search Mr. Gibbson's vehicle once they got a hit on his license plate number. Furthermore, Mr. Cooper, I think it's very suspicious that your client had his car repainted right after it was described fleeing away from a scene of a triple homicide. Therefore, motion for immediate dismissal of all evidence seized illegally is denied," Judge Hampton announced.

The court erupted in mayhem as Buck shook his head.

"But your Honor," Cooper stood before being interrupted.

"No *your Honor*. This matter is now adjourned," Judge Hampton stated, slamming down his gavel.

Before Buck could even express his displeasure, Cooper leaned over and whispered in his ear. "That's bullshit. I'm filing an appeal. This judge is an asshole. I'll be up to the jail to see you later on," Cooper assured.

"Man, be sure you come see me," Buck instructed before he was escorted away by the bailiff.

$$\longleftrightarrow$$

Sitting in the courtroom, stunned by the judgement Hampton handed down to Buck, Lamonte immediately hurried out of the room so he could call Desiree, who had to work that day, and give her the bad news.

"S'up, sis?" he said into his cellphone.

"Nothin', wha' happened?" she asked.

"It's all bad. Them crackas denied 'em."

"Fuck!" she blurted out. "Okay, talk to you later."

"Yep. I'm leavin' tha courthouse now. I gotta make a couple of runs and then I'll be at tha house."

"Uh huh," was all Desiree said before hanging up.

Later that night, Lamonte received a surprising phone call from Cooper's secretary, Jessica O'Neil. It turned out Jessica was a cougar. After talking for an hour, they made plans to hook up the following day.

CHAPTER TWENTY-FOUR

Red checked out to be good peoples, which was good because Lamonte hated to have to kill him.

After talking it over with the plug, Capone, he agreed to give Lamonte the bricks at a discount of $12,000 a brick, as long as Lamonte copped at least twenty a week. With a deal like that, Lamonte would have to come out of pocket $240,000 a week. But the going rate for a brick in the Bay Area was $18,500 and $30,000 back home in Chicago, so there was definitely a lot of money to be made.

Lamonte decided he'd wholesale the bricks for $16,000 in the Bay and $25,000 back home. Red insisted on meeting the connect, but Lamonte denied him that opportunity. In the end, Red settled for dealing with Lamonte as long as he promised to give him the same number as he was getting. Lamonte agreed. After all, he was using Red's money to help double his order a week, which resulted in him getting the $4,000 discount. Lamonte assured Red he was getting them for $14,000 a brick, which was far less than the $17,000 Red was used to paying. Red immediately agreed and it was on and popping.

After the first delivery from Capone, Lamonte knew he'd just upped his status to Kingpin. He was making big dollars back home, profiting $75,000 off every five bricks, and doubling his money off the Grapes. Bringing his net profit from the shipping operation to $88,000 after taking out $5,000 for Tony's cut for his role at Fed-Ex.

Lamonte and Tae-Tae split the profit down the middle.

In Oakland, Lamonte took to the streets like never before. In addition to selling hard, he wholesaled weight. Other than the turfs Red had on lock, the city belonged to him.

119

With so many hustlers copping from him, Lamonte decided to rent out a little house on the 7200 block of Bancroft Avenue and turn it into a trap. He gave his protégé, LiL Pookie the responsibility to run the trap house.

LiL Pookie introduced Lamonte to two young wild niggas named Murda and Lil' Trigg. They were straight up killas. Both were only seventeen-years-old, yet had already gained a reputation in the streets for delivering cruel and unusual punishments.

Murda was dark-skinned with long dread locks. He stood 6'1" and 210 pounds. Lil' Trigg, the wilder of the two, was light-skinned with little twists in his hair. He stood only 5'2", 140 pounds soaking wet. For every pound he lacked with his weight, he packed on his waist.

After getting to know them, Lamonte immediately took a liking to the youngstas. He could tell the little niggas were loyal so he offered them a job as security watching LiL Pookie's back at the house on Bancroft.

The months that came afterwards proved to turn out quite well for Lamonte. Not only was he eating, but so was everyone around him as long as they remained loyal. While Buck chose to limit his associates and kept his circle tight, Lamonte had put together a team of hustlers. Between Gino, Chop, E, Tina, and Pookie, he was running through four bricks a week easily. Tae-Tae was selling out fast back home, going through five bricks every two weeks. Lamonte's long list of clientele stretched far into West Oakland also. He had Glizz from Acorn, Pop from Ghosttown, and Green from M&M.

If you were copping and it wasn't from Lamonte, chances were you were copping from Red, which meant you were still copping from Lamonte. He was young and on the rise with a nice chunk of Oakland on lock. His operation was continuously growing.

As powerful as he'd became, you'd think nobody would try him. But there were still niggas plotting his demise. Those foolish enough to think shit was sweet would definitely find out.......

Anybody Can Get It!

After the third twenty brick shipment from Capone, Lamonte decided it was time for him to get his own spot and another whip. He'd been driving rentals for over six months and was ready to get his shine on again. He paid the white bitch Jessica to put a condo in her name for him. After giving her $3,000, plus all the money for the security deposit and the first year rent in advance, he was ready to move into his new spot.

He found a luxurious three-bedroom, two-bathroom condo in Hayward Hills, fifteen-minutes away from Oakland. He admired it one day while riding with Buck. He told himself then that one day he'd call the thirty-six story luxury highrise his home.

His dream came to reality.

The condo was fully equipped with two wood-burning fireplaces; one in the living room and the other in the master bedroom. The kitchen was gourmet style with a nice sized washer and dryer. It was definitely fit for a boss.

The condo received a lot of sunlight as the rising sun shined brightly through the floor to ceiling windows in the living room. Cocaine white plush carpet cushioned his feet throughout the apartment. Marble tile decorated the kitchen floor and bathrooms. Lamonte chose one of the few units on the 36th floor because it allowed more privacy and came with a larger enclosed balcony with double french doors.

Tae-Tae stayed with him whenever he came to town so he had a room of his own. Lamonte turned the other room into a gym equipped with mirrors all over the walls. From all the money he was making, he could have easily purchased a nice home in the Hills somewhere but a nigga of his status constantly needed security, and the highrise provided that.

One day, while surfing the net, Lamonte noticed a 2010 Porsche Cayenne twin turbo for sale by a private owner for $45,000. He called the number listed on the page and prayed nobody had inquired about the vehicle. Within the hour, he was on his way to Sacramento to meet up with the owner, go for a test drive, and hopefully purchase the vehicle. He took Candi along just in case she had to drive his Charger back for him.

The owner informed Lamonte that the SUV went to 60 miles per hour in 6.4 seconds, and could get up to well over 160 miles per hour. He showed Lamonte the rear entertainment system and told him about the dual air bags and low milage on the vehicle. Lamonte was visably pleased, so he began to negotiate a deal. He told the owner he had $35,000 cash on him. The owner shot back, saying it was a brand new

Porsche and worth far more than the $45,000 he was asking for. He drove a hard bargain but in the end, he agreed to accept $40,000 cash without notifying the I.R.S of his lucrative purchase.

With the paper work taken care of, and the vehicle fully paid, it was time to put the twin turbo to the test. Once Lamonte hit the freeway, he floored it, leaving Candi in the dust.

As soon as Lamonte made it back to Oakland, he went straight to his homeboy, Carlos, at East Bay Customs. He gave him specific instructions and Carlos was happy to comply because he knew Lamonte didn't mind spending for what he wanted. Lamonte became good friends with Carlos after he took him his Charger, which he coughed up close to $20,000 for the paint, rims, music, and stash box.

He assured Lamonte he'd have the Porsche ready by Lamonte's nineteenth birthday celebration, which was coming up in a couple of months. Candi was the only person that knew about the truck. Lamonte wanted to surprise niggas when he brought it out for his
birthday.

It would be another way of showing how big he was doing it in his newfound home of Oakland, California.

CHAPTER TWENTY-FIVE

Tae-Tae called him early Friday morning, waking him out of
his sleep.
"Yeah," Lamonte answered.
"Rise and shine birthday boy."
"Yeah, yeah, yeah, wha' time you gettin' in folks?"
"Shit, my plane land at 2 o'clock yo time."
"I can dig it. I'll be there," he replied.
"Nigga, wait 'til you see wha' I got cha fo' yo b-day. You gon' love
it," Tae-Tae claimed.
"Off top. You know tha clubs goin' to be packed ta'night, right? I
hope you're bringin' yo bling bling, 'cause Im' a set it off in that
muthafucka! You know how a real Chi-Town G do it."
"No doubt. I might just have to go see yo dude, Carl, over at
Highline to snatch up somethin' else."
"Yeah, who knows, I might just have to buy myself somethin'
special also," he suggested.
"Whatever nigga," Tae-Tae remarked. "Just make sure you're on
time picking me up. I ain't try'nah be waitin' 'round like last time with
over $100,000 taped to me."
"Nigga, that only happened once, and I told you I got caught up in
some shit," Lamonte said, thinking back to the day Tae-Tae was
referring to.
He had knocked this bitch name Jada coming out the gas station on
98th as he pulled in to get some gas. Needless to say, fifteen minutes
later he was circling the block while Jada gave him top and ended up
being thirty minutes late.
"Yeah, okay," Tae-Tae said sarcastically.

"Nigga, I'll be out front as soon as you get off the plane. Now let me go so I can get up and get in the shower," he replied, as he got out of bed and headed towards the bathroom.

"A'ight, one!"

"One!"

Lamonte hung up, took a quick piss, and started running his shower water. Moments later, after getting into the shower, Jessica appeared butt ass naked and entered with him. She stood beneath the showerhead with her back to Lamonte as she began to lather up her body.

Lamonte admired the view. Jessica was definitely a bad snow bunny. At thirty-two years old, her mildly tanned, white skin complexion glowed under the water while her hair looked like golden silk hanging down her back. She was Russian mixed with Italian. Not only was her face on point, but she also had body. She was Anna Kournikova with an ass and titties like Coco.

"You ready for your birthday present?" she teased.

"Wha' you got fo' me, Ma'?" he asked, pulling her backwards towards his dick. Lamonte then licked and kissed her neck while moving her hair to the side.

In between his kisses, Jessica turned around, got on her knees, and went straight for his manhood, taking it in her mouth. She spit on it and licked it before finally deep throating it. As she furiously bobbed her head back and forth, she snuck a glance up at Lamonte to make sure he was enjoying his gift. She worked her jaws even faster when she saw Lamonte's eyes roll to the back of his head.

"Damn Ma'," he said in a lustful tone. "You 'bout ta make me cum."

"Mmmmmm Mmmm, bust in my mouth baby," she said around his hard dick.

"Oh...oh…yeah… right there Ma', I'm 'bout ta Oh-ohhhh Shitttt." Lamonte tried to hold back but Jessica worked her jaw muscles to the extreme.

Jessica could tell he was enjoying himself from the way he was moaning and groaning. She worked some old school tricks on his young ass and Lamonte could no longer restrain himself as he felt the sensation in his balls about to erupt. All it took was a few more strokes before he emptied what seemed like gallons of sperm into her mouth.

Looking up at him, she smiled swallowing every bit of it. It felt so good Lamonte's knees got weak, and if it weren't for him holding onto the shower rail, he would have fell.

"Happy birthday baby," Jessica said, pleased with her performance.

"Good looking," Lamonte simply replied.

After showering together, Jessica got dressed and headed out the door to her own apartment in Castro Valley.

That's one bad ass snow bunny! Lamonte thought to himself as Jessica waved bye.

When she left the apartment, Lamonte rolled up a blunt and made his way to the balcony. After closing the french doors behind him, he took a seat in one of the lounge chairs. He opened up his C.D. case and rummaged through the selections. He'd been listening to Bay Area music more and more since coming to the Bay. Once he found what he was looking for, he popped it in the C.D. player on the table and reclined in his chair, waiting for the sounds that always motivated him. Within seconds, the speakers came alive.

Bitch, bitch, bitch, she sucked my dick, don't fuck wit' that...bitch, bitch, bitch, bitch, that's why E-40 and Too Short say, bitch, bitch, bitch, bitch...

E-40, the Ambassador of the Bay, was spitting some shit on his C.D. called *Day Shift.*

Lamonte fired up the blunt and let the smoke take him away. He thought about everything he'd experienced since losing his dad. He went from robbing, to killing, to locking down a whole city dealing. He definitely came a long way. Once motivated by the lifestyle of gang banging and repping G.D. everywhere he went, his motivation was now strictly dollars. He was lucky enough to have an opportunity to escape that lifestyle but never the one to forget where he came from. It was G.D. to the death of him.

He thought about his mom. He loved and missed her unconditionally. He thought about Buck's case and last but not least, his deceased dad and how he'd be so proud of the man he became.

As he smoked and reminisced, his cellphone rang. He hit the answer button on his iPhone.

"Sup."

An automotive voice came over the line.

"You have a collect call from...*Buck*...an inmate at Alameda's county jail, press 0 to deny," Lamonte accepted the call and waited for Buck to click on.

"Sup nigga? Happy Birthday!" Buck spoke.

"Good lookin'. Sup wit' you doe. A nigga ain't heard from you in a minute. What's crackin'?" Lamonte shot back.

"You know, same ole', same ole'. Another one like tha others. Tired of this county shit, and thinkin' 'bout taking' that five piece fo' tha burner. If so, they gon' drop tha homicides. A nigga just try'na get back ASAP, nah mean?" Buck said sadly.

Lamonte was stunned by the news of his uncle thinking about taking a deal. He couldn't be serious after all the money he gave Cooper.

Buck continued. "Shit, it's already been ova a year. With half time, I'd be home in no time."

He was listening while wondering if that was indeed the best idea. So he asked, "You sure that's wha' you wanna do?"

"Yeah, I'm ready to get up out this fish bowl. It ain't nothin' but another year and a half, so it's nothin'!"

"Off top. You ain't gotta worry 'bout shit either. It's all good in tha hood!" he assured him.

"No doubt. Anyways, I heard 'bout tha party tonight. Nigga, just make sho' you watch yo'self out there. You know how niggas be actin' after they've been drinkin'."

"I know. But I stay on point. Plus Im'a have my niggas there, so I'll be straight," he said while thumping ashes in the ashtray in front of him.

Buck was silent for a moment, then said, "Don't sleep on that nigga Red either. You know tha streets are talkin'."

Buck was referring to Lamonte's dealing with Red, and letting him know that he indeed knew about it. "Uh-huh, good lookin' fo' tha heads up."

"It ain't nothin', just keep yo' head up and eyes open. I'm 'bout ta get off this phone and go work out. Im'a hit you up later."

"Off top nigga. Get that money. Stay up and get at me."

"One love my nigga."

Lamonte ended the call and reclined in the lounge chair, smoking, and thinking about his conversation with Buck. Moments later, he phoned Carlos at East Bay customs while finishing his early morning birthday blunt.

"My man, Black! Happy birthday," answered Carlos.

"S'up Los, how's it lookin'?"

"It's all good. You gon' love it, watch! Wha' time your pickin' her up?"

"I'll be up there right befo' you close. So have me detailed up," Lamonte replied, anticipating its looks.

"I got cha, my man."

"A'ight, see you then."

"Later my friend."

CHAPTER TWENTY-SIX

Tae-Tae was back in Oakland. After retrieving his Louis Vuitton carry-on bag, he strutted through Oakland International Airport paranoid as usual because of the $120,000 he'd smuggled onboard. He bypassed the baggage claim, a lesson he learned on his first trip out. Then he had to wait with $50,000 on him for over twenty minutes before his luggage finally arrived on the conveyer belt. After that incident, he vowed never to travel with more than a small sized carry-on bag with him. He'd simply buy whatever he needed when he got there.

He was relieved once he made it to the exit. Lamonte's Chrysler 300 rental was parked in the drop off zone with its hazard lights on. He immediately went straight to the car. The whole way his eyes darting side to side, looking at every white person with shades on.

$$\longleftrightarrow$$

Tae-Tae arrived in Oakland right on schedule. He phoned Lamonte as he departed the aircraft and Lamonte assured him he'd be waiting out front in the dark blue Chrysler 300 he was pushing. As Tae-Tae approached the vehicle, Lamonte could tell he was relieved to have accomplished yet another trip.

Shit! With over $100,000 of Lamonte's money on him, Lamonte was relieved also.

Once he got inside the car, Lamonte pulled off.

"S'up with tha Gangsta? How was yo' trip?" he asked his old time friend.

"Shit, same ole', same ole'. Nothin'serious. Piece of cake," Tae-Tae said convincingly. Lamonte knew he'd been sweating bullets.

Pushing number seven on the C.D. changer, Jay Z's 'Empire State of Mind' came blasting through speakers.

In the passenger's seat, Tae-Tae was busy detaching the stacks of money from his body. After retrieving and storing the last stack into his Louis Vuitton bag, he pulled a gold box with a white ribbon on it. "Happy birthday, bruh!"

Surprised, Lamonte was eager to see what was in the box. He figured it was some jewelry. He opened the box and was overwhelmed by the sight of a ten caret black diamond chain and five caret black Jesus piece attached to it. He delicately removed the chain from the box, adoring it like it was the last piece of pussy on the planet.

"Now this is a muthafuckin' gift! This shit phat ass fuck! Good lookin' my nig....Love you," he said, putting on the necklace.

"Ah nigga, it's nothin'. You know how we do it. Besides, yo' real gift is right in this bag." Tae-Tae smirked, rubbing his hand over the Louis Vuitton bag, referring to the $103,500 that belonged to Lamonte.

As Lamonte cruised the streets, he kept his eyes glued to the rearview mirror, looking out for the police or anybody trying to follow them. Merging into oncoming traffic on 880, his cell phone vibrated. After turning down the volume on the stereo, he answered. "S'up wit' it?"

"Happy b-day bruh. What's crackin' wit' you today?" Lil' Pookie asked.

"Shit, just picked up Tae-Tae from tha airport, 'bout ta hit tha mall, then get somethin' ta eat. Wha' you got goin'? How we lookin' ova there?"

"Man, you know it's business as usual. Runnin' through this shit like laxatives. You might wanna drop by," Pookie said, indicating he needed to re-up.

"Off top. Give me a couple of hours and I'll be through there."

"Yep...One."

Lamonte hung up the phone and tossed Tae-Tae a bag of Grapes. "Roll up."

"I was afraid you weren't goin' ta ask." Tae-Tae smirked, snatching up the bag.

129

Twenty minutes after leaving the airport, they were pulling up in Southland Mall's parking lot. After grabbing a few stacks out of the Louis Vuitton bag, and locking it away in the trunk, Lamonte handed Tae-Tae a .9mm to stuff in his waistband before they headed inside.

They strolled through the mall popping tags like ball players.

Lamonte was shuffling through a rack of Christian Audiger jeans at Up Against The Wall, when a voice called from behind him.

"May I help you find somethin'?"

The voice had an accent that Lamonte couldn't place, and sounded super sexy. When he turned around, he came face to face with the baddest female he'd ever laid eyes on. She had long jet-black hair with gold streaks. Her face and skin was flawless with not a blimish in sight. She had eyes like Lala Vazquez and a body like Rosa Acosta. Lamonte couldn't tell if she was Puerto Rican or Dominican. What he did know was that she had indeed just helped him find what he'd been looking for.

Checking her name tag, he said, "I think you just have, Evelyn."

"Is that so? Because I was referring to tha' clothes."

"Well, since you helped me find tha' girl of my dreams, I guess it's safe to trust you wit my sizes." He smiled.

Evelyn peeped game and smiled back. "Well, what sizes are you looking for?" she asked.

"I need these, these, and those ova there. All in a 38, plus I want the T-shirts to match, in 3XL. And if you got that white Live Mechanics leather jacket ova there in 3XL, I'll take that also."

"Will that be it? Or would you like to buy the store too?" she joked.

"Nah, not tha' store. But I would like to buy you lunch."

That statement caught her off guard. "Thanks, but no thanks. I don't know you like that. How I know you're not some crazy lunatic." She shot Lamonte down smiling at the cat and mouse game she was playing with him.

But the mouse was definitely chasing that cat.

"Definitely not a lunatic. Crazy maybe. One thang fo' sho' is I'd be crazy not to try to get to know you," he said.

"Um-hum. Let me go get your stuff."

When she returned, they chopped it up for about ten minutes. He told her about his birthday party later that night at Club Sway in San

Francisco, inviting her to come. She agreed so he told her he'd put her name plus two on the list.

After purchasing his gear, and blowing over $2,000 in the store, he headed for the door with nothing but thoughts of Evelyn on his mind. She was a twenty-one year old Dominican Republic native who'd recently moved to the Bay Area on a student visa. She attended California Berkeley and majored in Corporate Law. She had two roommates in Alameda and was currently single with no kids.

As Tae-Tae and Lamonte walked through the mall, they stopped at Highline Jewelry store to see if Carl had any new pieces. Carl was in the middle of helping a customer when he saw them enter the store.

"My main man, Black. I'll be wit' you in one second," he said, before turning to one of his employees and telling them to finish helping his customer. "Black, what can I do for you, my friend?" he asked, extending his hand.

Lamonte briefly shook hands with Carl before saying. "You ain't got nothing new back there?"

"I actually just got some new watches and bracelets in. They're in tha back. Let me go get them."

While looking over pieces, Lamonte noticed the customer Carl was previously helping staring in their direction. He didn't think much about it. *Yeah nigga! You see it. Groupie ass nigga. Probably think we're ball players or something.*

Carl returned and once Lamonte laid eyes on the black and white diamond zebra designed Johnny Watch, and matching Boosie bracelet, he knew he was about to pop some rubber bands.

"This muthafucka's clean. I can rock this wit' my white or black pieces," he said, admiring the jewelry.

"Man, I'm feeling that gold and black one. Shid, I might just have to rock them shit's to tha party tonight," Tae-Tae added.

"Oh! Ya'll going out tonight, huh? Where to?" Carl asked, hoping his conversation would lead to a big purchase.

"Yeah, I'm having, a birthday bash tonight at Club Sway in tha city. That's why I'm thinkin' 'bout coppin' some new pieces," Lamonte replied.

As Lamonte looked over Carl's shoulder, he caught him again. That same nigga sneaking peeks in their direction. *Damn nigga! Wha' tha fuck you keep lookin' at?*

Lamonte was about to approach him and say something, but was side tracked by Carl saying, "I give you a good deal since it's your birthday."

The mentioning of a deal brought Lamonte back to the jewelry. He agreed and followed Carl to the counter.

By the time they paid for their jewelry, the stalker was long gone, as well as the $20,000 they paid a piece for the watches and bracelets. Since the mall housed a Hometown Buffet, they decided a quick meal would be right up their alley.

←——————————————→

When he answered his cell phone, he was ready to curse whoever it was out. "What is it? I'm busy!"

"Wacko...Man, check it out! You'd never believe wha' just happened. A nigga up here at tha mall and I stopped off in Highline to see how much they'll charge me fo' a grill. And guess who walks in?"

Wacko was concentrating on the blowjob he was receiving and didn't have time to play the guessing game. "Who nigga!" He'd already recognized the voice to be Rich.

"That nigga Black! That's who. Him and some nigga just came in there blowin' big chips on pieces." Rich was Wacko's goon and was eager to deliver the information.

With the mention of Black's name, Wacko immediately snatched his dick from the girl's mouth and started pulling up his pants. "Where...Where... where you at?"

"At Southland. I told you, I was at Highline-"

"Please tell me he's still there and I'm on my way right fuckin' now!" Wacko was hyperactive, impatiently ready to smash up there.

"Yeah, I just watched 'em go to Hometown Buffet. But you betta hurry up, 'cause that place is like a fast food joint."

"Damn! You shoulda called me as soon as you saw 'em!"

"I didn't know it was him 'til I heard the dude at Highline call out his name," Rich said.

"Nigga, I'm on tha way. Call me if he do it movin'!" Wacko ordered.

After hanging up the phone, Wacko grabbed his Tec-9 and raced out to his rented Camry.

Destination: Southland.

Objective: Kill Dat Nigga Pretty Black!

←——————————————————————→

The Hometown Buffet was packed with the usual crowd. After paying the hostess, Lamonte and Tae-Tae were escorted to their table.

As they walked through the crowded dining area to be seated, Lamonte's cell phone started vibrating. Looking at the caller ID, he saw it was Candi. After placing all the bags he'd accumulated in the mall under the table, he accepted the call.

"S'up pimp?" Lamonte joked.

"Happy birthday!" Her voice was bubbly and full of joy.

"Good lookin'. S'up wit' you? Yo nigga lettin' you come out to play tonight?" he asked, hoping she wouldn't be able to come.

"I'll be there," she simply replied.

Damn! he thought as his other line clicked.

"Hold on a sec," he said before glancing at the name on the screen. He clicked over.

"Los, what's good?"

Since Lamonte was occupied talking on the phone, Tae-Tae took the opportunity to go get his food while Lamonte watched their stuff.

"Black, somethin' came up and I gotta get outta here early. How soon can you get up here?" Carlos asked.

"Shit, I can be there in like thirty minutes."

"Okay buddy, Im'a be waitin'," Carlos said before disconnecting.

When Lamonte clicked back over, Candi had hung up. *Fuck her anyway!*

Tae-Tae returned and placed his plate full of food and drink on the table. After taking his seat, he immediately started tearing off into his food. When he noticed Lamonte laughing he asked, "What's so funny?"

"You nigga," Lamonte teased, before getting up and checking out the food selections.

133

Lamonte and Tae-Tae left the Hometown Buffet feeling rejuvenated. When they made it back to the car, Lamonte popped the trunk open and tossed their things inside. Driving out of the parking lot, Lamonte made sure to signal before he advanced onto the street. He glanced in both directions before he began to merge into southbound traffic. Before he could successfully complete the turn, some fool in a Toyota Camry sped into the mall's parking lot, cutting him off. He barely avoided a collision.

Honk! Honk! Hoooonk!

"Stupid muthafucka! You don't see my fuckin' turn signal!" he yelled more to himself than to the occupant of the other vechicle.

Frustrated, he floored the accelerator and the car shot towards the freeway.

$$\longleftrightarrow$$

Wacko gripped the steering wheel with one hand and dialed Rich's cell with the other. His adrenaline was pumping like he had nitro in his blood.

Pulling into the mall's parking lot, he barely avoided hitting a car, which caused the driver of the other vehicle to bang on his horn. Wacko thought to himself, *shut tha fuck up! You lucky I'm on a mission or I'd give you wha' ya looking' fo'.*

Rich picked up

"Nigga, I'm dippin' through tha parking lot by tha Hometown right now! Where that nigga at?" Wacko's tone was authoritative.

"Man, you just missed 'em like two minutes ago."

"Shit! Shit! Shit!" he cursed, punching the steering wheel. "Nigga, I told you to hit me if he left!"

"I was just 'bout ta call you!" Rich barked. "But don't trip, tha nigga is throwin' a birthday bash tonight and I know where at."

"Oh yea? And where is that?"

"It's gonna be at......"

After getting all of the necessary information from Rich, an angry Wacko peeled out of the parking lot. He'd just have to catch the nigga tonight.

Maybe this will be better, he thought. *Then I can give it to 'em raw and uncut.*

At this thought, he smiled and busted a u-turn, heading back to his spot. He had a cake to bake for a nigga whose birthday will be his last.

CHAPTER TWENTY-SEVEN

When they arrived at East Bay Customs, Carlos was standing out front waiting on Lamonte.

"Wha' you got goin' on here?" Tae-Tae asked as they pulled into the shop.

"I'm pickin' up my gift to myself," Lamonte answered, smiling.

They got out of the car and approached Carlos.

"Wasup wit it buddy? Thanks fo' gettn' here quickly," Carlos said.

"Aint' nothin'. This my man Tae-Tae, he's goin' to be needin' you to hook 'em up somethin' too real soon."

"Hey, how's it goin' Tae-Tae?" Carlos asked shaking his hand. "Anyway, a family emergency came up so I gotta split. But I made sure tha Porsche was nicely detailed and ready to go," he said, walking them to the back of the shop.

At the mention of the word Porsche, Tae-Tae looked at Lamonte with that I know you didn't expression on his face.

"Off top. Good lookin'," Lamonte said to Carlos as they continued to walk toward the back.

As they made it around the back, Tae-Tae's eyes bulged out of his head, and his mouth dropped open. "Oh shit! Nigga, no you didn't!" he shouted in amazement.

The Porsche was candy burnt orange on matching 28" Dub Floaters. A regular Porsche Cayenne demanded respect in the hood but a twin turbo candy burnt orange on matching 28" floaters? Now that was the ultimate.

"Nigga, this shits king! Where's tha keys?" Tae-Tae asked Carlos.

Carlos tossed him the keys and Tae-Tae immediately jumped behind the wheel and cranked it up. Too Short came thumping from the speakers and Tae-Tae turned the stereo up. The bass from the six 12-inch woofers viberated off the shop's windows.

The ride was super clean. The interior was peanut butter leather with burnt orange gator skin running down the center of the seats. The carpet was tan, but the floor mats were orange with the name *Pretty Black* embroidered in them. All four headrests were mounted with seven-inch TV monitors, and a big twenty-inch screen dropped from the backseat ceiling. To top it off, Carlos also installed a secret hidden compartment.

From the smile on Lamonte's face, Carlos could tell he was satisfied.

"Niggas definitely gon' hate when they see this shit! You already know," Tae-Tae said.

"Good! Im'a be like Maino, *Hi Hatas*!" Lamonte said smiling.

After confirming the code to the stash box and making sure it was working correctly, Lamonte gave Carlos the $18,000 that was owed and kept it moving. Tae-Tae jumped in the Chrysler and followed him back to the condo so he could park the Porsche until later.

Once they entered the condo, Lamonte went and put the things he'd bought at the mall away. Next, he put the remainder of the money he'd collected from Tae-Tae in his safe. With his business completed, they left to make a few drops in the hood.

The rest of the day was pretty much the usual; smoking blunts and dropping off work.

After dropping off the re-up to Pookie on Bancroft, Lamonte let the youngster know what time they'd meet. Next, he made a drop to Gino in tha ville before rolling through Funktown to see if he saw Red.

Lamonte spotted Red standing out front of one of his trap houses with a couple of his runners. He pulled over and hopped out.

"S'up wit' ya'll niggas?" Red asked, stepping to the car.

"Nothin much. Try'na see wha' time ya'll niggas headin' to tha city?"

"Shit, we probably gon' dip 'round 10:30. I gotta make sure I get a good parking spot, nah mean? Wha' time ya'll dippin'? By tha way Happy B-day."

"Good lookin'. Shid, we gon' dip 'round 11 o'clock. I'm bringin' my lil niggas, so I gotta make sure we all get in, nah mean? Im'a hit you up when we're on our way and see where ya'll at."

"Fa' sho," Red said.

"A'ight niggas, ya'll be easy," Lamonte said before getting back into the Chrysler and pulling off.

Later that night...

Lamonte and Tae-Tae exited the condo looking like they stepped out of a GQ magazine. Lamonte had on a white Gucci polo shirt with a red and green collar, blue True Religion jeans, and white Gucci loafers. The white, red, and green Gucci skully sat right above the two-carat diamond studs in each of his earlobes. The white Gucci leather jacket he wore cost him $3,500. He was also rocking his white diamond chain and cross, as well as the black diamond chain and Jesus piece Tae-Tae had gotten him. The black and white diamond zebra designed Johnny watch and bracelet set his outfit off.

Tae-Tae was Louie down to the socks. He sported black Louis Vuitton jeans, with a black and grey checkered designer sweater, skully, belt, and shoes to match. Not the one to be outshined, he also had on his tiger designed watch and bracelet, as well as three diamond chains. They were definitely ready to floss.

It was 10:45 p.m, so Lamonte called Pookie to inform him that they were on their way to the meeting spot. The youngster had stopped by a few hours before to pick up the Charger. He was surprised when Lamonte told him he could drive it. Once he reached Pookie, he told him that he was on his way out the door.

"Alright big bra'," Pookie said. "We'll meet you there."

The AM/PM gas station on Hegenburger Rd. was like a sideshow every night on Friday and Saturday. Anybody who was anybody would stop at the gas station to get gas, blunts, or simply show off their rides before hitting the clubs. The gas station was so thick, cars were lined up waiting to enter. Lamonte was in line behind a white BMW 745 waiting to gain entry when he called Pookie.

"S'up bra', where ya'll at? We up here and it's thick ass shit," Pookie answered.

Lamonte looked around trying to spot his Charger in the crowded parking lot, but he couldn't. "Shit, I'm 'bout ta be dip in a sec," Lamonte said. Making his way through the entrance, he immediately spotted Pookie, Murda, and Trigg standing next to his car, surrounded by girls. He still had Pookie on the line. "Look at ya'll. I see ya'll got bitches flockin' and shit."

"Where ya'll at?" Pookie asked, looking for a rental or something.

"Nigga, this me right here in this orange thang. So tell Trigg and 'em ta fall back."

"Oh shit! That's that nigga Black and Tae-Tae in there, be easy," Pookie shouted to Lil Trigg who already had his .40 cal out.

Lamonte hung up the phone and pulled beside the Charger. Although he loved seeing his little niggas stuntin', the Porsche was killing shit. Right now, he was stealing their spotlight.

Everybody at the gas station had their eyes on Lamonte as he parked and got out. He and Tae-Tae gave each of the little niggas dap as they circled the Porsche in amazement.

"Damn! Bra', when you get this? This muthafucka clean!" Pookie said.

"Hell yeah and it's tha twin turbo. So I know this bitch run," Murda added.

"Ya'll know I had to get me a birthday present fo' myself. I had it fo' a couple of months doe. It's just been in tha shop," Lamonte told them.

Pookie, Murda, and Trigg were all fresh to death. Each had on Christian Audiger outfits and brand new Creative Recreation tennis shoes with diamond grills in their mouths. The group kicked it at the gas station for another fifteen minutes, hollering at bitches and stunting on niggas before getting in their whips and rolling back to back to the club.

CHAPTER TWENTY-EIGHT

When the crew pulled up to Club Sway, they were greeted by the valet. Lamonte handed the man two hundred dollar bills and instructed him to park the Porsche and Charger right outside the door.

All eyes were on them as they strolled right past the enormous crowd; giving shoutouts to people they knew. Lamonte gave the bouncer at the door $1,000 and they breezed right through the door and security checkpoints.

The club was packed to its capacity as the group squeezed through the crowd. The spot was jumping. All the ballers were in attendance as well as the groupies. There was no denying Lamonte was that nigga. He was Oakland's new Lil'D and balling was an understatement. As they made their way to the stairs that led up to VIP, Ricks Ross' *Blowin' Money Fast* blared out of the speakers.

The spacious VIP section of Sway was located in the upper deck of the club, surrounded by glass and hanging right above the dance floor downstairs. It was furnished plushly with money green leather sofas and beds. Videos were being played on an eighty-inch flat screen T.V's in each corner of the room. The room had its own sound system that was pumping out Drake and Lil' Wayne's *Miss Me*.

As the group entered the room, Lamonte spotted Red sitting back amongst his crew, popping bottles. Chop and a couple of his goons were in the corner knocking back shots of Patron. Gino sat on a sofa with two groupies drinking Cristal and enjoying the atmosphere.

Lamonte decided to occupy the last sofa that sat in the back, the furthest from the door. As soon as they took their seats, he had a waitress

140

bring over two bottles of Patron; one bottle of Remy and two bottles of Cristal. Pookie, Murda, and Trigg immediately began rolling up blunts.

The bottles arrived as blunts were being passed back and forth. Tonight was Pookie's first time at a club, and Lamonte could tell he was enjoying himself. Murda and Trigg sat back calmly smoking while watching the scene with one hand rested in their laps. They never went anywhere without their burners and it cost Lamonte $1,000 to make sure they all got in without incident.

"Yo! Cheers to my nigga Black! Happy birthday nigga!" Red announced.

"Here's to us! Here's to getting money!" Another cat in Red's crew shouted.

"Cheers! Cheers! Cheers!" was coming from around the room.

"No doubt! Thank you all fo' coming. Town bidnezz!" Lamonte yelled.

They were all toasting and having a good time. Bitches stood around dancing and enjoying the free drinks. Bird Man's *Money to Blow* thumped through the speakers, and at the moment Lamonte felt like Birdman himself. He stood with a blunt in his mouth and walked to the glass that overlooked the dance floor in search of Tae-Tae, who had left VIP about thirty minutes ago and hadn't returned. Tae-Tae was nowhere in sight, but he did spot Evelyn and her friends by the bar.

Yes, she came, he said to himself.

Moments later, he spotted Candi walking through the crowd with Cristal; both were headed towards the stairs that led to VIP.

"Fuck!" he cursed under his breath.

⟵──────────────────⟶

The club was packed and jumping. All the local celebrities and video vixens were in the building. The dance floor was filled to capacity with people dancing and drinking.

Candi arrived in a black skintight Dolce & Gabana spaghetti strap dress with a slit down the side, revealing her curvaceous coke bottle figure. The Christian Louboutin peep toe pumps graced her feet as she made her way through the crowd.

141

Cristal was right by Candi's side wearing a Roberto Cavalli dress with gold Jimmy Choo stilettos. Both girls wore Christian Dior shades.

All Candi wanted to do was find Lamonte so she could parade in on his party. She immediately knew he was in the building when she spotted his Charger parked right outside the door. She could barely contain herself as she scanned the tables and bars looking for any sign of him.

Noticing the stairs that led to VIP, she said, "C'mon girl. I know where his ass at."

The girls turned their attention to the stairs and saw that a uniformed security stood guard. They maneuvered through the crowd, drawing flirtatious stares and occasionally brushing up against a few partygoers. At the entrance to the stairs, the security personnel asked, "Where ya'll think ya'll goin'?"

"To VIP, my mans throwin' his birthday bash here tonight, and we're definitely very important people," Candi happily replied.

Not sensing any danger from the two beautiful females standing in front of him, he allowed them to ascend.

The smell of Grapes hit the girls before they stepped foot inside of the room. Once inside, they were greeted by another packed crowd. Candi spun around to survey the room when her attention was drawn to a sofa in the far back. There Lamonte was sitting with three young men smoking blunts and popping bottles. A flock of bitches hovered around them.

Candi felt her temperature rising. She couldn't believe what she was seeing. Even though she had a man at home, and Lamonte wasn't hers, she was still visibly jealous. She stormed towards the sofa like a mad woman with a wild look on her face.

← ——————————————————————— →

As the night went on, bitches flocked around their table and sofa. Lil' Pookie helped himself to a red bone with a short Halle Berry haircut, but resembled Vanessa Simmons. Murda and Lil' Trigg both had voluptuous dark skinned cuties.

Meanwhile, Lamonte sat between two of the baddest bitches in VIP. Eva sat on his right, looking every bit like Kim Kardashian, while Tamera, sitting on his left, resembled Keri Hilson, but had a body like

Ester Baxter. Both females were dressed to impress as they sipped glasses of Cristal.

Fuck tha mayor. I got tha keys to tha city! he thought as he fired up another blunt.

He was in the middle of passing the blunt to Tamera when he was interrupted.

"Black!" Candi yelled out. "Wha tha fuck you doin' wit' these bitches 'round you like this!"

Out of nowhere, Candi stormed over towards him acting like he was her man. Tamera was the first to jump up ready to throw down. "Bitch! I got yo' bitch, bitch!"

Candi held her ground staring at Tamera with a screwed up face. "Bitch wha! Bring it! Bring it!" Candi shouted.

Before Tamera could get to Candi, Lamonte pulled her back down to the sofa while Pookie and Murda stood guard between the two. The girls were both hollering back and forth, and Lamonte couldn't tell who was the loudest.

He yelled, "Bitch, if you don't get up out my face wit' that bullshit! I ain't yo' muthafuckin' man!" He got up and pushed Candi away from him, causing her to fall. She looked up at him like he'd lost his mind.

"You put yo' hands on me!" she screamed. "Fuck you Black! I hate you! I hate you!"

For a brief moment, everyone stopped and looked. Niggas and bitches shook their heads at her.

Tamera grabbed Eva's wrist. "Black, you need to check that bitch! You got my number," she said as the two stormed off. Their stilettos clicking away with each step they took before they disappeared out of the room.

Fuck! There goes my menage a trios, he thought, mad as hell.

"I can't believe you Black! I hate you!" Candi was still shouting.

Lamonte looked down at Candi and all of a sudden, she disgusted him. "Look girl, I'on want shit to do wit' you again. Go home to yo' man!"

Lamonte strolled off, leaving Candi dumbfounded in the middle of the VIP area while everyone looked on.

←————————————————————→

The line outside of Club Sway was damn near around the block. Friday was always a jumping night at the club, but tonight it seemed as if the whole Bay Area had come out to celebrate with Black. He really made a name for himself when he decided to put out that mix tape. But his real claim to fame came from the dope he put out on the streets.

Wacko, Rich, and Dame drove past the crowded club and stared at the long lines. All three were dressed in all black and ready to kill.

"Damn nigga, it's poppin' up in that bitch," Dame stated as he checked and made sure the clip in the Tec-9 was full.

"Yeah, well...it's really 'bout to be poppin'," Wacko replied, checking the AK-47 and making sure it was locked and loaded. Once he saw it was, he rested it between his legs in the front seat. Next, he clicked off the safety on his .9mm and placed it on his lap.

Rich parked the Camry just up the street, giving Wacko a clear view of the club's front doors. Noticing security was on point at the doors, Wacko instructed Rich to go inside, keep his eyes on Black, then call and inform him when Black was about to exit.

Richard did as he was told and exited the vehicle, headed for the crowded club.

Dame jumped into the driver's seat and reached for the half-smoked blunt that was in the ashtray and fired it up.

Wacko pulled out a small plastic coke-filled baggie, dipped his pinky finger inside, and brought a fingernail full up to his nose. He sniffed and then closed his eyes as the dope worked its magic. Murderous intentions were Wacko's only focus as he awaited his prey.

←————————————————————→

Lamonte was sipping Patron out of the bottle while shaking his head and walking down the stairs. He was highly upset. He wasn't feeling Candi's drama queen act. He casually glanced in the direction of the bar and immediately spotted the butter pecan cutie he was looking for.

Lamonte smiled when he saw her and her friends laughing, having a good time. He walked over and greeted Evelyn with a hug and introduced himself to her friends.

"Hey beautiful. I see you made it," he said as he graced her cheek with a kiss.

Evelyn graciously nodded as she replied. "Hey, wha' can I say? You drove a hard bargain."

"And you play hard to get," he joked.

"Life has taught me that the things worth havin' come with a challenge," she said confidently.

"Well, I like challenges. And I'm very patient."

As Evelyn turned to place her drink on the table, Lamonte got a good look at her voluptuous ass cheeks, which jiggled through her Chanel catsuit. His imagination went into overdrive as he imagined fucking her from the back and watching her ass jiggle.

Evelyn turned to Lamonte. "Let's dance."

Without waiting for his response, she took his hand and led him to the dance floor. She began to grind to the beat of Trey Songz *Bottoms Up*. Lamonte was in full groove, holding his bottle of Patron while two-stepping.

$$\longleftrightarrow$$

Rich held a glass of Hennessy & Coke in his hand, the same drink he'd been sipping since he entered the club. He had to stay on point so he figured a one drink minimum would be best. He looked over at Black, who was dancing with a bad ass Spanish bitch, while holding up a bottle of Patron in the air. It was obvious Black was drunk, which meant he wouldn't be on his toes.

From where Rich was standing, he had a clear view of damn near every angle in the club. He could even see through the glass of the VIP window upstairs. Looking at the time on his iPhone, he noticed it was 12:30 a.m., only an hour and a half before closing. When the DJ stopped the music, Rich looked up and watched the nigga who he'd seen with Black at the mall make his way to the DJ booth.

"Bay Area, wha' is it!" the nigga said as he grabbed the mic. "I wanna thank everybody fo' comin' out and celebratin' my mans birthday

145

wit' 'em. Happy birthday Black! We love ya! Now everybody party tha rest of the night away."

The DJ started playing Nicki Minaj's *Your Love* and everybody resumed partying. Rich kept his eye on that nigga also. It was clear that he too was drunk from the slur in his speech. It was also obvious he was paid from all the Louie and diamonds he was sporting.

Yeah nigga, you can get it too! he thought to himself, before refocusing his attention back on Black, who was back dancing with the Spanish chick. Suddenly, out of nowhere, Candi and Cristal appeared.

Candi was visually upset, yet Cristal had a smile on her face as she approached the same guy who was on the mic. Rich watched Cristal engage in small conversation with the nigga before the girls headed to the exit and the nigga headed over in the direction of Black.

⟷

Lamonte smiled as he listened to Tae-Tae's slurred speech. Tae-Tae was definitely drunk. *Well, there goes my designated driver,* he thought as he reached for Evelyn and kissed her sloppily on the lips.

"Happy birthday, Black," she said regaining her breath.

"Thanks love. If it wasn't befo', it is now," he said as the DJ started the music back up, sending him and Evelyn back dancing seductively.

He was enjoying himself. The liquor had him cutting it up on the dance floor and dancing was something he never did.

The whole time Lamonte was dancing, he never once noticed the dude watching him from the bar.

"S'up wit' tha birthday boy! What's tha deal fam!" Tae-Tae screamed as he approached almost tripping over himself.

Lamonte raised his bottle at his homeboy and stopped dancing.

Tae-Tae said, "Bra, I need another bottle and you do too. C'mon let's hit the bar."

"Ohh no, yo' friend don't need no mo' drink... and you don't either." Evelyn laughed lightly while nodding her head to the song. "But I gotta check on my girls anyway, so let's head back over there."

Lamonte was having so much fun that he'd forgotten about the little episode with Candi. As soon as they made it back to their table, Evelyn introduced Tae-Tae to Monica, one of her roommates.

Monica was black mixed with white and resembled the model
Tammy Torres. She was super sexy in her Frankie B. skinny jeans and
Lela Rose top. Her open toe Gucci stilettos showed off her perfectly
manicured toes. From the way she was smiling, Lamonte knew she was
interested in Tae-Tae.

Lamonte was wasted from the Patron and blunts he'd smoked. As
he wiped beads of sweat forming on his forehead with a napkin, he began
to survey the crowd. He was scanning every face when, to his surprise,
he spotted one that stood out like a sore thumb. The same nigga who was
staring at him in the jewelry store was now seated at the bar acting all
nonchalant.

Lamonte immediately grew suspicious when he glanced in the
nigga's direction and saw him quickly look away.

"Yo, Tae-Tae. Don't look now," he said in a whisper. "But tha
muthafucka at tha bar, in the black button up been watchin' a nigga. I
noticed him earlier at tha jewelry store staring at us on tha slick. Now I
done spotted his ass over there staring from the bar. And his drink looks
watered down like he's baby sittin' it."

Tae-Tae scanned the bar until he found the dude in question. "Yeah,
I see tha nigga."

"Look, this wha' I want you to do. Go find Pookie and 'em and let
'em know we 'bout to roll out. I'm 'bout to tell Evelyn and 'em to dip.
After you head to VIP, I'ma dip to the bathroom. If that nigga get up and
follow me, Im'a body his ass."

"Nigga, you sure you don't want me to stay wit' you. We gotta stick
together in case he got company in here wit' 'em."

"Nah, nigga, it's good. Ya'll just meet me in the bathroom,"
Lamonte said.

Tae-Tae whispered something into Monica's ear before he got up
and walked directly to the stairs that led to the VIP area.

After saying goodbye to the girls, and promising Evelyn he'd call,
Lamonte got up and said to the bartender, "Excuse me, can you tell me
where the bathroom is?"

"Yeah, it's ova there in the back!" the bartender yelled over the
music.

"Good looking'," Lamonte said, making his way in that direction.

***

Wacko reclined his seat to make himself more comfortable in the car. They'd been sitting outside the club for over an hour and he was growing more impatient with every passing second.

He looked at the clock on the dash and read *12:30 a.m.* "It shouldn't be too much longer now."

"Nah, tha club will be lettin' out in a minute. Rich should be callin' any second," Dame said.

"This shit is crazy. All this waitin' 'round. A nigga like me ready ta go up in that bitch blastin' wit' this choppa," Wacko complained as he eyed the door in frustration.

Dame and Wacko sat in the Camry and watched as the silhouettes of awaiting partygoers stood in line, trying to make it in the club.

"This nigga got the nerve to park his Charger on front street. Bitch ass nigga ain't been in that car fo' months," Wacko spoke as he leaned his head back on the headrest.

Just as Dame was about to open his mouth to say something, he noticed Candi storming out of the exit door. Cristal was right on Candi's heels trying to keep up, but Candi was visibly fuming and moving too fast.

"Yo Wack, there goes yo' girl," Dame said as he eyed the two females waiting to get their car from the valet.

Wacko sat straight up in his seat and peered out his window. His temper rised even more when he saw Candi.

Wha tha fuck that bitch doin' here? Oh, she thinks it's a game, talking 'bout her and Cristal goin' to Dave and Busters for drinks, he thought to himself. *Yeah, I got somethin' fo' that bitch! Tha fuck she's doin' at this nigga's party?*

"Fuck that bitch! This nigga needs to hurry on up and call," Wacko said calmly, not wanting to reveal his true anger.

←——————————————————→

Rich watched the nigga sitting with Black whisper something into one of the girls' ear before heading up to VIP. Then he saw Black hug the Spanish chick he was dancing with, before her and her friends got up

148

and made their way to the exit. When Rich heard Black ask the bartender where the bathroom was, he figured it wouldn't be too long before Black left the club. He watched as Black headed toward the bathroom, and then discreetly followed him down the dark narrow hallway.

When Black entered the bathroom, Rich pulled out his phone and texted Wack.

He's on tha move now. He's in tha bathroom at the moment, but it looks like he's 'bout to bounce. Keep your eyes open.

<---------------------------------->

Tae-Tae, Pookie, Murda, and Lil' Trigg rushed down the stairs headed for the bathroom. Once in the hallway, Tae-Tae immediately recognized the nigga that was at the bar, typing away on his phone while trying to be discreet.

Tae-Tae looked over his shoulders to make sure the coast was clear before Murda and Lil' Trigg pulled their pistols from their waistbands and grabbed the nigga from behind.

"HEYY! he said getting caught off guard.

Murda, the strongest of the three, put his hand over the nigga's mouth while bringing his .9mm to his head, pushing him into the bathroom. When he got into the bathroom, he found himself face to face with Lamonte's .40 caliber.

"Wha' up folks...You know me or somethin'?" Lamonte asked flashing the cannon in his face.

"Nah, bra', I'on know you. Whaaaa...what's this aaall 'bout?" dude stuttered.

At the moment, the nigga's phone went off.

"What's that nigga? You wired or somethin'?" Lamonte asked.

"Nah, that's that nigga's phone. He was just outside the door textin' somebody befo' we snatched 'em up," Tae-Tae spoke.

"Oh really? Well, let's just take a look at that phone and see what's so important that you gotta be watchin' me and textin' muthafuckas in tha middle of tha club."

Lamonte grabbed the phone off dude's side and touched the screen, revealing the text.

149

It's all good, we waitin' out front. Hit me as soon as the nigga is making his way to tha door. Let me know how many niggas he got wit' 'em too.

Without warning, Lamonte cracked the nigga across his face with the .40, causing him to drop instantly.

"You bitch ass nigga! Wha' you call yo' self settin' me up!" Lamonte screamed. "You stupid muthafucka! You just committed suicide!"

Lamonte pointed the .40 at his head and let off three rounds, causing a couple of loud thuds to echo throughout the bathroom. Knowing there were niggas waiting outside to ambush him, Lamonte knew he needed a distraction to make it to the vehicles safely.

"We need a distraction," he said to his crew.

Exiting the bathroom, Lil' Trigg fired off three shots in the air, causing pandemonium to erupt throughout the club. It was a perfect cover. With guns drawn, the group ducked low and maneuvered their way towards the door.

⟵————————————⟶

Dame turned off the stereo, cutting Lil Boosie off in mid-sentence. Wacko strapped on his black Nike gloves as he studied the exit door in ritualistic fashion. He'd just received the text he'd been waiting on.

Now he awaited his target. Wacko felt that familiar surge of anxiety circulating through is veins; blood was about to be spilled.

Tucking the Tec-9 inside the pocket of his hoodie, Dame slowly exited the car. Wacko was stepping out with the AK-47 hanging by his side, when suddenly in a flash; pandemonium took control of the night. Partygoers inside the club came running and screaming in terror, looking for cover as if trying to avoid being hit by a stray bullet.

"Wha' tha fuck!" Wacko yelled, as he scurried to the nearest car to get a visual on what was going on across the street.

As Dame followed Wacko towards the car, gunfire exploded outside the club.

Wacko noticed someone shooting in the air. Then it dawned on him that Black had somehow figured out about the hit, and was trying to cause a distraction to get to his vehicle. Out of the corner of his eye, he saw the group running frantically with their guns drawn.

Not giving a fuck about innocent bystanders, Wacko positioned the AK-47 and rattled off a volly of bullets.

Pop! Pop! Pop! Pop! Pop! Pop!

The group fled for cover while squeezing off desperate shots as well.

Wacko's first issue of bullets disintegrated the outside of the club and chewed away at the partygoers, causing people to scramble in all directions. One bullet struck and flipped a chick trying desperately to sprint in some Red Bottoms. Another went through a car and instantly killed a valet attendant trying to park a Jaguar.

It was mass hysteria.

◄─────────────────────────►

Lamonte, Tae-Tae, Pookie, Murda, and Lil' Trigg were rushing to the vehicles. As they drew closer, a violent barrage of bullets rang out. Lamonte and Tae-Tae scrambled for cover behind a lime green H2, as bullets tore at anything in its path. Lamonte looked over at Murda and Lil' Trigg, who were firing in the direction of their attackers. Since they were trying to get a good bearing on where their targets were exactly positioned, Murdar and Lil' Trigg bullets missed.

Lamonte got on his knees and tried to peek across the street to determine the exact number of assailants that were shooting at them. He saw two, but didn't know if there was more roaming around.

The attackers continued firing; the explosions from each bullet fired were like rapid thunder, knocking huge chunks of concrete off the building. Plaster and other materials flew every and which way.

With agile speed, Murda and Lil' Trigg fled to a nearby BMW while firing the last of their bullets. They made it behind the car and knelt just as bullets tore huge holes into the BMW just above their heads.

Hearing the shooting stop, Lamonte figured the attackers were reloading and yelled out. "C'mon, I got ya'll covered!" Right before he sprang the .40 caliber into action letting off shots.

Pop!Pop!Pop!Pop!Pop!

Murda and Lil' Trigg ran rapidly towards the Hummer.

Meanwhile, Pookie hastily duckwalked towards the Charger, as bullets fired from across the street pulverized the cars he eased past.

Looking around, Lamonte noticed Pookie had made it to the Charger. He stopped shooting and shouted urgently. "Let's make a run fo' it!"

"But wha' 'bout them fuck boys?" Lil' Trigg spit the words out despite his intense exhaustion. "We can't just bounce."

"Nah bra', we just playin' it smart fo' now," Lamonte assured. "On tha count to three...one, two, three!"

They jumped up firing bullets in the direction of the attackers, while running to the vehicles.

While all this was going down, Pookie had made it into the front seat of the Charger. His heart was pounding as his eyes took in everything. He kept his eyes on the side and rearview mirrors, as he stuck the key in the ignition and cranked up the engine. Suddenly, through the sideview mirror, he saw Black, Tae-Tae, Murda, and Lil'Trigg running towards the vehicle. Within seconds, he had the Charger backed up with the doors open.

$$\longleftrightarrow$$

Wacko and Dame both reloaded their weapons and was about to continue their assault when more shots rang out.

Dame ducked just as a gust of bullets zoomed past his head, grazing his face. Within seconds, Wacko repositioned his AK-47, frantically looking for his targets. He saw the Charger reversing and upon closer inspection, he noticed figures fleeing to the vehicle. Thinking Black had made it behind the wheel of the Charger, Wacko opened fire spraying the whip with carefully aimed 223's.

As Murda and Lil' Trigg moved cautiously towards the car, Lamonte and Tae-Tae rushed over to the Porsche. Just as the two made it inside, their assailants opened fire, chopping away at the Charger and striking Murda in the back with several bullets. The youngster slumped in the passenger's seat, heaving rushed deep breaths. Then he rolled out altogether.

Pookie suddenly felt a scorching sensation as he slammed the gear into drive.

Lamonte and Tae-Tae returned fire as they watched Murda fall to the ground and laid motionless in a pool of blood. There was no doubt he was dead. Seeing the Charger speed off, Lamonte immediately floored the gas pedal while looking in the rearview mirror at the volly of flashes coming from the Ak-47 and Tec-9.

The sounds of sirens shook Lamonte loose from his galvanized state as he maneuvered through the San Francisco's streets.

Just that fast, a birthday turned into a day for the dead as bodies graced a scene meant for celebrating. *A-B-C-G was in full E-F-F-E-C-T*

CHAPTER TWENTY-NINE

WARZONE AT NIGHT CLUB
Leaves many DEAD and wounded

*N**ightclub in San Francisco turns into a nightmare as gunfire erupts, leaving three dead and eight others injured. Among the dead are, twenty-six year old Dionte Woods of Richmond, seventeen year old Derrick Johnson of Oakland, and twenty-three year old Richard Reed also from Oakland. Witnesses say shots rang out inside the club before two groups exchanged gunfire outside the nightclub injuring several innocent bystanders.*

The three deaths brought the number of homicides in San Francisco so far this year to 97. Last year at this time, there had been 76. Police and crime stoppers of San Francisco are offering up to $25,000 in reward money to anyone with information. Call the police at (415)87-C-R-I-M-E.

Lamonte shook his head with anger, rage, and something much stronger than fury as he read the front page of the Oakland Tribune.

Murda was dead; three shots to the back and a single shot to his head had killed him instantly. According to the article, two other guys had been killed as well. Lamonte knew one was the nigga he'd left stanking in the club's bathroom. He figured the other was just another innocent bystander.

The article further indicated that witnesses may have gotten a good look at the assailants. Now that's what bothered Lamonte the most besides Murda's death. He was concerned about cameras that might have been positioned outside the club, or witnesses describing them and the vehicles.

154

Pookie was hit once in the shoulder and he drove himself to Highland Hospital in Oakland, where he was released a short time later. Lamonte was still clueless as to who was behind the attacks. That had him so irked under the collar that he felt the blood vessels in his head throbbing as though any second they'd explode.

Somebody's tryin' to off me! Oh hell fuckin'no!

He wanted to react impulsively, but first he had to find out who was behind the attacks.

Tae-Tae was staying with Lamonte as he usually did whenever he came to town. Lamonte was on the balcony when Tae-Tae approached.

"What's good fam? Wha' that paper sayin'?" Tae-Tae asked, taking a seat and grabbing the newspaper before firing up a blunt.

"Man, nothing' really. I'm fuck'd up 'bout Murda. I really liked tha lil nigga. I swear, when I find out who's behind this shit, Im'a make it rain on 'em," he said reassuringly.

Tae-Tae inhaled the smoke and choked. "No doubt. A-B-C-G!" he said in between coughs.

"Damn nigga, that shit got you coughin' up yo' insides. Let me hit that shit," Lamonte chuckled, reaching for the blunt.

Tae-Tae handed off the blunt and watched as Lamonte puffed away. Reclining in the lounge chair, Lamonte thought about the situation.

After reading the article twice, Tae-Tae sat the paper aside and allowed his mind to reflect also.

Turning to his comrade, Lamonte asked, "Wha'day you leave on?"

"Shid, I'm 'pose to bounce Tuesday. But since it's ugly out here, Im'a have to reschedule that. Why?"

"Nah folks, you good. We still gotta get this money. I was just wonderin', 'cause I gotta re-up, that's all. I ain't too much worried 'bout no fuck boys."

Tae-Tae listened in silence while checking Lamonte's face for any signs of doubt. There was none. "Nigga, you sho'? 'Cause tha money can wait."

"Nah, can't sleep on tha bread," Lamonte responded with sincerity before passing the blunt

Lamonte thought about all the money he'd miss if Tae-Tae stayed any longer. Sure, he felt secure with him around, but with $88,000 back home to be made, he was more than sure it was worth him leaving.

"I'on know, Black. Shit just doesn't seem right." Tae-Tae couldn't grasp the reality that Lamonte was willing to put dollars over his safety. "Nigga, we both got well over enough money to chill fo' a while and see how this shit plays out."

"I know. But still, I'm not 'bout to let these niggas fuck off my program," Lamonte stated, reaching for the blunt.

⬅————————————➡

Two weeks after the club shooting, Wacko drove past the house on Bancroft Ave. He'd been watching the routine for three days straight. Now he was ready to make his move and with the street being dark, this was the best time.

Once he passed the house, he circled the block. There was an abandoned house located slightly behind the trap house one street over. Wacko scanned the houses and street, making sure no one was in their windows or outside before parking the stolen Acura Legend he was in.

Wacko and Dame stepped from the car, both wearing army fatigue pants, black hoodies and rolled up black ski masks on their heads. The duo moved quickly through the abandoned house's backyard and hopped a couple fences until they were directly in the back- yard of the trap house. Pulling out his weapon and rolling down his mask, Wacko positioned himself to kick down the back door.

Before holding up one finger, followed by two fingers, he whispered to Dame. "On tha count of three." When he held up his third finger, he followed it with his size 12 boots crashing against the door.

BLAM!

⬅————————————➡

Twenty minutes earlier...

Pookie and Lil' Trigg sat in the living room of the trap house smoking blunts, while thumbing their PS3 controllers back and forth, as they competed for the most kills in *Call of Duty*. It was close to 10 o'clock and it had been a good day. They ran through over 27 ounces and were sitting on close to $15,000 for Black to pick up.

Looking at his phone, Pookie realized it was that time. The house never operated before or after, 10 o'clock. The time restriction made it harder for the police to run up inside and catch them with any work. They never kept dope in the house after 10:00 p.m. Any work that wasn't sold by then was transferred and stored at another location around the block.

"Shid, it's 'bout that time. Ain't nothing but three and a half left anyway. You wanna run it 'round tha corner or you want me to?" Pookie asked.

"Shid, I ain't trippin'. I'll do it. I'm try'na hit up tha store befo' it close anyway. Nigga, you want somethin' back?" Lil' Trigg probed, placing the controller down on the coffee table and stuffing his glock .40 in his waist.

"Yeah, bring me a sprite and some sour worms. Oh yeah, grab another box of blunts too."

"Yep, I got cha," Lil' Trigg said, placing the zips into his Artful Dodgers jeans.

Once Lil' Trigg was out the door. Pookie double locked it before sitting back down and resuming his game.

"Oh, take that! Mu'fuckas! Bang, oh you think you slick, I see ya. Oh you try'na snipe a nigga, huh? Take that!"

The game had Pookie's undivided attention. It wasn't until he heard the loud sound of the back door coming off its hinges that he snapped out of the game.

BLAM!

Before he could reach for the P.89 that sat in front off him, he was looking down the barrel of Wacko's Tec-9. Meanwhile, Dame did a quick sweep of the house, making sure no one else was there.

"Reach fo' it nigga," Wacko whispered. "And you dead."

"Hol' on," Pookie started. "Ya'll don't wanna—"

"Nigga, shut tha fuck up!" Wacko threatened, slapping Pookie in the face with the Tec-9, causing a stream of blood to flow from his nose onto his shirt.

Pookie fell to the ground clutching his nose, forgetting about his sore shoulder.

"A-H-H-H-H!" he cried out in pain.

Wacko pulled out a roll of duct tape just as Dame reappeared in the room. He tossed the tape to Dame who proceeded to wrap it around Pookie's wrists and ankles. "Now, let's try this again. Where's tha dope and money?" he probed, placing the barrel to Pookie's temple.

"Fuck you!" Pookie shouted, trying to stall time. He knew Lil' Trigg would be returning soon.

"Word? You a tough lil nigga huh?" Wacko asked in disbelief right before slamming the Tec-9 back into Pookie's face, breaking his nose on contact.

Blood sprayed as Pookie's head snapped back again. "Ahhh!" he cried out.

"Yeah, tough guy. We can do this tha easy way or hard way. Either way, I'on give a fuck! But you are comin' off that work and loot, one way or tha other."

Dame ran off to rummage through the house, looking for anything of value, while Wacko continued to pistol whip Pookie.

Wacko jarred Pookie out of his daze after he passed out from all the pain that was being administered on him. "Wake yo' bitch ass up! Now you ready to tell me wha' I wanna know?"

Pookie disorienteldy looked around until Wacko raised his pistol again. "Okay! Okay! He pleaded, jerking violently as he lifted his taped hand up in attempt to stop the blow from coming. "It's inside the computer's hard drive box!"

Wacko moved over toward the computer and kicked the hard drive box over. "How tha fuck you open this thing?" he questioned, nudging Pookie with the gun.

"Y-Y-You just p-press together them two b-bottons and slide it O-O-outta tha slot," Pookie stuttered.

Pookie watched helplessly as Wacko took the stacks of money out of the box. He prayed that they'd be on their way now that they'd gotten what they came for.

"Okay nigga," Wacko smirked. "Now where's tha work at?"

"I-I-I swear...ain't no work."

Dame came running out of the room just as Wacko was about to slap Pookie again with the pistol.

"Somebody just pulled in tha driveway!" Dame announced.

Looking down at Pookie with vehemence in his eyes, Wacko stood over him and squeezed the trigger three times before he and Dame fled out of the back door and to their getaway car.

←————————————————————————→

Lil' Trigg was returning from dropping off the last of the dope and making a quick store run when he pulled back up in the driveway of the trap. As he tucked his glock in his waist, and reached for the plastic bag on the passenger's seat, three shots rang out.

Pop!Pop!Pop!

He immediately ducked down, while pulling for his glock. Not knowing where the shots were coming from, he feared exiting the vehicle.

After a few seconds of silence, he jumped out of his Mustang with the pistol drawn and ready. Pulling out his keys, he let himself inside the house. When he entered, he found bits of Lil' Pookie's skull and brains splattered all over the furniture. The rest of his body laid lifeless, partially blocked by the sofa.

CHAPTER THIRTY

Just when Lamonte thought things couldn't get any worse, the detectives investigating the club shooting had released footage from surveillance cameras inside and outside the club that night.

"Fuck!" he cursed as he watched images of Murda and Lil' Trigg firing weapons at several unidentified assailants. Luckily, for him and Tae-Tae, the Hummer they hid behind blocked them from the cameras. But it did catch a glimpse of the Porsche. Lamonte was already ten steps ahead of them though, dropping both vehicles back off to Carlos for re-painting.

Lamonte stood up from the sofa and made his way to his favorite part of the apartment, the balcony. Flipping through his cd case, he found the CD he was looking for and placed it into the CD player. He reclined in the lounge chair, fired up a blunt, and allowed his mind to reflect the past weeks' events.

Jadakiss' '*Why*' came pumping through the speakers as he smoked his pain away.

He was struggling with the loss of two close friends in just two and a half weeks. He was also worried about being apprehended for the scene at the club. To make matters worse, he was distraught about not being able to attend Murda or Pookie's funeral. Deep down he knew the places would be crawling with detectives and therefore he wouldn't be safe.

Due to the murder of Lil' Pookie at the house on Bancroft, he was forced to close up shop. He was now growing tired of his current lifestyle. Looking at the fact that he now had close to $500,000 saved up, he wondered if it'd be wise to move on to another city and enjoy life while he still had one. Even Tae-Tae had a nice chunk of change saved up. If they put their money together, there wouldn't be any limits to what they could accomplish.

He took a huge hit of the blunt and exhaled a cloud of purple smoke. The fact that he hadn't found out who was behind the attacks disturbed him. His phone started vibrating so he checked the caller I.D. Noticing it was Candi, he sent the call to voicemail, then sneered to himself when she called right back.

Candi had been blowing up his phone every day since the incident at the club and he really wasn't feeling her drama. By the fifth time she called back, he decided to pick up and give her a piece of his mind.

"Look. Candi...I already done told ya, I ain't fuckin' wit' you no mo'! All this blowin' up a niggas phone is uncalled fo'!" he said in a serious tone.

"Black, please...don't do this to me. I need to talk to you, it's important," she pleaded.

"Whateva! You don't need to talk to me. I already told you how I feel. Now if you don't mind."

"Black no! I'm...I'm..."

"Bitch, you wha!" he barked.

"Black, I'm pregnant."

"Pregnant?" Lamonte stated in disbelief. "Wha' tha fuck you tellin' me fo' –it ain't mine!"

"Wha' you mean, it ain't yours?" she was irritated. "I only been wit' you and my dude and the doctor informed us he's not able to have kids. I've been fuckin you unprotected for over eight months now, and I got pregnant!" she explained.

"Well it ain't mine!" he stated dramatically.

"Oh, I see...so you can make a baby, but can't take care of one, huh?" she growled.

"Bitch, this ain't Menace to Society! And I ain't Caine. So miss me wit' that bullshit!"

Click!

Just as Lamonte disconnected the call, his phone started to vibrate again. Thinking it was Candi calling back, he started to ignore the call. He quickly changed his mind, remembering Evelyn was supposed to be calling.

He looked at the screen and saw it was Red.

"S'up nigga?"

"Shid waitin' on you. A nigga dryer than a mu'fucka right now. When you think you gon' be ready?"

"Man, bra', I'on know. Shits mad crazy right now, nah mean? I ain't really tryin' to do too much, feel me? I'm just chillin' right now."

"Man, I feel you dawg. But shit, a nigga still gotta eat," Red shot back.

"I feel that. But right now I'm all fucked up 'bout my lil niggas. Not to mention, tha shit that's been all ova tha news. It's too hot right now fo' me to do anythin'."

"Well give me tha connect then since you ain't try'na make any moves."

"I already told ya, he ain't fuckin' wit' nobody but me."

"So a nigga supposed to wait 'til you finish grievin'and shit, befo' it's good. Wha' type of shit is that?" Red was obviously frustrated.

"You know wha', Red?" he said pissed off. "You ain't gotta wait fo' shit! I already told you I ain't doin' shit! Nigga, you buggin' me 'bout some work, while my niggas gettin' knocked down one by one! Nigga, you ain't called to lend a hand or nothin'. All you want is some work! Well nigga, it's bad!"

"Hold tha fuck up! Nigga, who do you think you talkin' to like that? You act like I got niggas gunnin' fo' you and shit! But whateva nigga!" Red yelled before hanging up.

Lamonte shook his head disdainfully and got up from the chair, pacing back and forth. They say when it rain it pours. Well shit, this was 'El Nino'.

As if on cue, his phone vibrated again and Candi's name popped up on the screen. He let it go to voicemail.

←——————————————————→

You know who you called. Leave a message after tha beep and I'll get back at cha......Beep!

Candi slammed the phone down. She was crushed. She was carrying the baby of someone who didn't want anything to do with her. It felt as if her world had come to an end. She couldn't tell Wacko about the pregnancy because they'd found out years ago from a specialist that he couldn't have any kids due to his outrageous drug habit. She'd been wanting a kid for so long and abortion wasn't an option.

In her emotionally unbalanced mind, depressed and delusional, Candi contemplated suicide. The pain she felt was unbearable. She was completely hollow and the pain hurt more than anything she'd ever experienced.

A broken heart paralyzed her state of mind as she walked over and retrieved the .9 mm handgun Wacko always kept in the nightstand.

Putting the gun to her head, Candi squeezed the trigger.

$$\longleftarrow\hspace{3cm}\longrightarrow$$

The next couple of weeks flew by without Red making any money and he was furious. Shit was getting hectic on his blocks without him having any work. He'd been making a killing off the yae he was getting from Black, so he hadn't tried to find another connect.

He had a few choices; sit back and wait for Black to come to his senses, find a new connect, or fuck with his old connect. He chose the latter and decided to call his old connect, Hector, out of San Mateo. He had no choice. He had niggas on hold.

"Hey Red, long time no hear," Hector said, picking up his cell phone.

"Huh? I can't hear you, you breakin' up," Red replied trying to get a good connection.

"Can you hear me now?"

"Yeah, I'm try'na see you 'bout somethin'. You good?"

"I'm getting' off tha bridge right now, so if tha call drop, hit me right back. But yeah, I'm good. Only thing is, I just came from over that way, so if you try'na get right, you gotta come to me."

"Shit, I ain't trippin'. Where you want me to come?" Red asked, hating that he was so desperate.

"How 'bout Hillsdale Mall? How long and how many?"

"Man, I hope it ain't the same shit as last time."

"No, no. It's that good, good you like, I promise," Hector assured.

"Well give me two fo' now, and if I like it, I'll get a couple mo'. Give me 'bout thirty minutes. I'm 'bout ta leave now. I'll call you when I'm gettin' off the bridge. Same price right?"

"Yeah, yeah. Just call me, I'll be waitin'."

"Cool, hit you in a minute."

After Red hung up, he went and got his money together. He hated that he was about to pay $3,000 more per brick than he usually would have fucking with Black. But shit, he couldn't wait any longer for Black. He had to get back to work.

←——————————————————→

Agent Mitchell sat in the unmarked van with earphones on listening to Hector's every word.

"Yes, we got this son of a bitch," Mitchell exclaimed.

"Oh really? What you got?" asked his partner Agent Gomez.

"The son of a bitch is meeting somebody in about thirty minutes at the Hillside Mall in San Mateo to sell two or more kilos."

Seeing the excitement appear on Gomez's face told Mitchell everything he needed to know. His big promotion was right around the corner.

Agent Gomez looked at his watch. "It's 2:30. I'm going to call in and have 'em set up surveillance at the mall ASAP. You said thirty minutes, right? Did he say what store they'd meet at?"

"No, but whoever he's meeting said he'll call 'em back when he gets off the bridge, so maybe he'll say then."

Gomez immediately got their boss on the phone and discussed the latest intercepted call to Hector.

←——————————————————→

Forty-five minutes later, Red was headed back to Oakland with two bricks in his possession. He'd met Hector in the parking garage outside of Macy's without an incident.

As he got on the San Mateo Bridge, he lit up a blunt that was in the ashtray. He was nodding his head to Big Rich's *Ballin*, and zoning from

164

the effects of the Grapes, he never noticed the highway patrol cruiser coming up his rear until it was only one car behind him.

"Fuck!" he cursed, reaching down to put the blunt out in the ashtray. He checked the speedometer of the Jeep Grand Cherokee to make sure he wasn't speeding. He wasn't.

Looking to the left, he could've sworn he saw the occupants of a black Tahoe with tinted windows looking his way.

Red wasn't sure if it was the bricks he was trafficking, the pistol he was packing, or the Grapes he'd consumed that had him paranoid. Sitting straight up, he put both hands on the steering wheel. He was hoping the highway patrol was on the Honda Civic behind him.

All kind of thoughts clouded his brain.

Damn! If they pull me over, they gon' smell this weed, so they gon' search tha truck. Man, if they find them bricks and this pistol, I'm through!

As Red passed the tollbooth on the Hayward side, the highway patrol switched lanes and zoomed past the Civic, jumping right behind him.

Now he was really sweating bullets.

He was coming up on the 880 exit, which would take him to Oakland. He decided not to get on that freeway, anticipating the cruiser going that route. Instead, he kept forward as the highway turned onto Jackson Boulevard and pulled into a shopping plaza. The cruiser followed him right inside the plaza where it finally turned on its red and blue lights.

"Shit!" he cursed, pulling up outside a Home Depot. Just as he was about to jump out and make a run for it, he noticed a swarm of unmarked vehicles speeding into the parking lot and screeching to a stop.

As he reached for the door handle, two all black Tahoe's skidded up and blocked his exit. His mind drifted quickly to his possibilities. The F.B.I agents raised guns indicated anything shy of surrendering would be suicide.

"Fuck!" he slammed his fist into the steering wheel. He was caught and there was no way for him to get out of it.

"Slowly exit the vehicle with your hands up!" an agent ordered with his .45 caliber drawn.

It was all over. He was busted.

CHAPTER THIRTY-ONE

The news of Red's arrest spread like a wild fire throughout the town. Word in the street was that the Feds intercepted a phone call Red had made to his former connect out of San Mateo. The Feds had been monitoring Hector's phone calls for thirty days and that day it paid off.

Red was arrested after agents followed him from Hillside Mall to a shopping plaza in Hayward, where they discovered two bricks in a Macy's shopping bag as well as a gun.

Had he just waited on me, he wouldn't be in this mess, Lamont thought as he maneuvered the rented Dodge Caravan down the freeway with Lil' Trigg riding shotgun.

"Man, shit is getting dumb ass hectic in tha town," Trigg started. "First Murda, then Pookie, now Red's caught up in some shit."

"Fo' real, "Lamonte agreed, passing him the burning blunt. "That's why I've been stressing getting you up outta here. With all tha snitchin' goin' on, it won't be long befo' somebody recognize you from that club footage and drop a dime."

"Man, fuck that! Where I'ma go? What I'ma do? I feel what you sayin', but tha town is all I know. If dem people come lookin' fo' me, they betta come correct. 'Cause on momma's, I'm goin' out blazin'! Plus them fools who knocked down Murda and Pookie is still out there. I ain't gon' rest, 'til they're in a box!"

"I feel you my nigga. But you still gotta be easy. You can't get revenge if you're locked up."

"No doubt. But I still ain't leavin' the town."

Lamonte looked over at the little nigga who reminded him so much of O-Dog from Menace to Society that it was scary. The only difference was that this wasn't a movie. This was real life, everyday hood living and in the hood, the A.B.C.G rule always apply.

Lamonte reached out for the blunt that Trigg was passing, took a deep pull, and continued on their littler journey.

←——————————————————→

Sitting at a table, playing a game of pinochle, Buck and his cellie, Fresh, battled against two chinos for $20.00 a game.

"Save it, it's game," Fresh said revealing the stats of the game.

After successfully saving their milt and winning their third straight game, Buck got up and headed for the top tier showers.

Under the stream of hot water, Buck mentally ran the circumstances of his situation through his mind. He knew all about the problems Black was facing on the streets and vowed to help anyway he could.

Since the jailhouses seemed to find out information quicker than the streets, Buck kept his ears glued to conversations. Niggas were always coming off the streets with stories to tell and Buck didn't have a problem ear hustling.

His thoughts were immediately interrupted by the noises the inmates made whenever new arrivals came into the pod.

"Fresh fish!...Fresh fish!"

"Welcome to Hell's Kitchen?"

"Aye Pimp, hope you got some rent money!"

Stepping from the shower, Buck got dressed before proceeding down the tier to see if the new arrival was somebody he knew.

Walking past cell 11, Buck glanced inside. Seeing a familiar face, he stopped and called him over to the door.

"S'up wit' it cus? Ain't you Jay and 'em peoples off 8-4?" Buck asked through the door.

"Yeah, that's my brother. S'up, you from tha 80's?"

"Nah, I'm from 9-0. But I fuck wit' a lot of niggas from over there. I'm Buck. What's your name?"

"D-Low."

"Yep, you hungry? I know you just got here and ain't got shit, so I'ma shoot you some hygienes and soups and shit. When they pop tha doors fo' door check I got' chu."

"Good lookin' my nigga. I was kinda hungry."

"Don't trip, it's nothin'. I got some magazines and urban books too. I'll shoot you a few."

"Yep, right on."

"It's nothin'!"

Turning away from the door, Buck noticed his cellie looking up at him from the card table downstairs.

"S'up Buck, he's from tha town?" asked Fresh.

"Yeah, that's Jay from 84th little brother. But now, deal out tha cards. I'm comin' right now."

CHAPTER THIRTY-TWO

L amonte nodded his head to Dem Hoodstarz, which was blaring from the speakers as he maneuvered his freshly painted Porsche Cayenne down 880 South headed for the Embassy Suites.

He smiled as the thoughts of fucking Evelyn for the first time invaded his mind. It was something about her conversation and the way she carried herself; not to mention the fact that she was super bad had him wanting to wife her.

Ring! Ring! Ring!

Lamonte turned down the stereo when he saw his cell phone light up in the cup holders.

"S'up Ma'?" he answered once he saw it was Evelyn.

"Nothin', just wanted you to know that I was here. The room number is 1237."

"Yep, I should be there in like fifteen minutes. Do you need me to pick up anythin'?"

"Nope, I told you I'm takin' care of everything."

"All right then, see you in a sec," he said, before smashing on the gas pedal, forcing the luxury SUV to get up.

Fifteen minutes later, Lamonte was pulling into the parking lot of the Embassy Suites. Before he got out, he put the SUV in park, turned the A/C on high, rolled the driver's side window halfway down, and then pushed in the cigarette lighter; which caused the passenger's floorboard to slide back, revealing a stash box with a .40 caliber and Mac-11 with a thirty round clip inside. He grabbed the .40 and stuffed it in his waist before he slid the floorboard back and got out.

Lamonte strutted through the hotel lobby and immediately made his way to the elevators. Once inside, he pushed the button for the 12th floor. Stepping back, he watched the door close and patiently waited for the elevator to reach the floor.

As he exited, he found suite 1237.

Knock! Knock! Knock! Knock!

Evelyn opened the door wearing a white lace camisole and matching thong. The first thing Lamonte noticed was the scented candles placed all around, dimly lighting the room.

"So you made it?" she greeted in a seductive voice.

"Wouldn't have missed it fo' my own funeral," he said as he walked inside, shutting the door behind him.

He walked over to the king-sized canopy bed, which was covered in white rose petals, and sat down.

Evelyn approached with a bottle of Cristal in her hands. "Pop this open for me, will you."

Lamonte nodded and popped the cork, causing the fine champagne to spill over the top. Evelyn returned with two champagne flutes and Lamonte immediately filled them.

"To us!" he said.

"To us!" she agreed as they raised their flutes.

While Evelyn tuned the radio to 106 KMEL, Lamonte pulled out a pre-rolled blunt and fired up. The strong scent of the purple haze instantly filled the room.

She returned to the bed where huge billows of smoke floated through the air.

When Trey Songz *Invented Sex* came blaring through the speakers, she decided to give Lamonte his own personal strip show.

He watched in amazement, puffing the blunt and sipping on Cristal, while Evelyn jiggled her voluptuous ass cheeks up and down.

"Mmmmm...You like wha' you see?" she whispered in his ear, letting her tongue wet his earlobe.

"Do I?" he asked, confirming how he felt as the scent of her perfume filled his nostrils.

Pulling off her camisole, Evelyn exposed her perky round titties and dark nipples. Lamonte finished the blunt, downed another flute of champagne, and then pulled Evelyn closer to him, putting her nipples in his mouth. He circled her areola with his tongue before trailing down the middle of her stomach to her belly button. She opened her legs, slipped her fingers in her panties, and played with her clit.

Lamonte couldn't help but stare at the lovely sight as Evelyn closed her eyes and worked her fingers in and out of her wetness. He licked her juices up as they flowed down her legs. Pulling her panties to the side, he went to work on her pussy. He licked and bit her clit gently, while his warm tongue wiggled in and out of her slit with skills.

She continued to work her magic on her clit as Lamonte gave her a tongue bath causing her to cum instantly. The only sound that could be heard was the radio, mixed with the grunting and gasps of their passion.

Reaching down, Evelyn massaged Lamonte's dick through his True Religion jeans, before dropping to her knees and unbuckling his Gucci belt. Pulling off his pants, she continued massaging his hardness through his Dolce and Gabbana boxers.

She planted kisses on his stomach before removing his dick and taking it in her mouth.

"Hmm," she moaned as she worked his manhood in and out of her mouth. "You like that Papi?"

"Yes! Yes!" he called out. "Right there Ma'! Yes, right there."

After putting her head game down, she was ready for Lamonte to go inside of her. "Please put it in me Papi," she moaned. "My pussy is on fire."

Pulling out of her mouth, Lamonte stood up, leaving his jeans on the floor next to his white tee. Picking her up by the waist, he carried her to the center of the bed.

They took off the rest of their clothes before Lamonte entered her slowly. Lifting her legs over his shoulders, he dug in, going as deep as he could go. The sight of her smooth-shaven pussy, as his dick slammed into her, turned him on.

"Ohh shit!" she called out. "Give it to me Papi!"

"Give me this pussy!" he called back.

"Yes! Yes! Fuck me Papi!"

"Whose pussy is this? Is this my pussy?" he asked pounding away.

"It's all yours, Papi...All yours! Oh my..oh shit," she moaned. "I'm 'bout to cum!"

171

Before she came, Lamonte pulled out, flipped her over, and entered her from the back.

"Oh my, ooh!" she screamed as he fucked the shit out of her. "I'm coming! AAAAH!" she screamed as a stream of pussy juices trickled down her inner thighs onto the bed.

When Lamonte felt himself on the verge of exploding, he fucked her so hard he could feel his balls slamming up against her wet thighs. "Ohh shit! I'm 'bout to...Ahhh!" he yelled as he shot his cum deep inside her.

"Damn, Ma', you tha best," he complimented once he regained his energy.

Evelyn cuddled in Lamonte's arms and they fell asleep.

←——————————————————→

Buck stood with his back against the rec wall, while D-Low stood in front of him talking about the latest shit that was going on in the hood.

A few yards away, inmates occupied themselves playing basketball, handball, volleyball, and working out.

Buck was listening to D-low go back and forth but kept his eyes on his surroundings. He'd been in jail for sixteen months now. He saw two birthdays slip by and numerous niggas coming in and out during that time.

Buck was laughing at something D-Low was saying before asking about his brother Jay.

"So s'up with Jay and 'em? I heard they got a machine goin' on 8-4 beyond imagination."

"Yeah, he and Dame got shit on lock over there," D-Low replied with a grin.   "Niggas got tha block rollin' for' real."

Buck felt like he'd been slapped in the face. Just hearing about all the money being made outside the walls almost pushed him over the edge. He decided to ease in with grace.

"So that nigga Dame finally gettin' his chips up, huh?"

D-Low sighed in frustration. "Yeah, that nigga came up from a lick and been doin' his thang ever since."

"Oh! So that nigga out there layin' shit down, huh?"

"Off top. He's been fuckin' wit' that nigga Wacko from Brookfield. Them niggas stay on one."

"So he's fuckin' wit' crazy ass Wacko, huh? Shid, I guess a nigga gotta eat one way or another."

"Fo' real doe. It's this young nigga from Chicago out there doin' his thang too. Got shit on lock! That nigga Dame and 'em already laid tha nigga down. This nigga actin' like he can come open up shop in Tha Town," D-Low said with a wicked grin on his face.

D-Low continued talking; not realizing Buck was steaming with anger.

"Yeah, shit is dumb ass ugly on the streets. Niggas gettin' knocked down left and right."

Buck struggled to contain his shock. "Yeah, I heard 'bout cus. Heard niggas tried to knock 'em down a couple of weeks ago at a club in Frisco."

"Yep, that was Dame, Rich, and Wacko. But somehow tha nigga Rich got smoked."

"Like that, huh?" Buck sighed inwardly and immediately got on another topic.

D-Low was rattling on about a new rap group in Tha Town and who flipped what latest whips. All the while Buck's head was somewhere else. A series of thoughts clouded his mind.

So that's who's behind tha bullshit wit' Black...I gotta get word to him ASAP.

CHAPTER THIRTY-THREE

Lamonte woke up to the feel of Evelyn's lips on his neck. He smiled, as his mind reflected on last night's events before adjusting his neck so that he could kiss her.

They'd been laid up all morning after a long night of lovemaking.

Sex with Evelyn was definitely different from the usual episodes he had with all the other bitches. It was deep and passionate. He didn't just rush to bang her out. He took his time and explored her body. There was something about their chemistry that was so intense. The thought of her being so independent also peaked his interest.

"What's good Ma'? Wha' time is it?" he asked in a groggy tone, attempting to kiss her on the lips.

"Ohh! Uhh-Uh...No you not try'na kiss me wit' that dragon breath," she replied with a burst of laughter before pushing him away.

"Oh, like that, huh? You got jokes," he said before blowing his breath in her face and throwing a pillow at her.

He got up and strolled to the bathroom.

Evelyn was laughing so hard she had tears in her eyes. Lamonte looked back at her.

Damn, she's super bad. Definitely a keeper! Let me go freshen up, so I can get some of that early morning lovin, he thought to himself.

"I'on know wha' you laughin' at, but we gon' see who's laughin' when I get out this bathroom," he told her.

Evelyn was still giggling while swinging the pillow he'd just thrown in her direction.

"Boy, I'm just playin'. Now put a move on it 'cause this kitty is callin' fo' you," she said placing two fingers inside her swollen lips.

Lamonte chuckled, but didn't verbally respond as he headed to the bathroom. Once inside, he noticed a fresh pair of boxers and wife beater laid out neatly on the counter next to all his toiletries.

Smiling as he put toothpaste on his toothbrush, he stood in front of the mirror brushing his teeth and thinking about that good pussy that awaited him.

After brushing his teeth, he ran some hot shower water while relieving himself of a much needed piss. Next, he slipped into the warm comfort of the shower stream.

As if on cue, Evelyn entered the shower and proceeded to wash Lamonte's entire body. Lathering his chest down with soap, he turned around and started smearing it all over Evelyn's breasts, while caressing them until both nipples got hard.

She moaned when he gently bit down on one of her nipples, while sliding his finger in and out of her pussy.

Dropping to his knees, he tickled her clit with his tongue then sucked it hard between his lips.

"Ohh my, Papi, please...."

Quickly working his lips back and forth, she grabbed his head and thrust her pussy into his face.

"Ohh Black! You 'bout to make me cum!"

Lamonte crawled further into Evelyn's sweet nectar, causing her walls to collapse like the levees in New Orleans, flooding him with her sweet juices.

Pulling Lamonte up away from her pussy, she sucked her juices from his lips. She reached down and caressed his soapy dick while rubbing it up between her slit.

When Lamonte couldn't take it anymore, he turned her around and entered her from the back.

Without hesitation, he pushed his way through her insides as she yelled out. The shower door shook as she yanked on the rail from his constant rhythmic banging. Her pussy was so tight it felt like heaven.

"Yes! Yes!" she moaned in between breaths. "Yes, Papi! Give it to me!"

Lamonte grabbed her by the hips and gave her long, deep strokes.

"Oooh! Baabby, I'm 'bout to cum!" she said in pure ecstasy.

Evelyn began to tighten her pussy around his dick, making Lamonte on the verge of exploding. Tilting his head back, he closed his eyes, enjoying the pleasure he was receiving.

Within the next few seconds, both of their floodgates were open.

Slapping her fat ass, Lamonte watched as it jiggled before kissing her on the neck. He was definitely addicted.

Lamonte had a bunch of runs to make that day so after washing up and ordering breakfast from room service, they both got dressed and parted ways.

←——————————→

Red paced back and forth in his cell staring at the ceiling, while kicking himself in the ass for getting busted. He blamed Black for his downfall. Had he plugged him, he wouldn't have reached out to Hector.

He'd been in Alameda County jail for over a month. Other than a couple phone calls to his baby momma, he had no contact to the outside world. Unlike state charges, being granted bail in the federal system could take him a couple of months. Red decided he didn't have a couple of months. He was restless and wanted out, now.

←——————————→

"I beat tha pussy up...up...up...up," Lamonte sang along with the music on his way to his condominium.

Today he was feeling good. All the stress from the previous weeks had disappeared the moment he was graced with Evelyn's presence.

Everyday somebody new was calling Lamonte trying to cop some work. Red was in jail and from the looks of it, he wasn't going anywhere soon. That gave Lamonte the opportunity to take over Red's blocks and stack some more change. If he was planning to call it quits, he was quitting with a shit load of money.

He had to give Lil' Trigg credit for stepping up and holding down the grind since the death of Lil' Pookie. For one, everybody in Tha Town knew about Lil' Trigg and his reputation so nobody dared tried to fuck him over.

Everybody was getting money. Even the niggas who used to fuck with Red were beginning to check more chips due to the low prices Lamonte threw out there.

The first thing Lamonte did was put the word out that he had $50,000 on the head of anyone who had anything to do with his misfortune. Whoever was behind those events belonged to him.

Naturally, it was assumed by this time in the streets, that whoever the individuals were had gotten ghost. The streets never slept. It always kept its eyes and ears open.

When Lamonte pulled into the underground parking garage of the condo, he noticed his neighbor, Robyn, cleaning her Mercedes CLS 500. He beeped the horn as he pulled in.

Getting out of the vehicle, he saw four missed calls on his phone. The numbers were all blocked. No voicemails neither.

"Fuck!" he cursed himself for not remembering to turn his ringer back on. He didn't want to be disturbed while with Evelyn so he turned it off. No sooner than he switched it back on, it started ringing.

"Yeah!" he said, activating the alarm and answering the phone at the same time.

"This is to collect call from...Buck! An inmate at Alameda County jail. To accept this call..."

Lamonte pressed zero, bypassing the rest of the recording, and Buck clicked on.

"S'up wit' it nigga?" Buck spoke.

"Shit. S'up wit' you. Why you ain't been callin'? I ain't heard from you in a minute...What's good?"

"You know, same ole' shit. Niggas comin' in left and right. But now, s'up wit' you doe? I heard it's been ugly, huh?"

"Yeah, but it's nothin' I can't handle, feel me?" he told his uncle confidently.

"Yeah, okay. 'Cause I'm hearin' a lot of shit I'on like, feel me?"

Lamonte knew Buck was referring to the situation at the club and at the house on Bancroft. Had he found out who was behind those events, they'd been dead a long time ago. He wasn't just avenging Murda and Lil' Pookie's deaths, but somebody wasn't respecting his gangsta and he knew his uncle was concerned.

"Yeah, it's been kinda ugly. But don't let that shit worry you, I'm good!"

"Yeah okay, I'on know everything that's goin' on out there, but I gotta good mind who's behind that bullshit," Buck said in a serious tone.

Lamonte listened as Buck went on about how he'd come across the information. He'd sucked up so much info about Dame and Wacko from D-Low without him suspecting a thing. He had the exact whereabouts on Dame. Wacko's whereabouts was a different story since he constantly kept it moving.

After Buck was finished relaying all the information to Lamonte, he said, "Good lookin'. And don't worry, I'ma have that surprise party waitin' fo' that ass."

Walking through the door of his condo, Lamonte tossed his keys onto the coffee table before flopping down on the sofa. He listened closely to every word Buck spoke. Honestly, he felt a whole lot better now that he finally had some names. Nevertheless, he hid his excitement as he changed the subject.

"Anyways, how yo' books lookin'? You 'on need no money or magazines or nothin'?"

"Nah, I'm good. Desiree keep a nigga straight."

"No doubt. Just makin' sho'."

"Off top. But look, I'm 'bout to get off this stress box and let you finish handling yo business. But keep ya head up and both eyes and ears open...one love nigga."

"Fa'sho... one love."

Lamonte disconnected the call and laid back on the sofa with a totally different mindset from which he had before talking to Buck. He now had the names of the perpetrators. Within an hour, he began to plot out a plan to snatch up Dame.

This was the break he needed. It was time niggas got a wake up call. *Apparently niggas didn't know who they fuckin' with*, he thought.

He jumped off the sofa. "A...B...C...G," he whispered with murderous thoughts on his mind.

CHAPTER THIRTY-FOUR

R ed laid across his bunk, staring up at the ceiling with both hands tucked behind his head. He was reminiscing about the streets when his name came across the PA system for a contact visit.

Ten minutes later, the cell door buzzed open. Red exited his cell and stood by the pod door where a big black bald headed C.O., who resembled Ving Rhames, came and escorted him downstairs. They walked in silence down the freshly buffed hallway.

"Walk through the metal detector, then follow me," the C.O. instructed before continuing down the hallway.

"Here we go," the C.O. said, stopping in front of what Red assumed was a visiting room for attorneys.

He unlocked the door.

"Have a seat; someone will be with you in a moment."

"Who the fuck comin' to visit me!" Red asked, as if he didn't already know.

"Shid, if I know. Maybe an attorney," the C.O. said, closing the door behind him.

After several minutes, two guys walked into the room Red was being held in. One was a lanky black man with broad shoulders who introduced himself as Agent Mitchell from the F.B.I. The second was a short Spanish guy, who looked older than his partner and introduced himself as Agent Gomez.

After taking their seats across from Red, Agent Gomez started. "So I received your letter last week Mr. Taylor and got up here as soon as possible."

179

After opening up his folder and pulling out Red's letter, he quickly scanned the pages before continuing. "It says here that you got some valuable information about a club shooting in San Francisco that left three dead and others injured a couple of months ago. And that you got information about a person who's supplying more than 80% of Oakland with cocaine and crack...is that correct?"

Red simply nodded his head before stating, "I got names, places, phone numbers, tha whole shebang! Question is, wha' can ya'll do fo' me?"

"Well that all depends on how good the information is. The only time the district attorney and federal prosecutors work out plea deals and full immunity, is if the person we're going after is big enough to spark their interest. Plus, you'd have to fully cooperate and truthfully answer any questions, regardless if it's pertaining to this investigation or not. You understand what I'm saying?" Mitchell spoke for the first time.

"Yeah, yeah, no doubt. Like I said, I got some heavy shit for ya'll. If ya'll can guarantee I wouldn't have to do any time for the charges I'm booked on, feel me?" Red looked at them as if he was running the show.

"Well first we got to hear what you have. I mean, we already got a slam-dunk case against you. Not to mention, we also got your connect. So whatever you got better be good," Gomez shot.

For an hour straight, Red ran off at the mouth like a faucet; exposing everything from the club shooting at Sway, the murder of Lil Pookie on Bancroft, to all the dope that was being flooded out in Oakland through Black. He even went as far to tell about other homicides he knew about. He purposely left out all names until he had a deal in front of him from the U.S Attorney.

Agent Gomez and Mitchell quietly took notes while Red sung a song that would have made Trey Songz proud.

After Red was done talking, Agent Gomez immediately got his boss on the phone.

$$\longleftrightarrow$$

After hooking up with Lil' Trigg, Lamonte got the rundown on Dame and Wacko. Dame was a hot-tempered nigga from 8-4, who had a reputation for playing with that iron. Word on the streets was that he had a nice little machine going on 8-4 with his cousin Jay. Wacko, on the other hand, was a known stick up kid from Brookfield. He used to pull capers with his little brother, Nine, throughout town. That was until Nine got killed.

Lamonte didn't give a fuck who they were or what they did. All he needed was a face.

"Yeah, it ain't gon' be nothin' to catch that nigga Dame. He stay out on that block," Lil' Trigg said, taking a pull on a blunt. "But that nigga Wacko is a different story. He stay in traffic."

"Yeah?" Lamonte said. "Well fuck it. I say we snatch up Dame and have 'em lead us to Wacko."

"I'm wit' that. But we gotta come correct 'cause that nigga stay strapped."

"No question. All we gotta do is sit on 'em. He'll slip eventually. Anybody can get it."

"No doubt, Black," Lil' Trigg said passing the blunt off. "Anybody-definitely-can-get-it!"

CHAPTER THIRTY-FIVE

Meanwhile on 84th Ave....

"Nigga, wha' they hittin' fo'?" Dame asked, approaching the dice game on his corner.

"S'up wit' it Dame? Niggas ain't seen you all day and it's biting like a mu'fucka out here," P.K. said, dropping a twenty dollar bill on the cement. "Bet you don't hit a dubb!"

"That's a bet, P.K.," Bone said before shaking the dice and letting them roll.

The dice landed on 11.

"Let me get that! Who got me?" Bone asked

"I got you!" Dame said, throwing down a fifty dollar bill. "And I bet you don't hit tha other thirty."

"That's' a bet Dame," Bone replied.

Bone rolled the dice again. They landed on 6.

"Bet fifty a piece on tha straight 6 and 6 or 8," Dame said, dropping a hundred dollar bill.

"That's a bet, Dame. We got eighty on tha straight 6 and fifty on tha 6 or 8."

Bone shook the dice again and rolled a seven. "Fuck!" he cursed before handing Dame $130.

"Now, who got me?" Dame asked, picking up somebody's twenty off the ground.

"That's me," Slim said. "Bet you don't hit a dubb too."

"That's a bet. Anybody else wanna lose some money. Bet fifty I hit," Dame said to everyone, as money continued to drop.

Dame placed five bets, shook the dice, and rolled a 7 out the gate. He picked up his winnings and yelled. "Fifty I shoot! Who got me?"

"Damn, Dame. You gon' raise tha game to tha 50's? We was havin' a friendly game," questioned Jay.

"Man, fuck that! Fifty, I shoot. Who got me?" Dame asked shaking the dice up good.

"Fuck it! Shoot tha 50's then," Jay said, throwing down two 20's and a 10.

Dame picked up the money and rolled a 10. "Taking all bets on tha 10 or 4," he said confidently.

After placing bets around the circle, it took Dame two rolls to come up with the 4.

"Bet back?" he asked, while scooping up the piles of money in front of his opponents fast.

Six rolls later he hit the 10; Five-Five.

"Whoever said, that was a hard fuckin' ten," Dame laughed as he continued to collect his money from everybody in the circle.

An hour later, Dame was up $6,000 and ready to quit.

"Good looking. Ya'll just paid fo' my re-up," he announced, stuffing money into his pockets.

As he turned to leave, Bone called out. "So you go' hit and run like that?"

"Just-like-that!" Dame replied smugly without even looking back.

Heading up the block to the dope fiend George's house, Dame strolled the concrete sidewalks. Everyone he walked by seemed to acknowledge him. As he looked around, he smiled to himself, scanning the flourishing drug organization he'd established. Dame was content with his hands on approach. He didn't mind serving fiends as long as their money was right.

Dame continued down the street, nodding his head. His swagger was through the roof. The brand new Air Jordan XI's on his feet squeaked with every step. He sagged his black Rocawear jeans, while the black hoodie concealed the .45 on his waist.

George spotted Dame as soon as he came into view. He walked over towards him like an employee does his employer on payday.

"S'up, nephew?" George greeted. "Ain't seen you all day."

"You know me; I stay makin' moves like a chess game. What's good doe? I heard it's been bitin'."

"Man, nephew, they been comin' left and right. I told you, you shoulda left me wit' a little something something. I been hitting that nigga Jay up all day wit' his stingy ass. I tell you...That boy ass so tight, I wouldn't be surprised if he could pick up a watermelon wit' it." George smiled warmly, flashing a jagged-toothed smile.

Dame let out a hardy laugh. Deep down he knew George was right about his cousin, Jay. That nigga would never come off anything unless the money was right.

"That's a good one, Unk. I tell that nigga all the time, in order fo' tha game to be good ta you, you gotta be good to tha game."

"Ain't that tha truth!" George laughed before moving closer to Dame. "Listen nephew, ya Unk need a wake up."

"Shit, it's 4 o'clock in the afternoon. If you ain't already woke, you ain't getting woke," Dame joked. "Nah, don't trip I got cha. Let's go inside."

When they got inside the house, Dame reached into his boxer briefs and pulled out a plastic zip lock baggie. Going inside, he grabbed two twenty dollar rocks and handed them to George.

"Good lookin' nephew. Im'a 'bout to go in tha back room and handle my business."

"I feel you. I'm 'bout to bounce up the block to tha store. Hit me if you need me."

"A'ight nephew, watch yo'self. You know them boys was shootin' up there last night so be careful."

"No question. Good lookin'."

Dame gave George dap and watched him disappear into the back room before he made his exit.

After leaving the crack house, Dame walked a short distance to the liquor store on the corner of 84th to put something in his system. It was a hot evening so he contemplated pulling off his hoodie although it helped to conceal the .45 on his waist.

Dame was completely unaware of the caravan occupied by Lil' Trigg parked up the block.

$\longleftrightarrow$

From a safe distance, Lil' Trigg watched Dame's every move. A few minutes elapsed before he pulled out his cell phone and gave Lamonte the rundown on the best place to make their move.

"Yo, we in luck. It looks like he's 'bout to go into this store on tha corner...And he's alone," Lil' Trigg assured Lamonte.

"I'm on it," Lamonte said, waiting in a parked car not too far away from the store.

"A'ight," he said. "Tell me wha' ta do?"

"Just stay put. When he comes outta tha store, dip up on 'em and distract 'em. I'll grab 'em from tha back befo' he knows what's goin' on," Lamonte said, exiting the vehicle.

⬅————————————➡

"Hey, Mo. Let me get two boxes of Peach Optimos, a pint of V.S.O.P. Hennessey and a ham and cheese sandwich. Put a lot of mayonnaise on that too. Gimme extra meat and American cheese. No onions," Dame requested.

"Okay, Buddy," Mo said, making his way over towards the sandwich area.

Mohammad was one of the coolest storeowners in East Oakland. The whole hood had love and respect for him. He was good to the people in the community. If you were short a dollar or two, he'd let you get away with it. If you needed store credit or a place to stash your sack, he was always cool with it.

"So how's business?" Mo asked genuinely concerned.

Dame shrugged. "It is wha' it is. I can't complain."

"That's good," Mo said, giving Dame a warm smile. "How's everybody on tha block? I heard 'em shootin' last night."

"Everybody cool. Some niggas came through bustin', but nobody got hit," he informed him.

"Well, praise Allah."

After Mohammad prepared the sandwich and rung up the rest of the items, Dame reached into his pocket and placed two twenty dollar bills on the counter.

"Keep tha change."

"Thanks Buddy."

185

"Sure thing. Later, Mo."

Dame gave Mo dap and left the store. He had no idea death was lurking right around the corner.

Dame exited the store, bag in one hand, and sandwich in the other. No sooner then he took a bite of his sandwich, a dark colored caravan skidded to halt a few feet in front of him, causing him to jump and drop his stuff. He tried to reach for his .45, but was met by a blunt force to the back of his head from Lamonte's Mac-11.

He collapsed to the pavement. "Ohh, wha' you was gon' do wit' this?" Lamonte asked, snatching the .45 from Dame's waist. "Get yo' bitch ass in the van!"

Lamonte put the Mac-11 to the back of Dame's head and pushed him through the sliding door of the van while getting in behind him.

Dame continued to struggle until Lamonte whacked him a couple more times across the head. He started panting heavily and gasping for air. "W-W-Where ya'll t-takin' me?"

"Shut-tha-fuck-up!" Lamonte lashed out.

"Bitch ass nigga, you know wha' it iz," Lil' Trigg added, before pulling off.

"I got 'bout $7,000 on me, it's yours," Dame pleaded.

"Nigga fuck that money!" Lamonte said, clenching his jaw. "Where yo' boy Wacko at? I hear ya'll niggas been lookin' fo' me."

"Man, I'on know where dude at."

BLAM!

Lamonte slapped him again with the gun.

Dame started convulsing as blood ran into his eyes from his head.

"Where-tha-fuck-is-Wacko!" Lamonte demanded.

"I'on-"

BLAM!

Before Dame could finish, Lamonte hit him again. "Nigga, lie to me again and I'm cappin' you right fuckin'here!"

"Listen, listen...I'on know where he's at but I can call 'em," Dame protested.

"That's exactly wha' you'll do. And nigga, you betta not try no funny shit!" Lamonte threatened.

***

Wacko was chilling at one of his spots, watching television and doing lines of coke. Suddenly, his cell phone started vibrated, causing him to jump and reach for his gun. Once he noticed the vibration was coming from his phone, he placed his pistol back down, took another sniff, and went to answer it.

"Yeah, what's good?"

"Where you at? You ain't gon' believe who I just seen," Dame said.

"Yeah, who that?"

"That nigga Black.... and guess where at?"

"Where! Where!" Wacko said instantaneously as he swiftly moved around the living room before sniffing another line.

"At this motel off A street in Hayward."

After hearing the exact location, Wacko said, "A'ight, I'm on my way." And ended the call.

He grabbed his pistol and gloves and threw a black hoodie over his black T-shirt. Finishing off the rest of the coke on the plate, he stepped out of the apartment. His adrenaline pumped double. He just knew this time he'd be successful in knocking down Black.

He jumped into his car and quickly made his way to the Motel 6 in Hayward.

CHAPTER THIRTY-SIX

The United States District Attorney, Paul Hire, was running late for his meeting, wearing one of his usual expensive suits. The last thing he looked like was a District Attorney. He was young and athletic looking, and resembled Tom Brady on draft day minus the cap.

He looked more like a college jock than a District Attorney. His Piaget Emperador watch, Armani suits, and the Aston Martin Rapide that he drove certainly made him look like a celebrity.

The gathered detectives and agents were called to the Oakland Federal building to discuss Lamonte Gibbson and his ongoing drug operation.

There were six agents present and three detectives. The group whispered in the room as they awaited the arrival of Mr. Hire.

"So he's a transplant of Chicago, huh?" Detective Matheson asked Agent Mitchell.

Mitchell nodded his head. "South Side Gangsta Disciples. Son of the late Jack Gibbson, a governer of the Gangsta Disciples until about eight years ago; he was gunned down in front of 'Ole Lamonte."

"Damn! Kid had to watch his pops get executed, huh?" Agent Li asked.

"Don't go feeling sorry for 'em too soon. I got in touch with detectives from Chicago who claims Lamonte was the main suspect in a home invasion gone bad, leaving six dead. The detectives thought they had him when they believed he'd left his blood at the scene after being shot in his shoulder. They questioned him at the hospital, but got nothing. He claimed to have been shot in a drive-by while walking a friend to the subway. But listen to this...He didn't give the detectives the name of the friend that was with him-"

"Sticking to the code, huh...Never give up a name," a young, Detective Carter said.

"But what about DNA? Surely they had enough grounds to arrest him."

"Apparently not. The blood was sent to a lab to be tested before an arrest warrant could be issued. And listen to this...Unfortunately, it got destroyed. This detective...detective...umm?"

Mitchell opened up his folder and scanned the notes.

"Bailey! This Detective Bailey said he tried to keep tabs on Lamonte's whereabouts when he was released from the hospital to no avail. He'd already abandoned the Windy City. Det. Bailey also suspected Lamonte was responsible for other homicides in the city."

Agent Gomez nodded his head. "We also got information from a confidential informant who's willing to testify that Lamonte was responsible for a club shooting a while back that left three dead and numerous others injured. He also claims not only is Lamonte supplying eighty percent of Oakland with crack and cocaine, but he's also shipping five to ten kilos a month back to Chicago. I don't know if any of you remember a sixteen-year old boy found shot to death execution style in a house on the 7200 block of Bancroft Avenue a couple months ago-"

"Anthony Dixon, friends call him Lil' Pookie. I remember that case," DEA Agent Lorenzo Frontieri said, cutting off Gomez.

"That's right...Well this C.I. claims the house was being rented by Mr. Gibbson, and used to sell and store drugs. Looks like the kid, Anthony, worked for Mr. Gibbson."

District Attorney Paul Hire walked into the room full of law enforcement officers and cleared his throat.

Immediately the room got quiet.

"Gentlemen, as most of you know, my name is Paul Hire, United States District Attorney. I know some of you personally and others I've seen yet have not had the opportunity to meet. Anyhow, I've asked you to come here today so we can discuss an ongoing problem that's affecting our community...And that problem is a Mr. Lamonte Gibbson A.K.A Pretty Black. Now, recently we've been able to get key information about Lamonte's operation from a confidential informant.

With your help gentlemen, we'll be conducting a full scale investigation."

Mr. Hire continued. "During the course of this investigation, you're entitled to pull off the gloves. I'm talking wiretaps, video surveillance, visual surveillance; the whole nine. Whatever you need."

Hearing this, all of the detectives nodded their heads, understanding what their next mission was. It was bad enough dealing with California dealers, but now they had to stop a visitor.

After all questions were answered, and everyone was fully briefed, Mr. Hire thanked everyone for coming before ending the meeting.

$$\longleftrightarrow$$

Lamonte and Lil' Trigg took Dame to a room that was rented by a dope fiend and tied him up with some plastic zip ties.

Keeping the Mac trained to the back of Dame's head, Lamonte instructed him to call Wacko and read exactly what he'd written on a piece of paper.

At first, Lamonte was reluctant that his plan wouldn't work. But after hearing the anticipation in Wacko's voice, he knew he'd show up; now all they had to do was sit and wait.

Dame was dazed and had lost track of how many blows Lamonte delivered to his head. He was reeling, still trying to come to grips with the realization that he was about to die.

"Just kill me, nigga!" Dame grunted as blood mixed with sweat rolled down his chin.

WHACK!

"That'll be too easy," Lamonte said, hitting him again.

Lil' Trigg smirked. He was getting a kick out of this shit. He wanted to walk over, pull out his dick, and piss on him. However, because of DNA and today's technology, he didn't exercise that thought very long. Instead, he walked over and swung his pistol with as much force as he could to Dame's face, knocking several teeth down his throat.

"AGGGG!" Dame tried to scream, but the sound was muffled by the old rag that was gagged in his mouth. "Fuck you!" he grunted.

"Nah, fuck you!" Lamonte said nonchalantly as he brought the Mac-11 down hard on his nuts.

"OWWWW!" Lil' Trigg cried out. "I know that had to hurt"

Dame was terrified. He couldn't believe he was caught slipping. Deep down he knew he'd never make it out of the motel room alive. His only regret was that he'd help lure Wacko to the room. He figured if he could buy himself enough time, he'd figure a way out of this mess.

His body ached all over and he shook uncontrollably every time the cold steel came crashing down on him. He smelled the scent of urine in the room and immediately realized he'd pissed his pants.

Lamonte had beaten Dame for so long; perspiration soaked his face and shirt. Completely out of breath, he decided to take a break, but not before walking over to the dresser and retrieving the bottle of Wild Turkey. After taking a big pulp, he doused Dame's bloody body.

"AGHHHHHHHHH!"

Dame's muffled scream was so frightening; Lamonte thought he was going to pass out.

The 80 proof alcohol felt like liquid fire on his open wounds. The last thing he remembered before passing out was reciting Mattew 6:9-13 in his head.

He knew he was destined to death. He just prayed they'd get it over with already. Dame mumbled something incoherent and passed out.

⬅——————————➡

Wacko drove like a maniac, dipping in and out of traffic. He pushed the pedal down and accelerated his speed down the 880 freeway.

Dumping a large amount of cocaine onto his fist, he brought it up to his nose and sniffed hard. Snapping his head back, he tightened his grip on the steering wheel as the grade A cocaine went straight to his brain.

"AAAAAARGH!" he yelled, shaking his head violently.

By this time, he had already exceeded the speed limit, leaving all the other vehicles behind. He felt his blood pressure rising. He'd consumed so much dope that day. It's a wonder his heart hadn't popped.

Minutes later, he arrived in Hayward at the Motel 6, a rundown piece of shit motel, which was ducked off and in the cuts.

The sun was going down when he pulled into the parking lot. After making sure the thirty-round clip in his Ruger P.89 .9mm was indeed locked and loaded, he tucked it in his waist.

Exiting the vehicle, he called Dame's phone as he made his way to the room he'd be waiting in.

⟵————————————————⟶

Lil' Trigg watched Wacko the moment he pulled into the parking lot. He'd been crouched down for ten minutes in the back seat of the rented caravan, awaiting his arrival. Once he was sure it was Wacko, and he was alone, he simply sent Lamonte a text.
Showtime!! He's in route to tha room, solo.
When Wacko stepped out of his vehicle so did Lil' Trigg. He followed Wacko from a safe distance all the way to the room. Had Wacko not been so occupied with his phone, he probably would've concentrated more on his surroundings.
Lil' Trigg gripped the weapon in his hoodie pocket as he waited for the perfect opportunity. Within minutes, that opportunity would arise.

⟵————————————————⟶

Wacko called Dame for the third straight time with the same result.
He'd been trying to reach his comrade since arriving at the motel, but didn't receive a response.
At first, he thought that Dame might've been laid up with a bitch. But that didn't make any sense.
He'd knew I was comin', Shit! He was the one who called me.
Wacko's instincts told him something wasn't right. He immediately pulled out his gun as he reached the room door. Proceeding with caution, he knocked.
Knock! Knock! Knock! Knock!
He stepped away from the door with the P.98 ready, while scanning the parking lot.
Moments later, the door opened. Wacko spranged into action like a marksman. He moved into the doorway, legs spread, gun aimed high, and looking for any movement. Before he could get a good look at the occupants in the room, an electrifying circuit sent shock waves throughout his entire body struck him, causing him to lose grip on the P.89 and drop to the ground.

He looked up wild-eyed as Lil' Trigg stood over him with a taser gun in one hand and a .45 in the other.

Suddenly, Black appeared in the doorway and retrieved the P.89 from off the ground, before half dragging him into the room. Lil' Trigg timidly brought up the rear, kicking him in his face violently.

When Wacko came about, he couldn't believe his eyes as Black and Lil' Trigg stood over him pointing guns. He looked over at Dame gagged and tied to a chair and vowed to kill him if they ever made it out of there.

"Aye!" Black said, kicking him in his side and stirring him from his thoughts.

"So you tha pussy that's been try'na off me huh? You called yoself comin' here to kill me, right?"

Black raised his foot up and brought it down hard against his head. "Well bitch, it's been a change of plans!"

Boom! Boom! Boom! Boom!

Lamonte's index finger squeezed off on the trigger and clicked off four rounds, all of which landed in Wacko's forehead, cracking open the back of his head. It sent blood and bone fragments splashing against the white wallpaper.

Wacko's upper body jerked off the ground twice before resting there as if he was sound asleep.

Lamonte handed the P.89 to Lil' Trigg.

Boom! Boom! Boom! Boom! Boom!

Lil' Trigg placed three slugs into Dame's chest and two into his head, answering his prayers.

The thought of torturing Wacko was very tempting. It crossed Lamonte's mind earlier as he awaited his arrival. Once he was in Lamonte's presence, it was a different story.

If it wasn't for the strong possibility of someone calling the police, due to the shots fired, Lamonte surely would've stayed around a little while longer to make sure the fire he set in the trashcan ignited properly.

CHAPTER THIRTY-SEVEN

B uck couldn't believe what he was seeing as his face became glued to the television. He listened as the news' anchorwoman reported.

"Good evening everyone. I'm Heather Holmes. In today's top story...Hayward police are investigating a gruesome discovery at a Motel 6 in Hayward. We go to our correspondent, Amber Lee, who's live at the scene...Amber?"

"Good evening, Heather. I'm standing in front of the Motel 6 in Hayward, off west A-Street, where fire fighters were called to the scene of a two-alarm fire a little after 7 o'clock this evening. Occupants in room 113 said they smelled smoke, and later located that source when they ran outside and discovered room 111 engulfed in flames.

"After successfully putting out the premature fire, authorities found the remains of two males shot multiple times. As you can see, scores of law officials are at the scene right now."

"Amber, is there any information surfacing about the identities of the two males found inside the room?" the anchorwoman asked.

"Well, Heather, an unnamed source has told Channel 2 news that authorities had indeed identified one of the victims, but was not releasing his name until family members could be notified. At this time, they're just ...Wait...Yes. Heather, the name of one of the deceased has just been released. The family has confirmed the body of twenty-four year old Damion Clark of Oakland was amongst the victims. Authorities so far have no clues as to what led to these senseless killings. This is Hayward's 28th homicide of the year. Anyone with information concerning this crime or others, are asked to call Crime Stoppers at (510)8-7-C-R-I-M-E.Reporting live from Hayward...Amber Lee."

"Thank you Amber...In other news today..."

Buck smiled to himself as he sipped the jailhouse wine in his cup. He knew that shooting had everything to do with the information he'd given Lamonte. His thoughts were later confirmed when a photo of Dame flashed across the screen.

He quickly made his way over towards the day room, where D-Low was getting a haircut.

After explaining to D-Low what he'd just seen on the news, D-Low immediately jumped out of the chair and ran to the phone.

$\longleftrightarrow$

Lamonte sat in front of his television watching the 10 o'clock news. No matter how many times he saw Heather Holmes on T.V., the irony of her beauty never ceased to amaze him.

He poured himself another shot of Hennessey and lit up a blunt. The smoke seeped from his nose and disappeared into the air.

Time to call it quits, he thought.

Now that he'd revenged Lil' Pookie and Murda's death, he could entertain the possibility of actually retiring from the game.

But wha' would I do? Open up some sort of business? Concentrate on my music? All I know is tha streets. Yeah, I could work on putting out an album but then wha'? With that thought, he took another pull of the blunt and sat back.

Lamonte didn't know shit about running a business. He didn't even have a G.E.D. The thought alone was laughable. Him being anything other than a hood nigga seemed like wishful thinking. The hood was where he belonged. Not once had he relished the thought of being a hard working individual. He was into the finer things in life and the streets provided him with the means of getting them.

A hustler's life wasn't indeed promising, but shit nobody's was. *Anybody Can Get It.*

CHAPTER THIRTY-EIGHT

Two months later...

Lil' Trigg darted in and out of stores at Richmond's Hilltop Mall, while Lamonte followed close behind. Lamonte decided to up the young nigga's status in the streets because of his loyalty and success with distribution of his work. With the extra money, Lil' Trigg treated himself to a new whip and lots of shopping sprees.

"C'mon, bra'. I wanna see if they got tha new Penny's!" Lil' Trigg shouted excitedly, walking into Shiek's shoe store.

Lamonte shrugged and followed.

They stayed in the store for about thirty-minutes as Lil' Trigg mulled over and tried different shoes. Lamonte picked up a pair of Nike Air Max 1's and signaled a sale's clerk for help. He didn't really need any new shoes; he already had plenty at home he hadn't worn yet. Still, he couldn't help but admire the purple and white classics.

After trying on the shoes, he told the clerk, "I'll take 'em."

"What'd you get, bra'?" Lil' Trigg asked, walking up to the counter with three boxes.

"Shit...just some Air Max's."

$$\longleftrightarrow$$

Agent Gomez lounged near Shieks with his partner, Mitchell, keeping a close eye on Lamonte and his friend. For two months he and his partner had been tracking the young kingpin's every move. So far, they hadn't noticed anything out of the ordinary, other than Lamonte's lavish lifestyle. Within the last ten days, Gomez and Mitchell observed Lamonte spending money like it grew on trees.

Agent Mitchell took snap shot after snap shot of Lamonte and his friend. "Look at the kid who's with Black. Does he look familiar to you?"

Gomez held the high power camera to his eyes and zoomed in to inspect the kid's face. "Nope, can't say he does." Gomez watched as the duo paid for their things before exiting the store. "All I see are two scumbags spending more money in a single day than I make in a couple of months."

The two watched as both hustlers exited the store.

Gomez handed the camera back to his partner with frustration. "Fuckin' assholes! Sometimes I wonder if we're in the wrong profession."

Mitchell shook his head. "All that glitters isn't gold!"

***

Glancing at his phone, Lamonte noticed they'd been at the mall for longer than he anticipated. The sun would be setting soon and they'd be needed in the hood.

Leaving the store, they made their way towards the exit.

As soon as they started walking, a chill went up Lamonte's spine alerting his warning system. He immediately stopped and looked around for any signs of danger.

"What's good, bra'?" Lil' Trigg asked, looking around suspiciously.

Not seeing anything out of the ordinary, Lamonte shook off the uneasiness. "Nothin' dawg, I'm trippin'."

Continuing to the exit, his eyes vigilantly swept back and forth. For some reason he couldn't shake the feeling of being watched.

Fuck it! He chalked it up as paranoia.

***

Gomez and Mitchell followed the duo towards the exit and watched as they suddenly stopped and looked around suspiciously.

Gomez had made a call in advance, so everybody was in place and waiting. The first person to identify Lamonte and Lil' Trigg when they exited the mall was Det. Matheson.

197

Matheson was standing out front smoking a cigarette while talking on his cell phone to his partner, Det. Thompson, when the duo walked past.

As the duo made their way towards the parking lot, Matheson informed his partner they were coming his way.

CHAPTER THIRTY-NINE

gents Gomez and Mitchell sat inside of an enclosed room watching footage from the night of the shooting at Club Sway. They looked on distracted as they watched several innocent bystanders get mowed down by bullets while others scrambled for cover. The gunmen were shooting from a location across the street, out of view of the cameras, so the tape didn't catch any images of their faces.

Mitchell stared at the screen with determination in his eyes. "I know it's here...I remember the first time we watched this film. It should be...Here! Here!"

When the club erupted in pandemonium with club goers fleeing from inside the club, Mitchell stopped the tape.

Zooming in on the faces of two individuals returning fire, Mitchell said, "You see that?"

"Yeah, that's Derrick Johson, A.K.A Murda, found dead at the scene from multiple gunshot wounds. It's believed he had a hand in the murder of Richard Reed, found shot to death in the clubs restroom...so?"

Mitchell opened up the complete file on Lamonte Gibbson. Going through the surveillance photos of Black, he found what he was looking for. After examining some photos, he passed one over to Gomez.

Gomez's pleased facial expression said it all without him saying a single word. "Holy shit! Look at the fleas on Fluffy."

Mitchell knew his partner too well. "Are you thinking what I'm thinking?"

Gomez smacked his chewing gum. "Uh-huh! I want this asshole brought in today. I wanna know his full name, street name, last known

199

address, girlfriends...any and everything we can find out on this scumbag."

Gomez peeked at the screen one last time.

"And I want it like yesterday...Damnit!" he re-emphasized

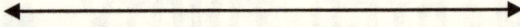

◄━━━━━━━━━━━━━━━━━━━━►

With the dismissal for Red, business prospered enormously. Lil' Trigg's life took a turn for the better. Just as Black had promised, his status in the streets was through the roof. With the extra money he was making, he was finally able to shine like the big boys. He tossed out all his old clothes and upgraded his wardrobe.

Lil' Trigg coasted down International Blvd. He had a blunt hanging from his mouth, while DJ Khaled's *All I Do Is Win* blasted from his six 15's.

He nodded his head and threw up his pinky finger as people admired his cocaine white '74 drop top Chevy Caprice on matching 28 inch Lexanis; one of the vehicles he'd flipped since coming up. The top was down, causing the sun to glare off the bone white dashboard as he turned onto 90th Ave. At 9-0 and MacArthur, he pulled into the liquor store.

After parking the Caprice and snatching his .45 off the passenger seat, he tucked it in his waist and hopped out of his ride. Nodding his head to a group of niggas who were posted outside the store, he made his way inside.

After purchasing a box of Swishers, a bottled water, and a 4X white tee, he exited the store just as a young lady was about to enter. She was light skinned, with bright red micro braids running down her back. She had on some green, army fatigue booty shorts that complemented her apple bottom. Just by how she looked, Lil' Trigg could tell she was a Bop, exactly what he liked.

As she strolled past, the double d's she kept packed under her tank top, pressed up against Lil' Trigg's arm.

"S'up wit' it Ma'?" he said, holding the door open for her.

"Hi," she said, looking him up and down. "How you doin'?"

"I'm good now that I've been blessed wit' yo' presence. I'm sayin' though, what's yo' name?"

"Angel."

"You so right. S'up wit' it Ms. Angel, I'm try'na see what's crackin' wit' you. Wha' you got goin'?"

"Wha' I got goin'? Boy, I'on even know yo' name!"

"I'm Trigg. But check it, I'ma cut to tha chase. If you ain't got shit goin' on, jump in, and hit a couple corners wit' ya boy," Lil' Trigg shot, nodding his head towards his ride.

She glanced over at the triple white Chevy sitting clean in the parking lot, and immediately soaked her panties. "Okay, but only fo' a minute. I gotta babysit my little brother in 'bout an hour," she said, looking at her watch.

That was more than enough time for Lil' Trigg. He walked over to his car and hopped inside, followed by Angel. By the time he made it to the 100's, he was topped down, getting topped down. No doubt, he was definitely winning.

Lamonte sat in the living room of his apartment and placed the duffle bag full of money on the sofa. Pulling out neatly rubber banded stacks; he prepared to recount all the money inside the bag. Popping the rubber band off the first stack, he sat back and prepared himself for a long night.

Four hours and numerous paper cuts later, the total was looking him in the face. *Is that right? It can't be,* he thought.

If it wasn't, he definitely wasn't about to recount it. The total on the paper in front of him was $948,000, just $52,000 shy of a million.

Damn! There's just 'bout a ticket here, he said to himself.

He knew he was sitting on something cool, but it'd been awhile since the last time he counted up all the money in the safe.

He picked up a ten G stack-all hundred dollar bills, and shuffled through it like a deck of playing cards. Grabbing two more stacks, he got up and walked over to the full body mirror behind the door. Posing from different angles with the money outstretched in his palms, he thought of the song *Make it Rain*, before tossing the bills in the air.

Lamonte watched as the bills floated through the air surrounding him like back when he was a kid playing with bubbles. All the years of

201

jacking and hustling had finally paid off. People spend their entire lives working and trying to move up the corporate ladder without seeing a fraction of the money he had stacked in just a couple of years.

He sat back down on the sofa with bills still scattered about. Again, he thought about the prospect of getting out while he still had a chance. Even with Red behind bars, he still had to maintain his 20 bricks a week purchase. For $12,000 a brick, why wouldn't he? But now that he was almost worth a million he was beginning to think about his future.

The streets were getting more complicated by the day. He'd already been a direct target of a couple of goons trying to get a come up and it was only a matter of time before the law started sniffing up his ass. So far, he'd beaten the odd by dodging death, the penitentiary, and poverty; that itself was a hard enough job. Looking back at the deaths of his Pops, Tres, Murda, and Lil Pookie, plus the incarceration of Buck and Red, he felt he'd been working pretty damn hard. Now he sat and contemplated calling it quits.

$$\longleftrightarrow$$

For the next two weeks, it was business as usual. Lil' Trigg was busting moves left and right, and basically took over all of Red's blocks. Gino had finally managed to lock down Tha Ville. Chop was doing his thing with Tha 70's, and parts of Tha 60's on smash. E from Seminary was steady struggling to get niggas to fuck with him. Lamonte couldn't figure that out. It seemed like no matter how low he dropped the prices, E just couldn't prosper. Tae-Tae was still back and forth from the Chi to Tha Town and Tina's spot was still being used to store work.

After the deaths of Wacko and Dame, the word was officially out that Black wasn't to be fucked with. But each passing day, Lamonte was getting more restless. He'd grown tired of looking over his shoulders and peeking around corners. He was ready to start enjoying the fruit of his labor.

$$\longleftrightarrow$$

Sitting in their cell, playing dominoes, Buck and Fresh were battling for 100 push-ups per game.

"15! And dominoe!" Fresh declared with a smug grin on his face, after slamming his last dominoe down. "Wha' you got?"

"Fuck!" Buck cursed. "I knew I shoulda got rid of this big six. Here, give yo'self

10."

"Too much," Fresh said. "That's game."

"Run it back, I let you win that one," Buck said, confidently as he took a sip from one of the many bottles of jailhouse wine he had stored in their cell.

"Shake 'em up—" The sounds of keys jingling alerted Fresh, cutting his sentences short.

"Shake down! Up against the wall!" yelled a big C.O. in riot gear.

Buck got a major surprise as he started getting too comfortable with his wine making. There were so many undercover snitches that he didn't know who was a friend or foe. Niggas was dropping kites left and right. For a month straight, the goon squad ran up in their cell searching for contraband.

Unfortunately, on this day, they would discover eight bottles of Pruno. After taking the rap for the alcohol, Buck was sent to the hole.

"Man, what's takin' so fuckin' long!" Red asked, heated. He was on the phone with Agent Gomez, inquiring about when he'd be released. Red had gone before the grand jury and testified against Black and a couple other people he knew. Once they completed their arrests, he'd be released pending the outcome.

After Gomez listened to Red's pathetic outburst, he shot back, "Listen here, Mr. Taylor! These fuckin' things take time! I'm not one of your fuckin' homeboys who come runnin' on your demand. Now, I know you're ready to get out that fuckin' place, and I don't blame you. But for God's sake, let me do my job. And quit calling me!"

Red hung up the phone. He had no choice but to wait.

CHAPTER THIRTY-NINE

Outside the parking lot of the Eastmont Police station, F.B.I agents Gomez, Mitchell, and Li, along with members of the D.E.A and O.P.D, geared up for the apprehension of Tarik Nelson A.K.A Lil' Trigg.

Their destination was an apartment complex on the corner of 98th and Bancroft Avenue, where the suspect was allegedly staying with his girlfriend.

Gomez, Mitchell, and Li rode in the Tahoe, followed by two Crown Victorians and numerous patrol cruisers.

The convoy of vehicles crept down Bancroft with the Tahoe in the lead and Mitchell behind the wheel. His eyes roamed around the neighborhood before he pulled over and killed the engine. From inside the truck, Gomez scanned the entire area through binoculars.

After concluding they hadn't been tipped off, Gomez gave the word. "Move in," he said into his radio.

Everyone exited their vehicles and made their way down the small path that led to the apartments. Breaking up into groups, they quickly surrounded the outer wall of the complex.

Mitchell unlocked a side gate and gained entrance. Det. Matheson, Thompson, and DEA Agent Frontieri came through a front gate and blended into the shadows of the complex until they reached the targeted apartment.

With the apartment completely surrounded, Mitchell quietly crept to a window. Peeking through, he immediately spotted someone sitting in the living room watching television. With his weapon positioned, he whispered.

"Now don't be fooled by this kid's youth. He has a reputation of being a cold-blooded killer. He's considered to be armed and dangerous. So be extremely careful."

Agent Gomez, being the officer in charge, said, "Okay, this is the plan. Matheson, you and Thompson cover the back. Li, grab some officers and make sure all the windows are secured and get some people to cover the garage as well. Mitchell, Frontieri, and myself will take the front door. Once everyone is in postion, we move on three."

They wore the faces of trained soldiers. This is what they lived for. This is why they represented the shield.

⟵―――――――――――――――⟶

Inside the apartment, Lil' Trigg sat with his feet up on the coffee table smoking a blunt in front of his flat screen TV, laughing his ass off as he watched *Friday* for the thousandth time. His trusty Mac-11, with the 30 round clip, sat on his lap as he blew rings of smoke into the air. Ki-Ki, the chick he'd been fucking with for a couple of years, came out of the back room wearing nothing but a T-shirt and a thong. She walked over and stood in front of the TV with her neck cocked and her hands on her hips.

Lil' Trigg looked at her, took a big hit from the blunt, and blew the smoke in her direction. "Wha' bitch!" he yelled, irritated.

He hated being interrupted while watching his movie.

"Wha', bitch?" she snapped angrily."Who tha fuck you got suckin' on yo' dick?"

"Suckin' on my dick!" he growled. "Bitch, you trippin'."

"Oh, I'm trippin', huh? Well, wha' tha fuck is this!" she hollered, holding up a pair of his boxers; red lipstick was smeared around the opening. "Mu'fucka. I don't wear lipstick! So...Who tha fucks been suckin' yo' dick, Tarik?"

⟵―――――――――――――――⟶

Agent Gomez followed as Mitchell and Frontieri made their way to the front door. The trio positioned themselves on the side of the wooden frame, while Gomez signaled to the officer holding the Bat-A-Ram.

205

Once the officer with the Bat-A-Ram was in position and ready to go, Gomez stated through the radio, "Eagle one in position."

"Eagle two in position."

"Three in position," they each said in unison.

Gomez took a deep breath and began to count. "On three...One...Two..."

←——————————————————————→

"Bitch, you trippin'-"

Blam!

"FBI! FBI! Everybody on the ground!" Mitchell yelled, coming through the door first.

Lil' Trigg immediately snatched up the Mac-11 and dashed across the floor, letting off a hail of bullets.

Tac-Tac-Tac-Tac-Tac-Tac-Tac

Mitchell tried to duck behind a wall when a bullet struck him in his neck, dropping him instantly. "AAAAAHHHHHH!" he screamed out.

Thinking fast, Frontieri dropped to his knees and applied pressure to Mitchell's wound, stopping the bleeding. He looked up at Gomez, who was signaling more officers into the room.

Jimmy, a big, country fed, white boy rushed into the room with his .9mm aimed high. Without hesitating to find a target, he let bullets fly.

Pop!-Pop!-Pop!-Pop!-Pop!

More officers quickly entered the room in striking position.

After getting Mitchell out of the line of fire, Gomez and Frontieri re-entered and spread out wide moving on each side of the room with guns drawn.

Tac-Tac-Tac-Tac-Tac-Tac

Jimmy was the next to feel the powerful impact from the Mac-11, as four slugs found its way into his vested chest plate, knocking him on his ass. "I'm hit!" he yelled out.

Lil' Trigg watched the big white boy go airborne, before he sprinted, zigzagging towards the garage.

Tac-Tac-Tac-Tac-Tac

He squeezed the trigger blindly, just to put space between him and the officers.

Gomez had his pistol aimed to kill as he took cover beside a wall. Noticing Lil' Trigg fleeing down a hallway, he fired.

Boom!Boom!Boom!Boom!

He riddled the wall with bullets, just missing Lil' Trigg's head, as he continued to flee. "Fuck!" Gomez cursed, seeing his shots were off.

Quickly raising her hands in the air, Ki-Ki rose from behind the sofa. "Please don't shoo-"

Pop!Pop!Pop!Pop!

Her words were cut short as four bullets entered her chest, knocking her off her feet instantly.

"Holy Shit!" Rookie officer, Fisher, quickly dropped his weapon and ran over to assist the wounded female. Moving fast while shots rang out, the only thing he found was a lifeless body.

He would forever be traumatized from that day's event.

Meanwhile, Lil' Trigg made his way through the garage door, pulling the trigger of the Mac-11 sub-machine gun.

Tac-Tac-Tac-Tac-Tac-Tac

Killing an officer in his path, as he moved toward his Chevy.

Gomez came from behind with his .45 gripped tight, cutting loose.

Boom! Boom! Boom! Boom!

As Lil' Trigg circled the rear end of the Chevy, a bullet grazed his ear. The next bullet hit him in his shoulder, causing him to drop the Mac-11 momentarily. He fell to one knee, clutching his shoulder before retrieving the machine gun.

Gomez smiled at the thought of victory. He moved quickly around the vehicle with his gun trained, when suddenly Lil' Trigg sprang into action.

Tac-Tac-Tac-Tac-Tac-Tac-Tac

He was making the chamber kick out shells until it was empty.

Click!

Bullets ripped through the lower side of Gomez's shirt, penetrating the outer coat of his bulletproof vest.

With Gomez on the ground, Lil' Trigg released the empty clip and slapped another one in with lightning speed before getting behind the wheel of the Chevy.

Putting the key inside the ignition, the Chevy roared to life before Lil' Trigg bolted through the garage door.

BLAMMM!

←──────────────────────────────→

    Agent Li heard an engine fire up, followed by tires screeching and hurriedly dove forward just as the Chevy came crashing through the garage door.

BLAMMM!

For him, this simple raid had turned into an all out war. The background check on this young hustler was right on point. He was armed and dangerous as hell and Agent Li knew he needed to get him before he got himself.

    Lil' Trigg sped down 98th, going way too fast for the 28 inch rims. Peering into the rearview mirror, he noticed the swarm of police vehicles on his ass. Holding the wheel with one hand and balancing the Mac-11 with his other, he fired at the pursuing vehicles.

Tac-Tac-Tac-Tac-Tac-Tac-Tac

Bullets covered the windshield of the first vehicle, causing it to veer to the right, slamming into a parked car.

BLAMMM!

Pop!Pop!Pop!Boom!Boom!Pop!

Officers returned fire.

Boom!Boom!Boom!Pop!Pop!

Tac-Tac-Tac-Tac-Tac-Tac-Tac-Tac-Tac

Lil' Trigg fought for control of the wheel, all the while yanking the Mac-11 and dodging bullets. He zipped through International Boulevard recklessly and rounded right onto the next street, the tires screeching as they gripped the pavement.

    Continuing to fire at the vehicles, he took his eyes off the road for a second, never noticing the Tahoe speeding up the street.

BLAMMMMM!

The black Tahoe slammed into the Chevy, dazing Lil' Trigg momentarily.

    When agents Gomez and Li collected themselves, they kicked open the doors and fired into the Chevy.

Boom!Boom!Pop!Pop!Boom!Boom!

Lil' Trigg caught two in his head, one in the neck, and a shit load to his body, killing him instantly.

CHAPTER FORTY

Lamonte was just pulling into his garage from yet another long night of being out with Evelyn. Grabbing his phone, he checked his voicemail while getting out of his vehicle. To his surprise, he had messages from everyone trying to score.

"Wha' tha fuck!" he said to himself as he listened to another nigga's message about not being able to reach Lil' Trigg. *Im'a kill this nigga.*

Lamonte called Lil' Trigg's phone three times as he made his way inside the condo. Once inside, he headed straight to the balcony to fire up. He tried Lil' Trigg's phone again and it still was going to voicemail. Ending the call, he placed his phone on his lap just as it began to ring.

He immediately answered, thinking it was Lil' Trigg calling him back. "Yo!"

"Black, nigga where you at? You gotta turn it to the 12 o'clock news! Lil' Trigg just got slumped!" E yelled through the phone.

"What!" he yelled back while running into the living room to turn on the television.

In the middle of E explaining all the details, Lamonte dropped the phone as he noticed a bullet riddled Chevy that looked like Lil' Trigg's on the screen.

Now all of a sudden the news had his undivided attention. Grabbing the remote, he turned up the volume.

"Good afternoon, this is Frank Summerville reporting live from the scene of what appears to be a quadrupled homicide. Details are still sketchy, but from what we do know, one FBI agent was shot and killed, as well as a veteran officer of the Oakland Police Department.

The officers' names have not yet been released because their families haven't been notified. The third person, an eighteen-year old,

210

Tarik Nelson of Oakland, was killed as he engaged in a shoot out with the officers on this street right behind me. From the information we've gathered, FBI agents as well as DEA and OPD staked out to serve a warrant on Tarik Nelson, who was wanted in connection with the triple homicide that occurred awhile back at Sway night club in San Francisco. Upon arriving at an apartment complex on 98th and Bancroft Avenue, shots immediately rang out as officers engaged in a shoot out with the suspect. A fourth person, a female acquaintance of Mr. Nelson, is believed to have been shot, and killed as well. Sources tell us Mr. Nelson somehow managed to make it to his garage, where he jumped into that white Chevy Caprice, before storming through the garage door, and the outer iron gate of the apartment, leading officers on a highspeed chase down 98th Avenue."

"Witnesses described the shootout scene like something only seen in a movie.

At this time, several officers are being treated at Highland Hospital for non-life threatening injuries. As always, we'll keep you posted on any and all news as it develops.

Reporting live from Oakland, Frank Summerville."

Lamonte immediately shut the television off and quietly paced back and forth across the floor, holding his head.

Damn, not Lil' Trigg', he thought. *First Murda, then Pookie. Buck and Red locked up. Damn! Anybody Can Get It. Who's next? Tae-Tae? Gino? Me?*

He stopped pacing when his cell began to ring again and quickly he picked it up.

"Hey Babe. I was just callin' to let you know I made it home safe," Evelyn said.

"How's yo' day goin' so far."

"Damn, Ma', it's dumb ass hectic out here right now. Im'a have to hit you back later."

"Oh, I'm sorry. Anything I can do to help?" she asked sincerely.

"Nah, I'm good, Ma'. I just gotta handle a few things. Im'a get up wit' you later though."

"Okay Babe. Have a good day and *please* be careful."

"I will," Lamonte said disconnecting the call.

No sooner had he put the phone down on the coffee table, it started ringing again. Looking down at the caller ID display, he frowned. *Cooper? Wha' tha fuck he want?* he thought to himself as he reached down to answer the phone.

CHAPTER FORTY-ONE

Mr.Cooper had called and informed Lamonte that he needed to see him A.S.A.P. He arrived at Cooper's office a little after 4 o'clock, just before the building closed for the day. He had no idea the purpose of the visit. Lamonte wondered if it had anything to do with Lil' Trigg's situation or if Cooper found some kind of loophole in Buck's case. Whatever the case, Cooper wasn't discussing it over the phone.

When Lamonte entered the lobby, Jessica was already gone for the day, so he walked straight into Cooper's office uninvited. Cooper was seated behind his desk, talking on the telephone with whom Lamonte assumed was another one of Cooper's clients.

Cooper acknowledged him with a nod as he took up a seat in one of the leather chairs at the desk.

Lamonte waited patiently as Cooper concluded his telephone conversation. Once Cooper hung up the phone, he greeted Lamonte with a handshake that instantly made Lamonte uneasy. Shaking hands was unusual for them. They were always straight to the point about everything.

After the *informal* greeting, Cooper stood and paced the floor while wiping thick beads of sweat from his upper lip and forehead.

After minutes of beating around the bush, Cooper got straight to the point. "Listen Black, some heavy shit is about to hit the fan. Now, I don't know how you conduct your business, but loose lips sink ships. If you understand what I'm saying?"

Lamonte was confused. "Look, if this got anything to do wit' that shit on tha news, I'on know nothin' 'bout it. I got an alibi! I was wit' my girl."

"News? What's going on in the news?" Cooper asked surprisingly, cutting Lamonte off. "I was talking about your name being implicated in a federal investigation."

"A federal investigation!" Lamonte asked outraged. Now he was nervous, a little too nervous. When he heard the words federal investigation, he knew then he was up shits creek without a paddle.

Cooper took a deep breath before continuing. "Yes, it seems like the investigation has already began due to a confidential informant and all the information he's provided."

Lamonte couldn't believe the words that were coming out of Cooper's mouth. He sat there overwhelmed and shocked with no idea if he was coming or going. Mentally, he was at a loss for words.

A confidential informant! But who? Gino? Red? Tina? E? Chop? Shit, it could be anybody. Was it Lil' Trigg before he got killed? Nah! Lamonte immediately crossed that thought out of his mind.

Lil' Trigg had gone out the same way he vowed to go out—guns blazin'! Nah, Lil' Trigg definitely lived by the death before dishonor code.

But who? And how much time do I have before the doors came crashing down?

Lamonte's mind was so occupied with a thousand questions; he hadn't heard Cooper calling his name.

"Black! Black!"

"Oh, my bad, I drifted off fo' a sec."

"You think? Son, are you alright?" Cooper asked concerned.

"Yeah, I'm good," he said confidently. "So, wha' do all this mean?"

Cooper repositioned himself back behind his desk and pulled a file out from one of his drawers before taking a seat.

Staring at the large manila envelope, Lamonte gestered for it and Cooper handed it over to him. Lamonte opened the file and at the top of the title page in big bold letters read:

THE LAMONTE GIBBSON DRUG OPERATION

Wha' tha fuck, he said to himself.

Continuing to read the rest of the papers, Lamonte damn near fainted. There were names of everybody in his circle and a couple others he didn't recognize.

Lamonte read about the triple homicide at Club Sway, the homicide of Lil' Pookie at the house on Bancroft, and other homicides that had nothing to do with him. He read about all the drugs he was allegedly dealing in Oakland and other parts of the Bay Area. It even went as far as his dealings back home in Chicago.

When he read about an unknown source from Mexico supplying him with kilos for $14,000 a piece, as long as he purchased at least twenty kilo's a week, he knew without a doubt who the CI was.

Turning to the last page, he confirmed what he already knew. There at the bottom of the page, signed next to US attorney Paul Hire's name, was Reddick Taylor...A.K.A Red Nose.

The nigga Red had officially turned into a hot boy, stool pigeon, rat, snitch...a mu'fuckin' informant!

Lamonte was speechless. Cooper could tell by the look on his face that he was highly upset.

He gave Lamote a few minutes to gather his thoughts before he spoke.

"I guess you already know this doesn't look good. I mean, how much does this fucker know about your operation?"

Guessing from the look of disparity on Lamonte's face, Cooper answered his own question. "We're fucked!"

"I can't believe this shit!" Lamonte slammed his fist on Cooper's desktop. "How could that nigga do me like that?"

"I tell you...The game just isn't the same anymore. These fuckers nowdays will tell on their own mothers to save their asses," Cooper declared.

"So wha' now?"

"Well, I got that information from a good friend of mine who works for the US Attorney's office. Right now, the indictment is presumed to be sealed. Now, I'm not sure when it's going to be unsealed, but unless you're ready to forfeit your freedom, I would suggest you get the hell outta dodge."

After discussing the matter a little longer, Lamont was ready to leave. He thanked Cooper again and assured him he would send a little something something in good faith for him, and his friend at the D.A.'s office.

Lamonte left Cooper's office knowing that it was only a matter to time before he'd be indicted because of a bitch ass nigga who couldn't do his time. He knew at that moment that the saying was definitely the truth.

Anybody can get it!

CHAPTER FORTY-TWO

B ack at the apartment, Lamonte paced back and forth in his living room smoking a blunt. His head throbbed vigorously from the massive migraine that'd been bothering him since he left Cooper's office.

This shit is really fuckin' me up. I've worked too hard for wha' I got to just lay down to tha law. If it ain't one then it's another. First, it's the situation wit' Lil' Trigg. Then tha' shit wit Red. I swear, shit's all fucked up. Fuck! They got the names of everybody. I'on need this shit in my life right now. Fuck! I gotta do it movin', he thought to himself as he stopped pacing long enough to answer his ringing phone.

"Yeah!" he barked in an irritated tone.

"Sor-ry, I guess it's still not a good time," Evelyn said.

"Oh, my bad Ma'," Lamonte softened his tone. "What's good?"

"You! I've been worried sick about you and just wanted to make sure everythin' alright."

"Shid, I'm good Ma'. Well actually I'm not, but I'll be a'ight. I just...just."

"You just what?"

"I just gotta get away fo' awhile."

"Black, is everything alright? I mean....get away for how long? When? Please talk to me baby. You scaring me."

Lamonte's first thought was not to tell her. Although Evelyn had a special place in his heart, and he'd miss her trememdously, he just couldn't bear the thought of hurting her. Then again, if he told her, she might decide to come with him. In the end, he opted for the latter, and allowed himself to tell her what was going on.

Two Days Later...

"Yo Red," somebody yelled, easing up behind Red. Red immediately jumped up from the card table ready to defend himself. But he became less tense when he recognized who was addressing him.

"Zoe, nigga you betta stop creepin' up on people. I damn near knocked yo' ass out," he said, sitting back down at the table.

"Yeah right nigga. If I was yo enemy, yo ass woulda been hit like good weed," Zoe chuckled.

"Yeah, whateva nigga. Wha' you want anyway? You see we ova here gamblin'."

"Aww nigga, don't get mad at me 'cause you losin'," Zoe said, ruffling a newspaper in his hand.

"Fuck you nigga, I ain't losin'! Anyways, what's good?"

"Nigga, check this shit out."

Zoe handed Red the Oakland Tribune. When Red read the headlines, his heart skipped a beat.

Teenager kills two officers and injures others before being gunned down by officers on East Oakland Street.

Tarik "Lil' Trigg" Nelson, 18, of East Oakland fatally shot two officers and wounded others as agents from the FBI, DEA, and OPD set out to serve an arrest warrant on Nelson at an apartement complex on 98th and Bancroft Avenue.

Nelson was wanted in connection with the triple homicide that occurred a while back at Sway Nightclub in San Francisco. Authorities converged on the residence shortly after 10 o'clock Thursday morning, and was greeted with hails of bullets. Special Agent Raymond Mitchell, 31 of the FBI, as well as veteran officer Lt. James Williams, 42 of OPD, were pronounced dead at the scene from multiple gunshot wounds.

A third victim, Ki'Moni Turner, 20 of Oakland, was hit by stray bullets, later died from injuries to her chest, and torso. Nelson was killed a short time later after he fled the apartment in a late model Chevy Caprice, taking officers on a high-speed chase down 98th Avenue, where he continued to fire his weapon. Authorities are still investigating these homicides.

"Damn, that lil nigga went out like Levelle," Red exclaimed aloud.

"Yeah, cus went out like a fuckin' G. Fuck dem crackas. They been killin' us fo' year."

Red's mind went back to what he'd just read.

Fuck! That was Agent Mitchell that got killed. Of all the officers, it had to be the one that was helping me wit my get out of jail free card, he thought, before getting up and heading to the phones.

←——————————————————————→

Mr. Cooper, shook his head. "How you holdin' up in here, Buck?"

"I mean...It iz wha' it iz. So wha' brought you up here today?"

Cooper smiled as he took a seat on the other side of the table.

"Thank you officer, I'll buzz when I'm ready," he told the C.O.

When the C.O. was out of the room, Cooper pulled out a folder from his Burberry briefcase. He took a deep breath before showing Buck the unsealed indictment on Black.

Buck looked down at the papers and couldn't believe what he was seeing.

"As you can see, it's not looking too good for your nephew," Cooper said, folding his hands on the table.

Buck shifted uncomfortably in his seat as he continued to read the papers. His face held a gasp of shock as he finished reading the last page. "Fuck! I told 'em not to trust that nigga Red. I need to get a message to him ASAP."

"I'm on it." Cooper assured, pushing over a pen and note pad. "In the meantime, you need to figure out what to do about Mr. Taylor. Without him, they don't have a case."

"Umm-Hmm, do you know where he's bein' housed?"

Cooper shifted through his notes. "2nd floor, B-8."

"Yep, good lookin'," Buck said sincerely.

"No problem." Cooper glanced at his Rolex before lifting his briefcase. "Look I got to be at the courthouse in thiry minutes. I'll be back up here when I learn something new."

Smiling, he shook Buck's hand before tapping the buzzer for the C.O. to open the door and let him exit.

Moments later, the C.O. came back and escorted Buck back to the hole.

← ———————————————————————— →

Back at the FBI headquarters, Agent Gomez let out a deep breath. He hated the fact that Black and his crew were still on the streeets. For nearly three months, he and his partner, Mitchell, had been building a case against Black. But Mitchell would never be able to see the day Lamonte Gibbson was apprehended and it was all because of the gun totting teen who took his life right in front of Gomez. A teen who was employed by this Chicago thug, Pretty Black.

Gomez knew that the look in his partner's pleading eyes before they glazed over would forever haunt him. He vowed to make every person who had anything to do with Black suffer.

They're all going down, one way or the other. And I'm going to do whatever it takes to bring justice for the death of my partner. Even if it kills me, he thought

CHAPTER FORTY-THREE

After driving around the apartment numerous times, Lamonte was finally satisfied that it wasn't under any kind of surveillance. It had been two weeks since the shoot out with Lil' Trigg and the news of Red cooperating. He gathered his thoughts and called Evelyn, telling her to make sure she was ready by 8 o'clock. Without waiting for a response, he hung up on her and stood on the balcony of his condo looking out at the beautiful sight for the last time.

His mind kept going back to the predicament Red had gotten him in. Buck had sent word from the jailhouse by the way of Mr. Cooper, assuring that Red was indeed a dead man walking. The situation had Lamonte so fucked up he hadn't eaten in days.

Flicking the Bic lighter, he lit the end of his blunt. As he took in a deep drag, smoke curled up in a small cloud in front of his eyes.

Lamonte leaned over the balcony's rail and exhaled the smoke as he stood in silence. Staring out at the cars and pedestrians moving freely caused a sudden tear to fall from his eyes. He was thinking about how much he was going to miss the Bay Area.

Looking at the time, he noticed it was shortly after 3 o'clock. He had less than five hours before he had to pick up Evelyn and make his way to Oakland's International Airport in time to depart their 10 o'clock flight to Miami. From there, they'd catch a one-way flight to Evelyn's homeland, Dominican Republic.

A week earlier, Evelyn had brought up the idea of them going back to her country. After listening to her tell him about the country and her family, Lamonte was all for it. He got them both fake ID's so they would be traveling under assumed names.

Stepping back inside the spacious condo, Lamonte went to his bedroom and grabbed the 1.1 million dollars from his safe and packed it in a suitcase. Feeling comfortable about all the cash, plus the new rental car, he proceeded to get dressed before heading through Tha Town for the last time.

After leaving the apartment, his first stop was Walnut St. to drop in on Desiree.

←——————————————————————→

The occupants of the Dodge Magnum had been watching Buck's house for two weeks awaiting their suspect. They figured he'd be paranoid after the death of Lil' Trigg so they made sure they stayed discreet.

The driver was getting really frustrated with the stake out but this was a personal vendetta for the passenger, who stressed the importance of the situation on numerous occasions. Besides, the passenger had already determined the fate of Black, and vowed not to rest until justice was served.

Taking down one of the biggest kingpins in Oakland, one who was responsible for all the pain the passenger felt would be well worth it so they sat and waited.

They prayed everything would go down smoothly and nothing would go wrong, although they both vowed to do whatever possible to bring Black down, even if it killed them.

Shortly after 4 o'clock that evening, surprisingly Black showed up alone which was perfect because neither one of them wanted to be up against several gun totting lunatics. Keeping their eyes on the prize, they continued to wait.

←——————————————————————→

Lamonte and Desiree sat in the living room smoking a blunt for old time sake. Desiree looked on in astonishment, impressed by Lamonte's nonchalant attitude about his situation. She also admired the loyalty he had for Buck.

Leaning his back against the sofa, Lamonte reached for the pre-paid cell phone he'd purchased a couple of days ago. Dialing a familiar number with his free hand, while clutching the blunt with his other, he let the phone ring four times before hanging up. His mother never anwered unfamiliar numbers, and today wouldn't be any different.

He finished the blunt, smashing the roach in the ashtray before reaching for the phone again. The voice on the other end responded on the third ring. Lamonte heard Tae-Tae grumble a "What's good," and waited.

Taking a deep breath, Lamonte's eyes searched around the place he once called home while gripping the receiver hard enough to crush it.

"I'm 'bout to bounce," he finally said.

Tae-Tae stayed silent on the other end. "Have a safe trip and stay in touch. Don't worry 'bout Moms, I got her."

"Yep. Love you folk and watch yo'self."

"Same here."

Lamonte hung up the phone, and walked slowly towards the open window and looked out on the street for the last time.

After chopping it up briefly, Lamonte handed Desiree a bag that contained the keys and titles to the Charger and Porsche, as well as $150,000 before making his exit.

The duo waited patiently in the Magnum parked across the street in full view of Buck's house. The plan was to follow Black once he left, then take him down the first opportunity that arised.

Just as planned, Black came strolling out of the house an hour later, looking around suspiciously before getting into his vehicle.

The mood inside the car was tense but eerily quiet as they followed Black from a safe distance.

The passenger reclined the seat, trying to relax while waiting for them to arrive where Black would lead them.

During the ride from Buck's house, Lamonte's mind raced back and forth about the whole fleeing the country scenario. He knew what he had to do. The thing was he just wasn't thrilled about being so far away. He knew if he didn't, he'd end up in jail for a long period of time. If not jail, the morgue. Although he wasn't thrilled about leaving, there was no way he'd sit around and wait to be apprehended.

Lamonte drove down MacArthur Boulevard. He was headed to the apartment complex on Alvingroom Court. Although the complex had recently undergone a complete renovation, the crime and drug activity was forever present. He was on his way to holler at Tina.

As always, upon arriving at the complex, Lamonte parked, got out, and was greeted with all the love he deserved. The complex was surrounded with young hustlers, loud music, hood bops, and plenty of smoke and drinks.

After returning the love, Lamonte headed up the walkway to Tina's apartment.

$$\longleftrightarrow$$

The driver sat slouched behind the wheel of the Magnum, smoking a cigarette while observing Black make his way through the building. The occupant in the passenger's seat was beginning to get agitated.

"Man, I hope this fucker don't be in there all day," the passenger said impatiently, looking through inconspicuous dark glasses.

"Yeah, I'll be glad when we get this over with. I swear, I'on know how I let you talk me into this," the driver responded, smashing the butt of the cigarette into the ashtray, before immediately lighting up another.

All of a sudden an argument erupted in the distance followed by the sound of glass shattering, causing the duo to sit bolt upright. A scene was unfolding through the windshield where two teens who had a little too much to drink had decided to engage in a fistfight.

"Fuck! That's all we need right now is a couple drunk assholes gettin' into it," complained the passenger.

"What do you wanna do?" the driver asked.

"Sit back. Them fools could kill themselves for all I care. Black's ass is getting it, and damnit, he's getting it as soon as he comes out!" the passenger fumed.

The duo watched as teens exchanged blows for what seemed like hours before the crowd dispersed into vehicles and fled out of the complex.

←————————————————————→

Lamonte sat on Tina's living room couch, nursing a blunt. The T.V. was turned to an old Raiders and Patriots' football game with the sound muted. Eighteen ounces of cocaine was piled in two neat rows on top of the glass coffee table.

Tina walked into the room with two ice cold bottles of water and sat on the far end of the couch. She reached for the lit blunt while placing a bottle in front of Lamonte.

"That's fuck'd up you gotta bounce, Black. But I know it's fo' the better. I still can't believe that bitch ass nigga, Red, did you bad like that," she said, taking a pull from the blunt.

Lamonte looked at her and smiled. "No doubt. These niggas ain't built Ford tough, Ma'."

"Who you tellin'. I swear these niggas mo' pussy than vaginas when faced wit' a lil' time," she replied, with a touch of sadness in her voice, before taking another hit and handing the blunt back to Lamonte.

"Ain't that tha truth," Lamonte reassured her, taking a huge drag while reaching for his small Gucci shoulder bag.

Tina watched as Lamonte slowly unzipped the bag. Her brown eyes gleamed when Lamonte flipped it over, emptying five thick stacks of cash over the coke.

"This is all you Ma'. On Momma's, you's a down ass bitch. This should keep you straight 'til Buck gets out," Lamonte said, placing the empty bag around his neck and shoulder.

"Oh, Black. You didn't have ta," Tina said, shaking her head.

"I know. But I wanted to," he said, watching Charles Woodson wrap an arm around Tom Brady forcing him to fumble in one of the most controversial calls in NFL history.

Looking at the time, he said, "Well, I gotta get goin' Ma'. I do got a flight to catch."

"Will I hear from you again?" she asked as he stood.

The force of her beauty now struck Lamonte as he stared down at her less than a foot away.

"Off top, Ma'. You know Im'a keep in touch," Lamonte leaned over and the two hugged for the first and last time.

$$\longleftrightarrow$$

About forty-five minutes later, after the drunken crowd departed, the passenger saw Black coming out of the building. Heart pounding and eyes twitching, the thoughts of that awful day was relived through the passenger's head.

Black was heartless and made a lot of people look like fools but he was about to pay for it.

"You sure you wanna go through wit' this?" the driver asked.

"Yep. I'm holdin' court in this fuckin' parkin' lot."

The passenger leaned forward to get a better look at their intended target before flicking the safety off the .9mm.

"A'ight, he's getting into the car," the driver nodded. "Go take care of it."

"I'm on it," the passenger said coldly, never taking eyes off Black.

"Be ready to move when I get back."

The driver looked at the passenger, but the passenger got out of the vehicle without turning to meet the gaze.

You were able to avoid the right side of the law, but you won't avoid this street justice, the passenger thought.

$$\longleftrightarrow$$

Lamonte made his way through the building and back towards his vehicle. Just as he was about to hit the button to unlock the door, he felt a tremendous chill. The little hairs on the back of his neck stood up, distracting and redirecting his attention.

He stopped short, turned around and surveyed the area. He thought he was tripping, but just couldn't shake the feeling of being watched.

Man, them Grapes got me paranoid like a mu'fucka! Let me hurry up and get up outta here, 'cause Lord knows I ain't strapped, he thought as he turned back around, hit the unlock button and immediately stepped into the driver's seat.

Just as Lamonte turned on the ignition and fiddled with the C.D. player, looking for his favorite song, he was interrupted by the sound of light tapping on the driver's side window. As he turned to inspect the sound, he came face to face with the barrel of a handgun pointed at his head.

The rest happened so fast, he couldn't believe it.

Pop!Pop!Pop!Pop!Pop!Pop!

Instinctively, he tried to shield his head with his forearms and hands, while desperately ducking for cover. The pain was unbearable as slugs entered his body. It felt like balls of fire was searing into him.

Within minutes, the rapid gunfire ceased and Lamonte looked up and noticed the assailant for the first time. He couldn't believe his eyes. She smirked as she brought the gun through the shattered window, leaving her sweet fragrance for him to feast on.

TI's *I'm Back* began to blare out of the speakers. *I never let you down, Im'a shine on sight, keep ya mind on ya grind, and off mine alright. Hard Im'a ball on them squares I float, quarter million dollar cars everywhere I go. I know I'm in the lead, it may seem it might be. But no matter what they doing, they don't do it like me. Like a G. I hold it down for the town I'm at, and I flash like that. Recognize I'm back!*

←————————————————→

She peered down at Lamonte, who was staring up at her while taking quick, shallow breaths. He couldn't help but wonder what would make her do something like this to him.

"Why....Candi, wha-"

Before Lamonte could complete his sentence, Candi raised the black handgun, and without saying a word, emptied the remainder of the clip into him.

Pop!Pop!Pop!Pop!Pop!Pop!

Then, with a cold-hearted passion, she stood and watched as his body convulsed until finally he laid slumped in the driver's seat.

"You hurt the wrong bitch," she said before hawking a loogy and spitting through the window.

No words could explain the pain she felt. After her botched suicide attempt, due to a malfunctioned firing pin, Candi fell into a depressed state. The stress caused her to have a miscarriage and this just compounded her depression. For weeks, she stayed in her apartment, until Cristal found her and cleaned her up from her musky state.

She had loved Black but now her love had turned to hatred and her scorn led to this. For weeks, she wrestled with the thoughts of revenge until it finally consumed her. She had to practically beg Cristal to help her. Once Cristal agreed, Candi found the motivation she needed to pull herself together.

It was the fuel of *get back* that motivated her, and now that Black was dead, she felt relieved. With one final look at his lifeless body, she turned. The only sound cutting through the apartment complex was the click-clack of her stilettos.

◄─────────────────────────►

Agent Gomez had finally caught up with Black. Word that he was trying to flee the country came to him that morning. He set out to track him down, despite his superiors unwillingness to grant him back up. He had been waiting for over 20 minutes for him to finally come out of the apartment and leave.

That's when the shooting occurred.

His first reaction was to jump out his unmarked car, with his pistol ready to fire. But flashes of his partner Mitchell's dying face came to his mind. It froze him in his seat. There was a part of him that wanted to see Black die for all the senseless killing he brought to the City of Oakland.

However, there was another part of him, the *protect and serve,* officer in him that told his conscious this wasn't right. He had wrestled with himself. Whoever this woman was, he bet Lamonte had done something he had no business doing.

The kid's karma came to haunt him like that, he thought as he watched her walk off.

It was right then that he decided not to do anything. This woudn't be the first or last unsolved murder in the Oakland area.

With that, he started his Crown Victoria, dropped it into drive, and bust a u-turn. For once, his superiors were right. He didn't need any back up at all.

EPILOGUE

"Taylor! Lawyer's visit!"

Red was laying on his bunk when he heard his name called. So much was going through his mind. He planned to be out by now but with Mitchell being killed, nothing was going how he planned. With hearing his lawyer was there for a surprise visit, he hoped the man had some good news concerning his release.

Jumping up, Red put his shoes on. Ever since he'd been at the north county jail, he never had a cellie. That was another request he had in exchange for the information he provided.

"You ready?" the officer asked coming to his cell.

"Yea."

The officer unlocked the door.

Red stepped out and took a good look at the C.O. "You look familiar," he said. "You from Oakland?"

With an expressionless look on his face, standing at 5'11", black, and sporting a short cut fade with waves, the 20 something year old officer brushed off the question. "I've been around."

Despite his response, Red never forgot a face. It was the first time he saw the officer. He figured that the regular, who worked in his unit, must've been off. "I swear I've seen you before."

"Stay against the wall and keep your hands behind your back," the officer ordered as a response.

The officer led Red to the elevator where they went down to the first floor. Once there, he took him to a small room with a table and two chairs opposite of it.

"Have a seat," the officer told him while removing his cuffs.

"I've never been handcuffed," Red told him. "When y'all start that?"

"It's our new policy," he responded while cuffing Reds left arm to the table.

"How long I gotta wait?"

"It won't be long."

As the officer turned to leave, Red caught a side profile and the feeling that he knew him gripped at him hard. For some reason he associated his face with Ghost Town, in West Oakland.

Nah, he thought. *What I need to worry about is checkin' this lawyer. He needs to get me out of here.*

The bullpins used for convicts going to and from court was along the same hallway as the room Red was in. When a loud commotion came, he turned in his seat, wondering what was going on.

Niggas probably fighting, he thought as the noise continued to get louder.

That's when he heard the door behind him open up. When he turned, he saw an inmate with a broom, an orderly obviously.

"Nigga, can't you see I'm on a lawyer visit," Red barked.

"Oh my bad," the man said with a smile.

That's when Red recognized the man was no other than Buck. Fear immediately gripped him as he tugged at the cuff seizing his wrist. "Hey Hey!"

Buck let the door close behind him. "Yea nigga, don't look scared now," he said breaking the broom across his knee.

SNAP!

"Help!" Red screamed but his cries were drowned out by the commotion in the bullpins.

Dropping the wisk end of the broom, Buck held the daggered side in his hands. Raising it high above his head, he aimed it; striking downward and plunging 12 long inches worth right into Red's throat. Once Buck was sure Red was dead, he exited the room. He grabbed the mop he'd sat against the wall and made his way down the hall. He stopped at the bullpin and looked inside. His partners, Al and Pistol, were in there waiting to go to court, along with a few more cats from town.

Al gave him a head nod.

"Good lookin'," he said.

"No pro'," Al replied.

Their commotion was the distraction he needed to drown out Red's call for help. Rounding the corner of the hall, Buck found Little Sean, who was all grown up now, and working as an officer at the jail. Despite his job, Little Sean was still a Ghost Town nigga right out the O.

"You took care of it?"

"Yea," Buck said. Little Sean's big brother, Dulo, was a nigga Buck served work to.

"Once I'm out I got'chu."

But Little Sean waved it off. "Fuck that snitch ass nigga," he said. "Let's say that one was for the whole town."

"That's right," Buck said as the youngster walked off.

And just like that, Buck dipped his mop inside the bucket, before sliding from side to side across the floor. His nephew was dead and he still had a little time to do. Although he wished he could've protected his brother's son a little better, he knew one thing about the cold-blooded streets of Oakland:

At any given time, Anybody Can Get It....

Book Order Form
Legit Styles Publishing
16501 Shady Grove Rd Suite #7562
Gaithersburg, MD 20898

Name: _____   Inmate ID: _____
Address: _____
City/State: _____

QUANTITY	TITLES/AUTHORS	PRICE	TOTAL
	KINGPIN, Byron Grey	15.00	
	The Wall Season 1, Don Twan	15.00	
	Confessions of A Cheating Heart, Donnie Ru and Don Twan	15.00	
	No TrustPassing, Hood & Face 1	15.00	
	Pay The Cost, Michael "Blue" Branch	15.00	
	A.B.C.G. (Anybody Can Get it) DeSean Gardner	15.00	
	Small Town Cemetery DeSean Gardner	15.00	
	Dinner Thieves, Zo Ali	15.00	
	COMING SOON!!		
	KingPin 2, Byron Grey		
	The Wall 2, Don Twan		
	No TrustPassing 2, Hood and Face 1		
	The Initial Investigation, Byron Grey		
	Murderland, Byron Grey		

Sub Total $_____   Shipping $_____   Total Enclosed $_____

Shipping & Handling (Via US media Mail) $ 3.95 1-2 book(s), $ 7.95 3-4 books, 4 books or more free shipping.

FORMS OF ACCEPTED PAYMENTS:

Certified or government issued checks and money orders, all mail in orders take 5-7 business days to be delivered. Books can be purchased by credit card at 1-800-986-0000 or on our website at www.legitstylespublishing.com. Incarcerated readers receive 25% discount. Please pay $11.25 and apply the same shipping terms as stated above.